WINDOWS NT SECURITY

Other McGraw-Hill NCSA Guides

Cobb   *The NCSA Guide to PC and LAN Security*
Kabay   *The NCSA Guide to Enterprise Security Protecting Information Assets*
Miora   *Enterprise Disaster Recovery Planning*

In order to receive additional information on these or any other McGraw-Hill titles, in the United States please call 1-800-822-8158. In other countries, contact your local McGraw-Hill representative.

WM16XXA

Windows NT Security

A Practical Guide to Securing Windows NT Servers and Workstations

Charles B. Rutstein

McGraw-Hill
New York   San Francisco   Washington, D.C.
Auckland   Bogotá   Caracas   Lisbon   London
Madrid   Mexico City   Milan   Montreal   New Delhi
San Juan   Singapore   Sydney   Tokyo   Toronto

Library of Congress Cataloging-in-Publication Data
Rutstein, Charles B.
    Windows NT security : a practical guide to securing Windows NT
servers and workstations / Charles B. Rutstein.
        p.   cm. — (McGraw-Hill NCSA guides)
    Includes index.
    ISBN 0-07-057833-8 (pbk.)
    1. Windows NT.   2. Operating systems (Computers)   3. Computer
security.   I. Title.   II. Series.
QA76.76.O63R895   1997
005.8—dc21   96-37593
                                                CIP

McGraw-Hill

A Division of The **McGraw·Hill** Companies

The views expressed in this book are solely those of the author, and do not represent the views of any other party or parties.

1 2 3 4 5 6 7 8 9 0   DOC/DOC 9 0 2 1 0 9 8 7

ISBN 0-07-057833-8

The sponsoring editor for this book was Judy Brief, the editing supervisor was Bernard Onken, and the production supervisor was Pamela A. Pelton. It was set in New Century Schoolbook by Priscilla Beer of McGraw-Hill's Professional Book Group composition unit.

Printed and bound by R. R. Donnelley & Sons Company.

For Tom Gillard and John Vaughn
who showed me the way

CONTENTS

vii

Contents

Contents

Contents

ACKNOWLEDGMENTS

The completion of a project of this magnitude is rarely due to the effort of a single individual; this project is no exception.

I'd like to thank those who spent long hours both researching data for this book and providing technical reviews of the draft. Any errors that remain are mine alone.

The review team included Ken Amann, Dennis Cherry, Tom Cooper, Clarke Ferber, Carol Hadas, John Ponchock, Anne Spanos, Jay Subramanian, Jude Sylvestre, and Scott Thomas. A special thanks goes to Tom Cooper (ECNE) for his work on producing the "NetWare Notes" sections of the text and to Jude Sylvestre for his work on Passcrack for NT.

Thanks to Ken Moss and Scott Armanini at Microsoft for their assistance in obtaining information regarding NT security and architecture.

Also, thanks to my editor, Jennifer DiGiovanna, and to all the people at McGraw-Hill for their patience and contributions during the production process.

And finally, a very special thanks to Suzanne and Sebastian for helping me get through it all. You're the best.

CHARLES B. RUTSTEIN

Introduction

Security is a game in which the final goal is never quite in reach.
—Laurence Martin, 1928

Welcome! By token of reading this book, you're about to enter the ranks of users and administrators who understand the secure configuration of Microsoft's Windows NT and Windows NT Server products. To date, little has been written on the topic—and even less has been written which is actually useful to real-life system administrators. This book aims to change all that. In the process, we're sure you'll learn things you never knew about the Windows NT products.

In reading through this book, you'll see every level of Windows NT—from the very foundations of the operating system right to the highest-level system administrative tasks. As a part of this process, you'll be given the tools you need to understand how the operating system works and how to make appropriate system configuration choices. Perhaps even more importantly, you'll be provided the background knowledge required to understand the implications of all your potential configuration choices. This, in turn, will enable you to make the right decisions for your particular Windows NT environment.

Of course, it's not all up to you. Throughout the book, we'll provide our best recommendations regarding system configuration options.

By now, some readers are probably wondering "Who's this 'we,' anyway?" Throughout the book "we" represents the collective knowledge of a core group of expert Windows NT users and administrators. These NT experts, many of whom are mentioned by name in the Acknowledgments, deliver pragmatic hands-on solutions to a variety of clients on a daily basis. As a result, the experiences they share are based on real-world problems and solutions.

Indeed, that's very much what this book is all about. Too many computer security texts are written with little regard to the real-life day-to-day needs of system users and administrators. Many fail to reach their target audience because they employ high levels of abstraction or theory. Others, it seems, are written to obfuscate security, rather than to explain it in clear, simple terms.

Our goal is simple: to provide the reader with a practical understanding of the mechanics of Windows NT, to clarify the potential weaknesses in the Windows NT architecture, and to make simple, easy-to-understand recommendations regarding secure Windows NT configuration. After all, Windows NT security is hardly rocket science, although it may appear that way at the beginning. We strongly believe that administrators need not be computer security experts in order to provide a reasonable level of security to their systems.

At the same time, this book won't simply tell you the configuration changes to make to your NT system to make it secure. Rather, we'll explain each step and provide detailed examples. Even nonprofessional Windows NT administrators can and should understand the implications of each operating system change recommended throughout the book. Of course, this isn't to say that securing a Windows NT system is necessarily trivial. Rather, it means that success is eminently possible, provided that the administrator invests the required time.

Indeed, a wise person once said that success is in the details. Arguably, this statement referred to Windows NT security. As with much of computer security, the successful Windows NT security administrator is extremely detail-oriented. Put another way, patience pays off with respect to computer security.

A Bit of History

Although Windows NT has only recently become part of the popular computing landscape, it has been in development and limited deployment for several years. The Windows NT project really began in late 1988 with the arrival of David Cutler at Microsoft.

For some time, Bill Gates, chairman of Microsoft, had been fascinated by the concept of creating a portable operating system. Cutler, one of the principal architects of Digital Equipment Corporation's VMS, was to be the person who would make it happen.

From the very beginning, Cutler knew that the operating system had to be portable—that is, able to run on multiple hardware platforms with minimal changes. Security also made the principal list of features, although it was considered by many on the project team to be a bit of an afterthought for about the first year of the development project.

By 1990, however, the importance of security to the rest of the operating system became apparent. In January 1990, Cutler asked Jim Kelly to take over development of the security features of NT. From that point, security progressed rapidly onward, often driven by demands from above. Eventually, the security architecture found its place within the greater NT operating system.

It was not until late July 1993, however, that development of the first release version of Windows NT (3.1) was completed. Finally, 5.6 million lines of code later, Microsoft had its portable operating system.

The next version of Windows NT, code-named Daytona, was both faster and more full-featured than the previous version. More importantly it was even more stable than its predecessor. With the arrival of Daytona (version 3.5), Windows NT began to be recognized as one of *the* up-and-coming operating systems in the computer industry.

The release of Windows 4.0 in mid-1996 has taken Windows NT to an even higher plateau. The addition of the Windows 95 user interface has finally brought ease of use to this most powerful of desktop operating systems.

So, What's to Protect?

Before delving too deeply into the details of Windows NT–specific security, it makes sense to take a moment to reflect on the role of computer security in general and its changing goals and targets.

In the past, corporate computer systems were monolithic hulks of computing hardware, hidden away behind glass walls and impenetrable hordes of white-jacketed attendants. In more recent times, computing power has moved out to the masses in the form of networks of personal computers running operating systems such as Windows NT, which are often, in turn, connected to heavy iron still residing behind closed doors.

During this transition, the location of the data being used by computer users has become indeterminate. As computing power has moved from the basements to the desktops of corporate IS users, it has become less and less apparent precisely *where* the data resides. More importantly, it has become almost impossible to protect.

Traditional mainframe security can be likened to the high walls surrounding medieval castles and villages. By placing all data within the protected walls of the memory and storage space of the mainframe, corporate data has been considered safe from unauthorized users, from both inside and outside the organization.

When that information moves outside the protected castle walls to local area network (LAN)–based operating systems such as Windows NT, however, it becomes vulnerable. Unprotected data moving throughout the enterprise may be subject to unauthorized access, data corruption, and denial-of-service attacks.

At the same time, however, the movement of the data closer to those who need to use it often makes both organizational and business sense. These organizational and business benefits usually outweigh the security and management concerns that are always a part of any distributed computing infrastructure.

The movement to more distributed architectures utilizing operating systems such as Windows NT now seems to be inevitable for many organizations. Given such a foregone conclusion, it is up to information system (IS) departments to determine (1) where data resides, (2) how to protect it, and (3) how to manage the security over time. It is a herculean task.

So, Now It's Secure, Right?

One further word of caution is also probably appropriate. Although this book contains gobs of information regarding the secure configuration of Windows NT, it doesn't cover everything that you'll need to provide a secure computing environment. Nor does it provide up-to-the-second information regarding the latest and greatest security breaches and patches.

Rather, the book is meant to provide a strong foundation on which to build the security of your Windows NT workstation or network and, more importantly, to provide a context for understanding the potential risks associated with NT such that you will be equipped to respond to future NT security issues.

Remember also that proper configuration of an operating system does not ensure the security of an enterprise. Indeed, policies and procedures—in addition to proper system configuration—are critical to ensuring that an enterprise remains secure against attackers from both inside and outside the organizations' boundaries.

In short, this book is not a panacea—nor is it meant to be. When used in the proper context, however, it will help bring a sense of order to the chaos which is Windows NT security.

1

Security Architecture

How can we expect someone else to keep our secret if we have not been able to keep it ourselves?
—François, Duc de La Rochefoucauld

Unlike the Microsoft operating systems which came before it, Windows NT was designed from the very first release with security as one of its principal foundations. By building the security subsystems into the core of the operating system, Microsoft intended to create an operating system which was fundamentally—although not necessarily—secure.

This means that while Windows NT has the *potential* to provide significant security, much depends on the quality of the configuration and implementation details.

Put another way, the NT operating system can be made to be secure; there are no significant known flaws in the underlying security model. It is not, however, secure immediately after it is installed. Rather, administrators must take the time to utilize the security which has been provided by the operating system architects.

Fundamental Components

The Windows NT security architecture is made up of five fundamental building blocks, which represent an entity commonly referred to as the *security subsystem*. Other pieces of the security architecture interact with these building blocks in order to provide the full security architecture. Understanding these building blocks is essential to an appreciation of the security architecture.

SECURITY ACCOUNT MANAGER (SAM). The *Security Account Manager* (SAM) is responsible for maintaining all local user and group accounts (and domain user accounts in an NT server environment). In addition, the SAM contains authentication data—generally passwords—which allow it to act as a one-stop shop for user identification and verification. In doing so, it interacts regularly with the Local Security Authority to validate users' requests.

LOCAL SECURITY AUTHORITY (LSA). The *Local Security Authority* (LSA) acts as a hub for much of the behind-the-scenes security activity. It is responsible for:

- *Generating access tokens.* Once initial logon is complete, all users are identified not by their usernames, but by their security IDs (SIDs) and associated access tokens (see discussion later in this chapter). The LSA is responsible for building the appropriate access tokens.

- *Holding the system security and audit policies.* The *Security Reference Monitor* (SRM) queries the LSA in order to validate security requests. In turn, the LSA consults the Security Policy Database and returns the appropriate response.

- *Logging the audit results received from the SRM.* When an audit alert is generated by the SRM, the LSA is charged with writing that alert to the appropriate system log.

SECURITY REFERENCE MONITOR (SRM). The SRM is the primary element of the security infrastructure. Significantly, it runs in kernel—not user—mode. The role of the SRM is to act as the primary authority for enforcing the security rules of the system.

When a user wishes to access a named object, the SRM provides services to check whether the user has the right to access that object. It then provides information on success or failure, and generates any necessary audit messages to be logged by the LSA. Note that while it runs in kernel mode, it responds equally to both user and system authorization requests.

OBJECTS. Objects represent the fundamental unit of measure for the security architecture. All security functionality is built around the premise that Windows NT can identify discrete elements within the system; these are termed *objects*. Objects may include any resource which can be discretely identified and protected. This may include resources which are obvious within the user interface, such as files and printers, as well as behind-the-scenes resources such as threads and processes. More specifically, objects may include the following:

- File and directory objects (when using the NT file system)
- Thread and process objects
- Semaphore and event objects
- Named-pipes objects
- Port objects

The reasoning behind the objectification of resources is to provide a common methodology for interacting with them. One element of this interaction, of course, is security. More specifically, objectification allows us to

- Create and explicitly name given resources
- Place access controls on who is or is not permitted to use that resource
- Track and log the users who interact with that resource
- Track and log the resources which are, in turn, used by that resource

Also, note that objects may function as "holders" for other objects; that is, objects may be an entity unto themselves (noncontainer objects) or may be a repository for other objects (container objects). Container objects allow for a simplification of object security, in that all objects within a single container may be assigned the same security restrictions.

LOGON PROCESSES. The logon processes are the users' window into the security architecture. They provide the shell through which users are able to identify themselves to the LSA. Note that the logon processes include both the interactive logon with which NT users are familiar as well as remote logon processes to Windows NT servers.

These five building blocks work in conjunction with other system elements to provide the robust security for which Windows NT is known. In the paragraphs that follow we discuss these other system elements and how they interact with the building blocks.

Objects and ACLs

As was noted above, an object can be any discretely named resource within the system. As might be expected, the user rights which may be associated with these objects vary greatly depending on the nature of the object itself.

For example, the following rights are associated with file objects:

- *Read*—users can read the file
- *Write*—users can write to (append or modify) the file
- *Delete*—users can delete the file
- *Change permission*—users can change the permissions on the file
- *Execute*—users can execute the file
- *Take ownership*—users can take over ownership of the file

Therefore, each user has specific attributes for each of these respective rights for each file object. The combination of object, object rights, and user attributes allows the Windows NT system to permit or deny object access requests.

Access Control Lists

Each object has a pair of access control lists (ACLs) associated with it: a *Discretionary ACL,* representing rights which may be assigned, and the *System ACL,* which is set by the system security policies. For the purposes of discussion throughout this book, the generic term ACL refers to the Discretionary ACL.

The ACL is a list of the sets of attributes associated with the object and the users [or SIDs (Security Identifiers)] who may exercise these attributes. The list of attributes and users is represented in a structure known in Windows NT as an *Access Control Entry* (ACE). Therefore, an ACL is a list of ACEs. Each ACE contains the attributes and rights associated with those attributes, represented in either specific form (i.e., an explicit list of the rights) or in generic form (i.e., utilizing a generic attribute, such as file write).

In order to simplify the process of assigning rights to objects, Windows NT generates a set of generic rights which map to the specific rights associated with specific types of objects. This reduces complexity by using generic terms to refer to attributes when possible.

For example, both file and directory objects have similar rights referring to the ability of a user to read data. Both file and directory objects therefore have a generic attribute type called `FILE_GENERIC_READ`.

Other, more specialized attributes are also present in the ACE. For any given object, the ACE may contain up to 16 specific attributes. These are commonly used in more complex objects, such as semaphore and thread objects.

Let's examine a sample ACL/ACE for a hypothetical directory object within an NT file system. Suppose we have a directory called "NeatStuff." The NeatStuff directory has an ACL as follows:

Discretionary ACL

- User Suzanne has full control of the directory (i.e., read, write, delete, change permission, execute, take ownership).
- User Sebastian has read and execute permissions.
- User Hacker has read and execute permissions.
- Group BadBoys is explicitly denied access.

System ACL

- Audit all file reads.

Now, let's examine what happens at a high level when a user attempts to access this directory object. We'll dig into greater detail later in the chapter.

First, the security subsystem will examine the relevant ACEs within the ACL for the NeatStuff directory. Suppose that user Suzanne wants to access the directory. According to the ACL above, she is both permitted access and not explicitly denied access. Therefore, her request is permitted. The same holds true for user Sebastian, with the exception that he is permitted only the read and execute attributes of the object.

User Hacker is in a different position. While he is permitted access to the directory for read and execute attributes, he is also a member of the Bad-Boys group. As is noted in the ACL, the BadBoys group is explicitly denied access. Because most Windows NT ACEs are ordered with deny rights first, user Hacker will be denied access in this case. Note that this will hold true, even though Hacker's user rights explicitly allow him access.

The following are some of the significant implications of the way that Windows NT handles object security assessment:

- Access to objects is denied, unless it is specifically authorized in one of the ACEs associated with the object.
- Access to objects is denied if there is *any* ACE which denies access before all requested access is granted. This holds true even if there are other ACEs which allow access. The result is a highly secure system, though one which may be difficult to troubleshoot. Note that audits may be helpful in this case.

Inheritance of ACLs

Creating an explicit ACL for each and every object in a Windows NT system is a long and tedious task. Indeed, it's a task that few would tackle, given the choice. In order to make the process easier, NT supports the notion of *inherited ACLs,* which allow objects to take on the ACLs of their parent object. As we discussed earlier, some objects function as container objects. The objects which reside inside these container objects are termed "child objects." The container object itself is known as the "parent object" of its children.

Consider the example above (in DACL/SACL list); each user was granted specific rights to the directory called NeatStuff. No mention was made, however, of rights to specific files within that directory.

In this case, the directory object functions as a container object for the files which reside in it. Without defining an explicit ACL for each file within the NeatStuff directory, we already know what the file rights will be. Because the file objects are children of the directory objects, they inherit the same ACLs as the parent (to the greatest extent possible). In the preceding example, the user rights shown are granted for both the directory and for the files which reside inside it.

> **NetWare Note**
>
> How does ACL inheritance compare with NetWare's Inherited Rights Filter?
>
> Under NT, ACLs define the rights that users have to resources (including files and directories). Unless explicitly set otherwise, files in a directory have the same access restrictions as the directory itself. This is automatic.
>
> NetWare allows the administrator to determine on a directory-by-directory basis how the rights flow through the file system. NetWare supports a concept of an IRF (Inherited Rights Filter). This sets the default access privileges that will pass through to the files and directories below the current directory. Just like ACL inheritance, the IRF is the same for all users across the system. It's different in that NetWare gives more control of what permissions automatically pass through to other objects.

Security Identifiers (SIDs)

Within the Windows NT security architecture, users are discretely identified not by their usernames, but by unique Security Identifiers (SIDs). At the time of account creation, the security subsystem generates a unique SID for the new account.

The generated SID is (nearly) guaranteed to be unique across both time and space. This means that no other user in the system—or any other system—currently has or will have the same SID. Unlike UNIX, where User IDs can be reused, SIDs are entirely unique.

In order to generate a unique system SID, Windows NT uses a proprietary hashing function based on three relatively unique factors: the current system time, the amount of execution time the current process has used in the user mode, and the computer name or domain name. The latter factor is dependent on whether the account is created within the User Manager or the User Manager for Domains. Note that future user accounts created on this system will be formed relative to this general SID. These three relatively unique factors in concert with the hashing function provide an SID which is almost guaranteed to be unique. This has significant implications.

Multiple identical usernames are permitted. Because all authentication takes place using the SID and not the username, the username itself is almost irrelevant. In fact, it serves merely as a more human-understandable version of the SID. However, it is not as specific as the SID. This means that multiple users within a Windows NT system (or a Windows NT network) may have identical usernames over time (although not concurrently). Because usernames and SIDs are not synonymous, we need not worry about accidentally granting rights previously assigned to another user. Consider the following example:

Imagine that we have a user in our personnel department named Suzanne User. Suzanne's username is SuzanneU, and she has access to sensitive records about individuals who work for our company. Some months from now, Suzanne leaves the company. Some months later, Suzanne returns to take a position in the sales department.

On her departure, the Windows NT system administrator deletes Suzanne's account. When she rejoins the company, a new account is created for her using the same original username: SuzanneU. Fortunately, we need not worry about Suzanne retaining her rights to sensitive personnel records. When the new account is created, Windows NT generates a new unique SID. The rights which were assigned to Suzanne's old SID do not apply.

There are a few SIDs, however, which are not generated using this algorithm. These are the so-called well-known SIDs, assigned generically across all Windows NT implementations at the time of installation. These well-known SIDs belonging to built-in user accounts cannot be removed from the system.

Of course, not only users have SIDs assigned to them. Windows NT also supports the notion of "groups" of users logically bound together by identical access rights (for more information on groups, see Chap. 2, *Managing User Security*). Each group which is created is assigned a similarly unique SID. From that point forward, the group acts as a container object, functioning only to assign specific security rights to the members of that group through their common SID. Note that users maintain their own unique SID in addition to SIDs for any groups of which they are a member.

Access Tokens

Access tokens are the run-time equivalent of a driver's license. Much as a license allows the authorized holder to drive a car, the access token is the user's license to access the system resources. Also, much as the driver's license indicates the restrictions on the driver [requirements to wear corrective lenses or drive only during daylight hours, Class C license restrictions (not to drive large trucks, etc.)], the access token indicates restrictions on what the user may or may not do to system resources.

Access tokens are generated during the logon process (see section on the logon process later in this chapter). Primarily, they consist of data gathered from the Security Account Manager during the authentication process. This includes

- The user's SID
- The SIDs for each of the groups of which the user is a member
- Special privileges granted to the user
- Default ACL for the user
- The "owner" assigned to newly created objects

"Special privileges" may include the right to perform certain system functions, such as shutting down the system.

Note that once generated, the access token becomes the primary security link between the user and the Windows NT system. Each time the user attempts to access a protected resource, the Windows NT security subsystem will verify the user using the access token. Moreover, the same access token will be used to identify and authorize all processes which are created by the user or by other processes created by the user. In this way, the system can track a user's rights through an infinite number of spawned processes.

Impersonation

In order to understand how the system tracks user rights across multiple processes, we must first understand the underlying architecture. Within Windows NT, rights to access specific objects are transitive across a user's processes. Put another way, each process a user spawns becomes an impersonation of the original user. Similarly, the processes spawned by that process are impersonations of the original user.

Windows NT refers to the combination of a user's access token and the program which is called by the user as the *subject*. On initial logon, the system creates an initial subject consisting of the user's workspace and desktop (formerly Program Manager). For each successive program spawned by the user, Windows NT creates a new subject.

There are two primary types of subjects: simple subjects and server subjects. *Simple subjects* are those created in the manner noted above—by the system upon initial logon. They can act only within the security context of the user's access token. *Server subjects,* on the other hand, are far more flexible. They are able to act as servers for other subjects in that they can take on the role of another subject and perform some processing activity.

To illustrate the performance of server subjects, consider the problem of spawning a process to be executed by the system itself. To perform the task in question, the system process may require the use of the security rights of the user. Unlike some other operating systems, background processes in Windows NT are not necessarily all-powerful; rather, they inherit the rights associated with the user who creates them. By passing the valid security token from the user's subject to the server subject, the user can effectively hand off both control and authority.

NetWare Note

How much power do processes have?

Until NetWare 4, there was no concept of logging into a NetWare server at the console. Processes running on the file server (Netware Loadable Modules, or NLMs) have full access to all files and directories on all mounted volumes.

Under NetWare 4, it is now possible to log into Netware Directory Services (NDS) for access to NDS objects. The file system is separate from NDS, and so users who have access to the NetWare console can still access any file or directory, but cannot make changes to the NDS security database.

Under NT this is not the case. Processes running have the rights of the user that started the process. This is similar to the idea of setuid in UNIX. UNIX typically has a file attribute called setuid which causes a program to run with only the privileges assigned to a particular user. This allows administrators to control how much power each process has over system resources.

Logon Process

The logon process provides the embarkation point for users interacting with the Windows NT system. All users must be authenticated before they are allowed to access any system resources—this is a fundamental tenet of both the Windows NT security philosophy and one of the requirements for C2 security (see below, section on C2 security).

Secure Attention Sequence

The first step in the logon process is to initiate the secure attention sequence (CTRL-ALT-DELETE). It was Microsoft's intention that this sequence be impervious to trojan horse-based attacks. Such attacks have been successful in the past on other operating systems by presenting the user with a phony logon screen which serves to capture the user's username and password before terminating and sending control back to the real logon screen.

Unfortunately, the architecture of Intel-based computers (where over 90 percent of Windows NT implementations are run) does not allow for this attention sequence to be totally secure. Because the user cannot be certain that NT is presenting the logon screen—and not, for example, an MS-DOS-based trojan horse, it cannot be completely secure. Indeed, even if it is Windows NT which presents a logon screen, the user still cannot be certain that another process hasn't tampered with the keyboard driver in order to fake a logon screen.

In short, the secure attention sequence is as secure as is realistically possible, although it is not quite foolproof. However, Microsoft notes that while there have been extensive attempts to find holes in the secure attention sequence, none have succeeded to date. In any case, users should be reminded to always press ctrl-alt-delete before logging in, even if there is a logon screen already displayed.

Authentication and Authorization

Once the user has initiated the secure attention sequence and has typed in her username and password, the logon process passes the appropriate information onto the LSA. In turn, the LSA calls on the proper authentication software in order to authenticate the user.

By default, NT relies on an authentication mechanism built into the operating system. Utilizing a standard one-way hash function, the NT authentication package provides simple username-password verification.

Unfortunately, experience has shown that simple username and password combinations are rarely sufficient to provide significant security.

The problems with passwords are both well documented and widely known. While system administrators have some control over password policy, there are still fundamental problems, including the following:

- *Poor password selection.* By and large, users tend to choose poor passwords, opting for their dog's name, their birthday, or other such simple data.

- *Insecure password storage.* The safest place for a password to reside is inside a user's head. Of course, many users find it impossible to remember their passwords, and write them down on paper (often near their computers).

Fortunately, the architects of Windows NT provided a hook for those who wish to use some alternative authentication package. The choices available are quite varied and provide similarly varying levels of security. Nearly any authentication package which utilizes a dynamic link library (DLL) for authentication may be adapted for use as the authentication method for Windows NT. (See Chap. 2, *Managing User Security,* for more information.)

If the default authentication package is unable to identify the user account in question, it automatically passes control to the alternate authentication package. If neither is able to identify the account, a message is returned to the user, indicating that the attempted logon was failed. At the same time, the LSA may make an entry in the audit log (per the system security policy) regarding the failed logon attempt.

In the case of a failed logon attempt, NT gives no information to the user regarding the specific cause of the failure. The user is not told whether the username entered is, in fact, a valid username, nor whether the password is invalid. Rather, the message given simply indicates a logon failure, notifies the user that passwords are case-sensitive, and prompts the user to try again. NT administrators can limit the number of attempted logon attempts for all NT accounts except for the administrator account—this is to prevent a potential denial-of-service attack.

Note, however, that other, third-party authentication mechanisms may not exhibit the exact same behavior. The Win32 API set for Windows NT can provide information regarding the presence or absence of a named user account. Therefore, we recommend that administrators who elect to use third-party authentication libraries should ensure that the libraries maintain the security features described above.

To determine whether the account name and password are valid, the system consults the Security Account Manager (SAM). Note that the SAM may reside in several places, depending on the exact configuration of the Windows NT system or network:

- If the system is a standalone Windows NT workstation, the SAM is on the local computer. The same holds true for Windows NT workstations in a workgroup configuration.

- If the system is a Windows NT workstation and a Windows NT domain is specified, the SAM will reside on both the primary and backup domain controllers (servers). Alternately, if the account is a local account, the logon process will forgo the domain logon process and consult the local SAM.

If the account name is valid, the SAM responds with a valid SID for the user, as well as valid SIDs for any groups of which the user is a member. This information is passed to the LSA, which, in turn, creates an access token (as described above).

The access token contains the valid SIDs and their associated ACLs and ACEs. It then passes the token to the Win32 subsystem, through which the user will interact with the Windows NT system. As a part of the introduction to the Win32 subsystem, the LSA creates a new subject for the user. Finally, if the logon is an interactive logon (i.e., at the system console), the Win32 subsystem will automatically start the windows shell (formerly Program Manager) for the user.

Single Sign-on

Windows NT networks provide a *single sign-on* (SSO) capability. This means that users need only to authenticate themselves once to their Windows NT domain, after which they are free to access resources to which they have rights across the domain. Those resources may exist on the Windows NT server to which they originally logged in, or they may exist on another server altogether. That other server might be halfway across the world—NT doesn't care, as long as the user can be authenticated to the proper NT domain.

SSO does not come without some increase in potential risk. By providing only a single logon to access multiple resources, more reliance is placed on that logon. The question to be answered, then, is whether the standard Windows NT logon is sufficiently secure to rely on for the security of the entire Windows NT network. For detailed information on SSO in general and on the Windows NT implementation of SSO in particular, please refer to App. D, *Single Sign-on Security*.

Security Authorization Process

The preceding sections provided the foundation to understand the entirety of the Windows NT security architecture. In this section, we put all the pieces together to understand the process by which Windows NT provides security to all the resources under its control.

The process proceeds as follows:

1. Users authenticate themselves to the system. Note that this authentication may take place either locally, in the case of a Windows NT system acting in a workgroup or as an independent system, or on the Windows NT Server acting as the domain controller for the given domain. Alternatively, the local domain controller may pass the request to the domain controller for a foreign domain in order to authenticate a logon request from a trusted domain. Assuming authentication is successful, the LSA grants the user a valid access token. This token contains valid SIDs for their user account and for any global groups of which they are a member, in addition to the privileges which have been granted to them.

2. When a user attempts to access an object, the SRM compares the ACEs of the object to the user's subject. The user's subject, in turn, is made up of the SID for the user and those of her respective groups.

3. The SRM proceeds through the list of ACEs, stopping if it finds an ACE which explicitly denies access. If no denial is found and there is at least one ACE which grants the rights requested, the access is permitted. Note that the order of the ACEs is significant; if a deny is found before a permit, access is denied.

4. If no ACE which permits access is found (or if there is an explicit denial of access), an error is returned to the calling process and a message sent to the LSA. The LSA may then place an event in the audit log, according to system audit policy.

Services and Drivers

Within Windows NT, services and drivers may be run with the privileges (i.e., under the auspices of an access token) of a named user. Note, however, that unlike other processes, services may run under the system account, rather than under a standard user account. Doing so allows them nearly full access to all the resources in the system (similar to daemons running as root in a UNIX system). As a result, services and drivers which run under the system account must be carefully monitored to ensure that they do not abuse their role in the system.

By default, most Windows NT OS services run under the system account. For example, the Windows NT Scheduler Service (AT command) is used to schedule batch jobs for selected dates and times in the future. By default, this service runs under the Windows NT system account, and can therefore be assumed to have full access to any resource in the system.

The obvious solution to this problem is to either (1) limit the access of these services by running them under nonprivileged accounts or (2) disabling them entirely. We recommend disabling those services which are not currently required; note that this doesn't mean that they need to be removed from the system, just temporarily disabled in the Services dialog box.

For those services which are required, however, it is often difficult to determine precisely which access rights are required. If you can determine the requirements through trial and error, it is probably worthwhile to limit access accordingly. Unfortunately, Microsoft has not (and will not!) make the source code to these services available to end users. Indeed, even if they did, most users probably wouldn't have a sufficiently deep understanding of these services to make a reasoned assessment of their relative security.

In a greater sense, this debate over the relative security of proprietary pieces of the Windows NT operating system is unlikely to ever be settled. Many former (and current) UNIX administrators seem to be appalled by the fact that Microsoft will not release the source code for its operating systems. After all, most of the popular UNIX operating systems have freely available (or at least available) source code. The availability of this code, in theory, allows a user to check for security holes.

In any case, this book is clearly not the proper forum for this debate— and in the end, the debate is probably completely without merit. Microsoft has not—and will not—release source code. Therefore, if you wish to use Windows NT workstation or server, you'll just have to trust Microsoft's security architects. Note only the fact that Windows NT is a departure from previous Microsoft OS security efforts; it inherits neither significant design considerations nor source code from previous efforts.

For most users, however, the NT native OS services are probably safe enough to be run under the system account. Having said that, however, we strongly recommend that Windows NT system administrators keep up with all the service packs (patches) which Microsoft publicly releases on a periodic basis.

C2 Security

Ever since the early days of computer security, system architects have tried to build strong, robust security into their programs and operating systems. In order to help formalize the process of providing adequate security, the National Computer Security Center (NCSC) of the National Security Agency (NSA) published a series of guides to computer security requirements. These books, known as the "rainbow series" because of their distinctive colored covers, set out the requirements for various levels of security in information systems.

The most well known of these books is the *Trusted Computer System Evaluation Criteria*. Alternatively, this book is known by the color of its cover: the "Orange Book." The Orange Book spells out the requirements and criteria for several levels of computer security. These levels are rated from the highest (A) to the lowest (D).

From the beginning, Windows NT was designed to roughly comply with the C2 level of NCSC security. In order to meet this level of security, NT is required to have several critical features, including the following:

- Each user must be clearly and uniquely identified. The system must be able to distinguish absolutely between the actions of different users and be able to verify that specific users are who they say they are. NT meets these criteria through the logon process.

- The system must provide discretionary access control. This means that an owner of a resource must be able to effectively limit others' access to that resource at her discretion. NT meets these criteria through its object access methodology.

- Administrators must be able to track the security-related activities of all users in the system. Moreover, the audit trails that track these activities must be protected against tampering. NT meets these criteria through the LSA logging process and by shielding the security log from all but administrative users.

■ The system must prevent against resource reuse. This means that resources (such as memory or disk space) which are no longer in use by a user must be cleared of all traces of the previous user before being used by another user. This prevents a user from capturing bits of information from another user's activities. NT meets these criteria by clearing memory immediately after it is freed by a process and disallowing the recovery of information in disk clusters which have been allocated from another user.

■ The system must be protected against external tampering with either the system files in memory or on disk. NT meets these criteria through effective memory and disk space barriers.

Unfortunately, designing the system to meet these criteria and actually determining that it does are two separate activities. The process of assuring that the criteria have been met falls to the NCSC. The process of evaluation for C2 security is both long and cumbersome.

In 1992, Microsoft signed a letter of intent with the NCSC to evaluate NT versions 3.5x at the C2 level. In 1995, a basic C2 evaluation was granted.

Note, however, that the C2 designation has significant strings attached. The evaluation does not include either network support (found in the Red Book criteria) or subsystem components (found in the Blue Book criteria). While both of these evaluations are now in progress, neither had been completed at the time of writing.

Moreover, the C2 evaluation is granted for only a specific configuration of the operating system running on a very specific class and configuration of hardware. This runs contrary to one of NT's intrinsic values—that it runs efficiently on a wide range of hardware configurations. This has led some to question the value of C2 evaluation. It is simply too expensive to evaluate the infinite combinations of system components that users may desire.

So, What Does C2 Really Mean?

Not much. For most users, the fact that the NCSC has approved the underlying design of NT is probably sufficient. In reality, this probably means that the foundation of the operating system is sufficiently secure for all except the most demanding (government) users. European users should note that Microsoft has also applied for a similar rating from European security authorities (E3).

The rainbow series books are extremely detailed in their descriptions of how to build secure systems. Unfortunately, they're not terribly well thought out in terms of utility and administration. As we will note throughout this book, selecting the proper level of security involves a simple series of tradeoffs between security and utility. Put another way, putting a C2-class Windows NT system in your organization may make your auditors happy, but it's unlikely to make either you or your users jump for joy.

Should you wish to build a C2-capable Windows NT system (note that you cannot build a real C2 system unless it is an exact duplicate of the evaluated configuration), Microsoft provides some support in the form of the C2 Configuration Manager.

C2 Configuration Manager

The C2 Configuration Manager is included with the Windows NT 3.51 (and later) resource kit. It provides a step-by-step checklist of items which must be reconfigured in order to provide the C2 level of security. The filename of the C2 manager is C2CONFIG.EXE.

When the C2 manager first runs, it examines the system for both known C2 configuration details as well as other potential security weaknesses that may not be addressed by the C2 criteria. The user is then prompted to make the required changes from within the manager itself. In this way, the C2 manager is a useful one stop shop for evaluating the security of your Windows NT system.

Consider the C2 configuration manager screen shown in Fig. 1.1.

The C2 manager provides the following guidelines regarding system security. Refer to Chap. 5, *The Registry,* for the registry keys which control the following activities:

File systems.   The manager provides the capability to convert any FAT volumes to NTFS. This provides the discretionary access control required by C2. For more information on Windows NT file systems, consult Chap. 3.

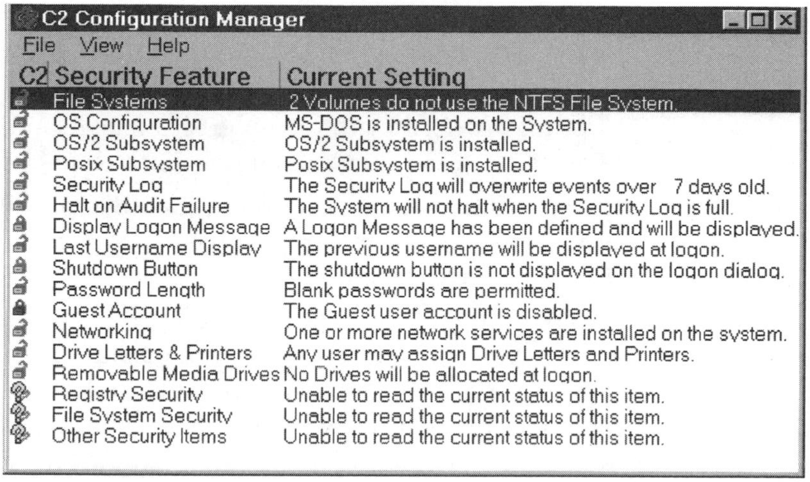

Figure 1.1
C2 configuration.

```
C2 Configuration Manager                              _ □ ×
File   View   Help
C2 Security Feature    │Current Setting
    File Systems         2 Volumes do not use the NTFS File System.
    OS Configuration     MS-DOS is installed on the System.
    OS/2 Subsystem       OS/2 Subsystem is installed.
    Posix Subsystem      Posix Subsystem is installed.
    Security Log         The Security Log will overwrite events over  7 days old.
    Halt on Audit Failure The System will not halt when the Security Log is full.
    Display Logon Message A Logon Message has been defined and will be displayed.
    Last Username Display The previous username will be displayed at logon.
    Shutdown Button      The shutdown button is not displayed on the logon dialog.
    Password Length      Blank passwords are permitted.
    Guest Account        The Guest user account is disabled.
    Networking           One or more network services are installed on the system.
    Drive Letters & Printers Any user may assign Drive Letters and Printers.
    Removable Media Drives No Drives will be allocated at logon.
    Registry Security    Unable to read the current status of this item.
    File System Security Unable to read the current status of this item.
    Other Security Items Unable to read the current status of this item.
```

Other operating systems. The C2 configuration requires that NT is the only operating system on the computer and that the boot timeout is set to 0. This allows Windows NT to start immediately without pausing for the user.

Subsystems. Because the Blue Book evaluation (for subsystems) has not yet taken place, the C2 configuration requires that the OS/2 and POSIX subsystems be removed.

Security logging. The C2 configuration requires that the security logs never overwrite events, regardless of their age. The security logs must be cleared manually by an administrator.

Halt on audit failure. The C2 configuration requires that if events cannot be written to the security log, the system should be halted immediately.

Logon warning message. Although not required for C2 compliance, it is recommended that systems display a warning message before logon, indicating the private nature of the system about to be entered.

Last username display. By default, Windows NT displays the username of the last valid user to log on to the machine. Although it is not a C2 requirement, we recommend that the previous username not be displayed.

Shutdown without logon. By default, Windows NT workstations allow the user to shut down the system without logging on. While not a C2 requirement, this is a potential security hole. Windows NT servers, on the other hand, are by default configured to not permit shutdowns without logging onto the system. See Chap. 5 for more details.

Password length.   The C2 configuration requires that blank passwords not be permitted.

Guest account.   The C2 configuration requires that the default guest account installed by the setup program be disabled. Note that in Windows NT 4.x, the Guest account is disabled by default.

Network.   Because the networking (Red Book) evaluation has yet to be completed, the C2 current configuration requires that all networking functionality be removed from the system. Obviously, this will significantly limit NT's functionality within many organizations.

Driver letters and printers.   By default, any user may assign printers and drive letters. Prudence dictates that these tasks be limited to administrators, although this is not required for C2.

Allocating removable drives.   While not required for the C2 configuration, some administrators limit users' access to removable media devices (e.g., floppy drives, CD-ROM drives).

Power-on password.   The C2 configuration requires that the system use a power-on password. The C2 manager cannot assist in setting up this configuration; it must be set in the BIOS (basic input/output system) of capable machines. This is required for the C2 configuration.

Secure system partition.   For RISC (reduced instruction set computer)-based Windows NT systems, the administrator should secure the system partition. This is required for the C2 configuration.

User Manager for Domains.   The User Manager for Domains is intended for Windows NT networks; the User Manager is intended for standalone Windows NT systems. Because the Red Book evaluation is not yet complete, the User Manager for Domains should be replaced by the standard User Manager. This is required for the C2 configuration.

Finally, Microsoft also includes with the C2 Configuration Manager a series of text files which describe the ACL activities performed by the C2 manager. The file C3REGACL.TXT describes the registry ACLs which are required for C2 compliance; note that these may be modified in the text file in order to make changes using the C2 manager. Doing so, however, will obviously mean that the configuration no longer conforms to the tested C2 configuration. The same holds true with respect to the file C2NTFA-CL.TXT for file system ACLs.

CHAPTER 2

Managing User Security

Three may keep a secret, if two of them are dead.
—*Benjamin Franklin, 1735*

Effectively managing the user security of a Windows NT system is perhaps one of the most important of the skills NT administrators must master. Indeed, few factors contribute as directly to the overall security of the Windows NT system as does user security.

Fortunately, Microsoft has provided excellent tools for managing user accounts, rights, and relationships. These tools are equally effective for 1, 10, or 10,000. Unlike some other operating systems which require the administrator to memorize obscure commands and manually edit configuration files, the Windows NT user management system is completely graphics. In keeping with the point-and-click design of the rest of the operating system, the User Manager allows first-time users to quickly understand and appreciate the breadth of choices available to NT administrators.

User Manager and User Manager for Domains

The User Manager and User Manager for Domains are the primary user configuration tools in Windows NT. User Manager for Domains is used only in a Windows NT server environment in which there is an active NT domain; in all other cases, the standard User Manager should be used.

By default, the User Manager is found in the *Administrative Tools* group within the *Programs* choice in the Start menu. By default, the User Manager main screen is divided into two major windows, as shown in Fig. 2.1:

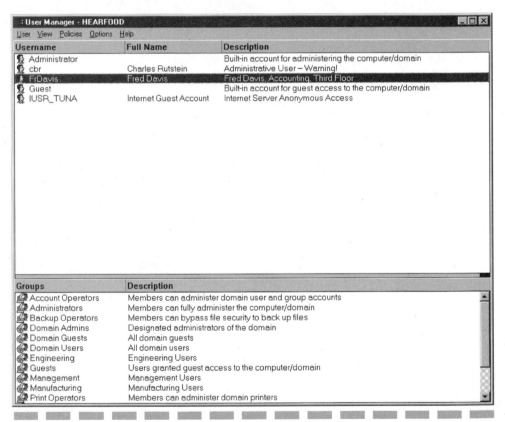

Figure 2.1   The User Manager main screen.

The top window shows a list of all user accounts currently known to the Security Account Manager (SAM). In the case of the User Manager, this view represents the SAM on the local machine; in the case of the User Manager for Domains, it represents the SAM on the primary or backup domain controller.

This top window shows the username in addition to other background information about the user. Because some organizations have username standards that are difficult to translate into real names, this screen may be very useful for some administrators. For example, consider the following view of the User Manager in Fig. 2.2:

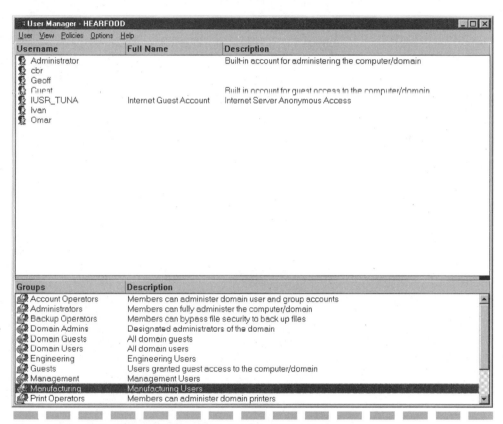

Figure 2.2   Descriptive fields within the User Manager.

In this example, the username FrDav tells us little about the user. The full-name column, however, shows us the full name of the user (Fred Davis). Finally, the description field tells us that the user is Fred Davis, who works in accounting on the third floor. We recommend that administrators use these descriptive fields for all users; one of the most common security blunders is to assign incorrect rights to a user due to a mistake in identifying usernames. The use of these fields will help reduce this potential security risk.

Groups and Group Descriptions

The bottom window shows all the valid group names into which users may be grouped. In the case of the standard User Manager, these are all local groups; in the case of the User Manager for Domains, these groups exist at the domain level.

Much like the top window, the lower window has a field for group description. Once again, we strongly encourage the use of the group description in order to reduce the chance of administrative mistakes. The group description should indicate to the administrator the general security rights which are granted to that group.

The descriptions of the default groups may or may not be sufficient for some administrators. For example, the default group "Domain Administrators" contains a description which reads "Designated Administrators of the Domain." Many administrators will want to flag this group with a more descriptive header, such as "Warning! Members of this group will have significant security rights!"

User Manager for Domains

Unlike the standard User Manager, the User Manager for Domains can be used to administer a large number of accounts across a range of domains. Selecting the User menu and the *Select Domain* option allows administrators to select the domain they want to administer.

Note that only one domain can be administered at a time from a single instance of User Manager for Domains. However, multiple instances of the manager can be opened concurrently, allowing the administrator to examine and administer users in several domains simultaneously. This is useful for administrators who must maintain several different domains, each with different sets of users. In fact, a single administrator at a single NT workstation could potentially administer all users across an entire enterprise.

Of course, this functionality brings with it the potential for a security breach. Administrators should keep in mind the fact that all Windows NT users by default have a copy of the User Manager on their desktop, although NT security prevents them from operations beyond their level of security.

Groups

The notion of groups in Windows NT is much like that in other operating systems. Rather than set user and file rights for each and every user, the administrator can give rights to various groups, then place users within those groups. Each user within a group inherits the rights associated with that group.

In Windows NT parlance, the *group* is a container object; the users associated with that group are user objects which reside in the container. In many cases, users will be members of multiple groups.

Unfortunately, this can lead to confusing situations if a user is a member of multiple groups with conflicting security rights. In such a case, administrators should be aware that groups which explicitly deny rights are usually processed first; therefore, if a user is a member of a group which is explicitly denied access to a particular resource, any request to use that resource is likely to be denied. This denial will occur regardless of the users' membership in other groups which may explicitly allow access.

Groups also exist within a specific context. On a standalone Windows NT workstation, the groups exist within the local context; they are therefore termed *local groups*. In a Windows NT domain environment, however, groups may be created in the domain context. These groups, then, are available to all users in the domain, regardless of where the user resides. These groups are termed, rather unimaginatively, *domain groups*.

By default, the Windows NT setup program creates several groups. Each is designed to perform some particular system function. The groups installed by default are listed in the following table.

Group Name	Description
Account Operators	The Account Operators group exists only on Windows NT servers acting as primary or backup domain controllers. Members of this group can administer both user and group accounts for systems and domains. No users are placed into the Account Operators group by default.

(*continued on next page*)

Group Name	Description
	The rights granted to Account Operators include the rights to create, modify, and delete all accounts, except those accounts which were created by members of the Administrators group. Also, Account Operators can modify or delete all global groups, except for those described below. However, Account Operators cannot assign user rights directly.
	In addition, Account Operators may not modify groups with higher or different security privileges, such as the Administrators, Server Operators, Account Operators, Print Operators, and Backup Operators groups.
	Finally, Account Operators in a domain environment have the right to log on locally at server consoles, to add computers to the domain, and to shut down servers from the server console.
Administrators	Administrators represent the highest authority within the Windows NT hierarchy. The Administrators group exists on all Windows NT systems, including workstations and servers.
	The administrators have all rights granted to them (or have the ability to grant them to themselves). This includes everything from creating, deleting, and modifying users to locking, shutting down, and reconfiguring servers.
	Unlike some other operating systems, however, Administrators do not, by default, have access to all files. Rather, they have the ability to take ownership of all files; once this takes place, they may grant themselves rights to the files. However, they cannot do so without alerting the original owner of the file. This is because the right to take ownership of a file does not grant the right to *assign* ownership of the file to another user. Therefore, an administrator could take ownership of a user's file in order to access it, but could not then reassign ownership rights back to that user.
	Because accounts in the Administrators group are so powerful, we recommend that they be limited to a few trusted personnel. By default, the Administrator account is a member of the Administrators group.

(continued on next page)

Group Name	Description
Backup Operators	Backup operators represent a curious security hole in the Windows NT operating system. Although Windows NT has no "superuser" with default access to all resources, most users and administrators are aware that the Administrator account is privileged with taking ownership of resources at any time, and therefore, of obtaining access to them. Few users or administrators, however, are aware that backup operators are nearly as powerful in a certain respect: backup operators are effectively able to read and write to any file in the system, regardless of the rights assigned to it.
	The Backup Operators group is found on all Windows NT workstations and servers. No users are added to this group by default. Users in the Backup Operators group are empowered to back up and restore any file in the system, regardless of the ACLs which protect those files.
	In addition, backup operators may also shut down the system from a system console, log onto a server console, and maintain a local profile.
Domain Admins	The Domain Admins group exists on Windows NT Servers functioning as either primary or backup domain controllers. Members of this group function as administrators for the entire domain.
	User accounts with membership in the Domain Admins group should be extremely carefully controlled; they are among the most powerful in the entire Windows NT hierarchy. By default, the Domain Admins group contains the Administrator account for the domain controller.
Domain Guests	Domain guests are found only on Windows NT servers which are acting as either primary or backup domain controllers. Members of this group have extremely limited privileges—like the guest account, they have only the right to log onto the system. In this case, however, interactive logons are not permitted; all access by domain guests must be across the network.
	By default, the guest account on the domain controller is a member of this group. For optimal security, we recommend that the Domain Guests group and the guest accounts be disabled.

(*continued on next page*)

Group Name	Description
Domain Users	Domain users are only found on servers which are acting as primary or backup domain controllers. The Domain Users group is similar to the Guests group in that it provides a very low level of access to the system.
Guests	The Guests group has a very limited set of functionality, which is less than that found in the Users group. Guests are permitted only to log on locally or via the network to a workstation or via the network to a server. They are not, by default, permitted to log into a server from the console. By default, the Guest account is a member of the Guests group. For optimal security, we recommend that both the Guest account and the Guests group be removed from the system.
Power Users	The Power Users group exists only on Windows NT workstations and Windows NT servers which are not acting as either primary or backup domain controllers.
	Members of the Power Users group have rights which are a slight superset of the Users group. In addition to all the rights granted to Users (log on, lock, shut down, maintain profile, etc.), members of the Power Users group are permitted to manage user accounts which they create. Moreover, they are permitted to create, delete, and modify shares for both directories and printers, and are able to move users into and out of the Power Users, Users, and Guests groups. By default, there are no user accounts which are members of the Power Users group.
Print Operators	The Print Operators group is found only on Windows NT servers which are acting as primary or backup domain controllers. By default, no users are added to this group. Members of this group may create new shares for printers, may delete shares for existing printers, and can change the parameters of existing printer shares.
	Members of the Print Operators group are also empowered to log on locally to workstations and servers, shut down systems from the system console, and maintain a local profile.
Replicator	The Replicator group exists on all Windows NT servers and workstations. By default, no users are members of the Replicator group.

(continued on next page)

Group Name	Description
	Members of the Replicator group are permitted to replicate files within directories with other authorized systems. To do so, they are granted the advanced system right to log on as a service. Because accounts which are capable of logging on as a service may be extremely powerful, accounts in this group should be strictly limited in number.
Server Operators	The Server Operators group exists only on Windows NT servers which are acting as primary or backup domain controllers. By default, no users are placed in the Server Operators group. Server Operators can perform nearly all server management tasks with the exception of modifying the system security policies and starting or stopping services. These tasks are reserved for members of the Administrators group. Server Operators are permitted to log on to server consoles, back up and restore files (see discussion above on backup operators), lock the server console, and shut down the server from the console. In addition, Server Operators may create, modify, and remove both printer shares and disk shares, and may format the server disks. Finally, Server Operators may also change the system time. *Accounts in the Server Operators group should be carefully controlled.*
Users	The Users group exists on all Windows NT workstations and servers. All users of the respective systems should be members of this group. On Windows NT workstations, there are no users who are assigned to this group by default. On Windows NT servers acting as primary or backup domain controllers, the Domain Users group and the Administrator account are default members of the Users group. The rights assigned to members of the Users group are dependent on whether the system in question is acting as a domain server or is an NT workstation. On NT Servers acting as domain controllers, members of the Users group are not permitted to log on to the console. They are permitted, however, to log onto the server across the network.

(continued on next page)

Group Name	Description
	On Windows NT workstations, members of the Users group are permitted to log into the console, maintain a local profile, lock the workstation, and shut down the workstation from the console. In addition, members on NT workstations may create and delete local groups on their particular workstation.

We recommend that administrators use both the groups which are built into NT as well as those of their own construction in order to provide group-based rights for as many users as possible. While there are likely to be some users who must be managed individually (i.e., outside the groups), the number of these users should be minimized.

System Groups

The groups listed above are those groups which are created by the system on setup. Other groups, however, exist but are not displayed from within User Manager. These so-called system or special groups are created automatically by the system. Some are available to administrators when assigning rights to resources; others are not.

Group Name	Description
Interactive	The Interactive group has as its members all users who log onto a Windows NT system locally (at the console). It does not include users who connect to NT servers across a network or are started as a server.
Network	The Network group has as its members all users who connect to Windows NT resources across a network. It does not include users who connect to NT resources through an interactive logon.
Creator/Owner	The Creator/Owner group is created for each sharable resource in the Windows NT system. Its membership is the set of users who either create a resource (such as a file) and those who take ownership of them. It is especially useful for setting access rights to files; using the Creator/Owner group, a directory owner can allow users to create files inside the directory, then retain ownership and full control of them.

(continued on next page)

Group Name	Description
Everyone	Another standard group which will appear regularly is not listed in the User Manager. This group is called *Everyone* and has as its members all users who access the system, whether locally, remotely via the Remote-Access Service, or across a network. It is not possible to create a user who does not have membership in the Everyone group. As a result, the Everyone group can be quite useful for setting systemwide policy and rights. For example, an administrator might wish to share a directory of common help files with everyone in the system. By sharing the directory and granting access rights to the Everyone group, all current and future users will be able to access the files.

Administrators should be aware that, by default, *Windows NT assigns full control rights to the Everyone group for all new file shares.* This means that until the administrator makes explicit security settings for file shares, all users will have full read, write, modify, delete, etc., rights to the files. Administrators must always be cognizant of the risks of this default; and we believe that Microsoft should change this default for all future releases. Although Microsoft has been aware of this problem since the first release of NT, there has been no effort to change the default.

Account Policies

By selecting the *Policies* menu, then the *Account* option within the User Manager, administrators may set account policy for the system or domain in which they are working. These account policies apply to all users within the system or domain. (See Fig. 2.3).

The system account policy choices available to administrators are described in the following paragraphs.

MAXIMUM PASSWORD AGE. With this option, administrators may choose how often users' passwords will expire. On expiration, users will be forced to choose another password before they can continue to use the system. One choice for this option is "Password Never Expires." *We strongly recommend against this choice; instead, we recommend that passwords be set to expire about every 45 days.* For more information about passwords, see section on user security risks below.

Figure 2.3
The Account option
under the Policies
menu.

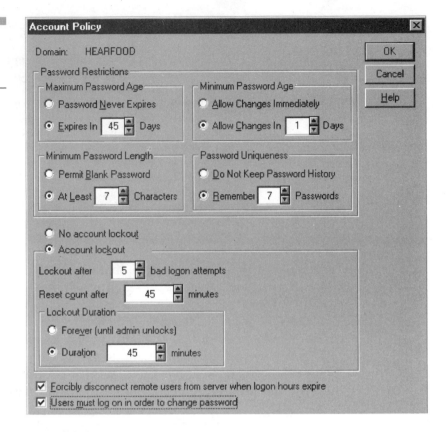

MINIMUM PASSWORD AGE. The Minimum Password Age option allows administrators to limit the frequency of password changes. Because most administrators would like to prevent users from using the same passwords over again in a short period of time, this option will help prevent password overuse. We recommend that administrators set the minimum age to 1 day.

MINIMUM PASSWORD LENGTH. Password length is a critical factor in determining the overall security of password-based security. For proper security, we recommend passwords of at least six or seven characters; longer passwords are even more attractive. The Account Policies dialog box permits a policy entitled "Permit Blank Password." *This is an unnecessary security risk and should never be used. All accounts should be forced to have a password of at least six or seven characters.*

PASSWORD UNIQUENESS. This option allows administrators to limit users' ability to reuse the same passwords time after time. NT supports a password history of up to 24 passwords. We strongly recommend that NT be set to remember and disallow the use of six to eight previous passwords. We do not recommend disabling the Password Uniqueness Setting.

ACCOUNT LOCKOUT. The Account Lockout features function as an ever-present watchdog. Because administrators cannot be present to monitor the security logs at all times, Windows NT provides the ability to lock out accounts for repeated logon failures. Once locked out, the administrator may decide whether the account will be reinstated after some measured period of time or must be manually unlocked by the administrator.

We recommend that the Account Lockout feature be used by all Windows NT systems. Accounts should be locked out after five failed logon attempts, and should be locked out for at least 45 min. The failed logon count should be reset every 45 min, as well.

These recommended settings provide a scenario in which it is not possible to attempt more than five unsuccessful logon attempts within 45 min. All failed logon attempts should be audited and reported in the security event log.

Note that we strongly recommend against locking out accounts indefinitely. Doing so opens up the system to denial-of-service attacks in which an attacker may purposely create multiple failed logon attempts for large numbers of users. This would effectively limit the ability of these users to use the system until the administrator unlocked the accounts manually.

Note that regardless of the system security policy settings, *the Administrator account is the only account which is not bound by the Account Lockout policy.* Put another way, it is impossible for the Administrator account to be locked out as a result of failed password attempts. Unfortunately, this means that while denial of service attacks are impossible against the Administrator account, the account is vulnerable to brute-force password guessing.

FORCIBLY DISCONNECT USERS. This option permits administrators to disconnect those users who are still logged into NT during system lockout hours. This is a useful option for those administrators who wish to keep everyone off the system while batch processes (e.g., system backups) are taking place. For organizations that do not require round-the-clock access for users, we recommend that users be locked out during the backup time period (often early morning). Users should be forcibly disconnected at the beginning of that period. For organizations which operate 24 hours a day, however, such a configuration is obviously unfeasible.

LOGON TO CHANGE PASSWORD. This option designates whether users must log into the system before changing their password. If this setting is enabled, users must first log into the NT system before changing their password. If their password expires, they must contact an administrator to change the password. We recommend that users be required to log into the system before changing their passwords in all NT implementations. Although this configuration setting may increase the administrative load for system administrators (especially on weekends!), it also provides a greater degree of security.

Audit Policy

For information and recommended settings for audit policy, please refer to Chapter 4, *Security Logging and Auditing*.

Creating a User

This section will step the reader through creating a user in a Windows NT system. Figure 2.4 represents the User Manager for Domains on a Windows NT server. The procedure is identical, however, on Windows NT Workstations or Servers running the standard User Manager.

In order to create a user, first launch the User Manager. By default, the User Manager icon resides in the *Administrative Tools* group within the *Programs* option in the Start menu. Then, select the *New User* option from the *User* menu. This will bring up a dialog box similar to that shown in Fig. 2.4.

There are several fields of this dialog box which are required. The first, of course, is the username for the new user account. Note that at the time of logon, usernames are not case-sensitive. When viewing the username via NT standard tools, however, the case entered here will be displayed.

The next two fields, Full Name and Description, are not required. We highly recommend, however, that administrators take advantage of these fields in order to more closely identify users. This helps reduce the poten-

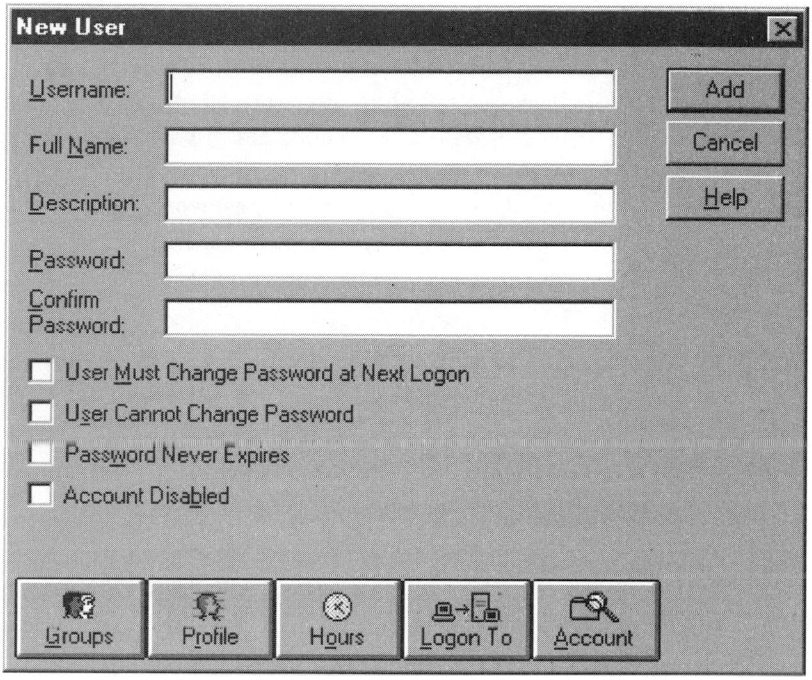

Figure 2.4
The User Manager
for Domains.

New User

Username:	
Full Name:	
Description:	
Password:	
Confirm Password:	

[ ] User Must Change Password at Next Logon
[ ] User Cannot Change Password
[ ] Password Never Expires
[ ] Account Disabled

Add   Cancel   Help

Groups   Profile   Hours   Logon To   Account

tial for administrative mistakes in the future and the potential security risks associated with them.

The following two fields contain the password for the user. When initially creating an account, many administrators choose to assign a password in order to provide security until users can choose their own. Like most other operating systems, NT requests that you type the password twice to limit the risk of a typing error. Note that when typing the password into the User Manager, the characters will not be displayed on the screen. Rather, they are replaced by asterisks, much as they are when you initially log onto NT.

Also, note that the length of the password is not necessarily indicated by the number of asterisks. In order to help hide the password, NT does not indicate the number of characters in the password to casual observers. You will see the number of asterisks displayed change after you create the user.

Next, the dialog box contains four checkboxes. The first indicates that the users must change their passwords at the next logon. When these users log on, NT will notify them and prompt them for a new password. It will not let them proceed without picking a new password. This function is often useful for administrators creating new accounts.

The second checkbox indicates whether users are permitted to change their passwords. In some circumstances, such as when a number of users are sharing a single user account, the administrator might not wish to allow the users to change the password. In our view, allowing multiple users to use a single account limits the administrator's ability to maintain accurate audit trails. Hence, we do not recommend this practice.

The third checkbox indicates that the users' passwords should never expire. *Because passwords provide such poor security, we recommend that this option never be used.* All users should be required to change their passwords on a regular basis—thus limiting the potential for unauthorized access. For more information on password weaknesses, refer to the section on user security risks in this chapter.

The final checkbox indicates whether the account is temporarily disabled. This is a useful function when a user will not be able to access the system for a long period of time (e.g., an extended vacation). By disabling the account, the administrator can reduce the chance of that account being hacked while not in legitimate use.

Moreover, some administrators choose to disable the accounts of users with excessive security violations. This forces the user to contact the administrator in order to have the account reinstated.

Group Assignment

Below these checkboxes are buttons which enable the administrator to assign further rights to the user. The first button is labeled *Groups*. Pressing this button will bring up a dialog box with two listboxes.

The first represents the groups of which the user is already a member; the second shows the groups of which the user is not a member. The administrator may choose to add or remove the user to or from a group with the *Add* and *Remove* buttons. Finally, the bottom of the dialog box contains a button which permits the administrator to assign the user's primary group.

The primary group is used when a user logs into a Windows NT system using the NT services for Macintosh, or when a user utilizes the POSIX subsystem. Note that users may not be removed from their primary groups.

Assigning Profile Logon Scripts and Home Directories

The second button on the New User dialog box is labeled *Profile*. This button allows the administrator to set up the user's personal profile, logon script, home directory, and drives to connect on logon. Consider the following choices available.

PROFILE. Windows NT supports individual user profiles for most users. These profiles contain information on the user's system preferences when logging into NT interactively or across a network from a Windows NT workstation.

Profiles can be useful for securing Windows NT workstations in that administrators can configure centralized profiles with environmental restrictions placed on them. These profiles can then be assigned to users as they log into a Windows NT domain from Windows NT workstations.

The specific user settings that are saved in the user profile are listed in the following table.

NT Object	Description
Control Panel	The user profile contains all user-definable settings for those control panel applets which support end-user configuration. This includes mouse, screen colors, cursors, sound, and international settings. In addition, the profile stores all user environment settings.
DOS Command Prompt	The user profile contains all user-definable settings for the DOS command prompt, including buffer settings, fonts, and colors.
File Manager	The user profile contains all the user-definable settings in the File Manager, including network drive mappings.
Help System Bookmarks	The user profile contains all the bookmarks that the user places in the Windows NT help system.
Print Manager	The user profile may contain all the user's settings in the Print Manager, including network printer connections.

(continued on next page)

NT Object	Description
Program Manager	The user profile contains all the user-definable settings in Program Manager (or Desktop and Start menu), including the user's personal program groups and icon layout.
Third-Party Applications	The user profile may contain information on Third-Party Applications, if the applications were written to support user profiles.

Note that the use of mandatory profiles in a Windows NT domain environment can help enforce restrictions on users' freedom within their own workstations. For example, some administrators may wish to restrict users from making changes to the group files on their desktops. Alternately, an administrator might wish to disallow any changes to the properties of common icons; this might help limit the possibility of a user unknowingly executing a trojan horse program. Each of these settings is possible by making the appropriate changes to the file manager (through the Registry Editor), then saving the user's profile on the domain controller.

LOGON SCRIPT. In Windows NT, unlike in Novell's NetWare, logon scripts are external executable files which are executed on user logon. These files may be batch files, .CMD files, or standard executables. Administrators should be aware that there is significant potential for system penetration if the right to assign logon scripts is compromised. In such a case (such as when an intruder user gains control of an Administrator class), the attacker could conceivably set any file to be executed on the logon of any user, including a user in the Administrators group. At that time, the file would run with the privileges of that administrator— and the audit trail would lead back to that user, not the real attacker. We recommend that accounts with the ability to change this parameter (see discussion of user rights below) be very strictly protected.

HOME DIRECTORY. The home directory is the user's main location for storing data on an NT workstation or server. All users should be granted Full Control rights to their respective directories; all others should have no rights to that directory. We recommend that directory rights be checked carefully before assigning home directories in this dialog box.

NetWare Note

How does the NT logon script compare with a NetWare login script? What does this have to do with denial-of-service attacks?

In both operating systems, scripts processed at login can run any type of executable file. These are almost identical, with one significant exception—it is not possible for a user to log into NetWare from the console. Therefore, it is not possible to start a process which runs on the console of the server (using server CPU and memory resources). There is not necessarily any prohibition against login on an NT system console, so users are able to start processes which use CPU and memory resources on the server itself.

It's not possible for a user to deny service on NetWare by consuming all of the CPU, because users cannot allocate CPU time. This is a risk under NT if users are allowed to log in at the system console.

Like NetWare, it is possible for an ordinary NT user to create a denial-of-service attack by consuming all the disk resources. While NetWare allows a certain level of control through disk space restrictions, this is not possible through NT because NT does not support disk quotas.

A denial-of-service attack is possible under most operating systems by filling the print queues with huge print jobs that fill the spool directories if the spool directory is on the same file system as the system files.

If the system file systems (root, %SystemRoot%, and SYS:) are filled up, Unix, NT, and NetWare all behave unpredictably, right up to the point where they crash. It's a good idea to locate the spool directories on a volume other than the system partition, or perhaps on a dedicated volume.

Another thing to think about is the unintentional denial-of-service attack created by a user who likes the OpenGL screen savers. These screen savers, and others like them, consume huge amounts of CPU power to rasterize the three-dimensional images for the screen saver. This is not typically an issue on an end-user machine, but on the console, it can bring your server to its knees.

Note that in a Windows NT network, home directories may exist either on the local disk or on a network server. Either may be assigned through the User Environment Profile dialog box.

Assigning Time and Station Restrictions

The next button on the New User dialog box, *Hours,* allows the administrator to assign restrictions on the hours which the user is allowed to use the system. Many administrators choose to limit users' access to the system during batch processes such as backups, which often occur during the early-morning hours.

Note that simply limiting users' logon hours in this dialog box will not necessarily limit their ability to use the system during off-hours. Rather, this box controls only hours permitted for logons. In order to actually remove previously logged-in users from the system during off-hours, administrators must click the appropriate checkbox in the Account Policies dialog box. For more information on this option, refer to discussion of account policies above.

The next button in sequence—available only on Windows NT systems acting in a Windows NT domain—allows the administrator to limit the user to specific workstations. The administrator may choose to allow access via all workstations (the default choice), or may identify between one and eight specific workstations which are acceptable. The names of these workstations must be placed in the boxes on this dialog box.

Note, however, that this is not a foolproof security restriction. Names are assigned in Windows NT networks on a first-come first-served basis. Therefore, a user may rename any computer with any other name, assuming that the new name has not yet been registered on the network. As a result, administrators should not rely on this function for realistic security.

Account Expiration

The final button in the window allows the administrator to enter two further pieces of data: when the account should expire, and whether the account is intended for local or domain use (only in Windows NT domain environments). With regard to account expiration, we recommend that administrators use the expiration fields when possible. Although the default is for the account to never expire, there are many circumstances under which the administrator might wish for an account to expire.

For example, consider the case of temporary workers within an organization. An administrator might assign valid user accounts to temporary workers in order to grant them rights and audit their activities, but would want to limit their accounts over time. In this case, the administrator could set a date for the account's expiration.

On the right side of the dialog box are two radio buttons. These allow the administrator to choose whether the account is a Global or a Local user account. Most user accounts within a domain are termed *Global* accounts—these are accounts which allow authentication and authorization throughout approved computers across the domain. This is the default setting for all new accounts in an NT domain environment. *Local* accounts, on the other hand, are intended for users from other, untrusted domains.

Note that local accounts may be used to access domain resources across a network; they may not, however, be used to log directly into Windows NT systems within the domain. Moreover, local accounts created within a domain cannot be used within other trusting domains.

User Rights (Standard and Advanced)

This section documents all the rights—both standard and advanced—which may be assigned to users. Administrators should be familiar with these user rights; the correct assignment of these rights will have an enormous impact on the overall security of a Windows NT implementation. The following table lists the NT user rights.

User Right	Type of Right	Description
Access computer from the network	Standard	This right allows users to access NT resources over a network. By default, this right is assigned to the Everyone, Administrators, and Power Users groups.
Act as part of the operating system (SeTcpPrivilege)	Advanced	This right is one of the most powerful in the NT hierarchy. It permits the user to act as a trusted portion of the operating system and therefore be granted all rights to the system. By default, this right is assigned to only some of the Windows NT subsystems. We strongly recommend against granting this right to any user.
Add workstations to the domain (SeMachineAccount Privilege)	Standard	This right is required at a domain level to add a new machine to that domain.
Back up files and directories (SeBackup Privilege)	Standard	This right permits users to circumvent the file access restrictions present on Windows NTFS disk drives for the purposes of backup and restore. *This right should be granted only when there is a clear need for it; even then, it should be limited to only a few trusted users.* Although users with this right cannot read the files they back up directly, they can move those files to another system in order to access them. As a result, this is one of the most powerful rights in the system. By default, this right is granted to Administrators, Backup Operators, and Server Operators (on Windows NT servers acting as domain controllers). See companion right, *restore files and directories* entry later in this table.
Bypass traverse checking (SeChangeNotify Privilege)	Advanced	In most cases, rights to files and subdirectories flow downward; that is, users who do not have rights to a specific directory will also not have rights to

(continued on next page)

User Right	Type of Right	Description
		traverse the subdirectories below that directory. The Bypass Traverse Checking user right allows a user to traverse subdirectories, even if that user has no rights to the parent directories. While the use of this option may complicate an administrator's understanding of how security rights flow within the system, it is useful for certain situations.
		Note that removing this right will limit functionality, but will simplify security. By default, this right is granted to Everyone.
Change the system time (`SeSystemTime Privilege`)	Standard	This right allows the user to set the NT system time. Because NT provides extensive logging capabilities, having the correct system time is important to providing an accurate audit trail. Without an accurate time benchmark, other security functionality (e.g., account lockout) may be adversely affected. By default, this right is granted to Administrators on Windows NT workstations and servers and Power Users on NT workstations.
Create a page file (`SeCreatePagefile Privilege`)	Advanced	This user right is designed to permit users to create page files within a Windows NT system. *In our experience, however, this right is not required to create a page file.* By default, this right is granted to members of the Administrators group. Note that this right has been made obsolete in the latest version of NT.
Create a token object	Advanced	This right permits the user (or process) to create security access tokens. There should be no reason for any user to have this right.
		In most organizations, this right should never be assigned to any user. By default, no users are granted this right.

(*continued on next page*)

User Right	Type of Right	Description
Create permanent shared objects (`SeCreate Permanent Privilege`)	Advanced	This right allows users to create special permanent shared resources. These include resources which represent system devices (`\\Device`) which are used by Windows NT. By default, this right is not granted to any user or group. However, administrators need not have this right.
Debug Programs	Advanced	The Debug Programs user right allows users to do extremely low-level (process/thread) debugging of executable code running on Windows NT. This right is extremely powerful and should be protected accordingly. By default, this right is granted to members of the Administrators group.
Force shutdown from a remote system (`SeRemoteShutdown Privilege`)	Standard	This right is designed to allow users to shut down a Windows NT system remotely. It has no effect, however, in the current releases of Windows NT. By default, this right is granted to Administrators on Windows NT workstations and servers and to Power Users on Windows NT workstations.
Increase Quotas (`SeIncreaseQuota Privilege`)	Advanced	This user right allows users to increase the object quotas. It is available only in the latest release of Windows NT Server. By default, this right is granted only to Administrators.
Increase scheduling priority (`SeIncrease BasePriority Privilege`)	Advanced	This right allows users to increase the processor priority of a given process. Mostly used for tuning, this right has few direct security—but many system performance—implications. It could, however, be used in a denial of service attack. It should be given only to those users who have a need to tune the Windows NT system. By default, this right is granted to Administrators on Windows NT servers and workstations and Power Users on Windows NT workstations.

(continued on next page)

User Right	Type of Right	Description
Load and unload device drivers (SeLoadDriver Privilege)	Advanced	This user right allows the user to load and unload device drivers from memory. Administrators should be aware that device drivers have no security restrictions placed on them and thus may be used in an attack against NT security. As a result, we recommend that the right to load and unload device drivers be limited only to fully trusted users. By default, this right is granted only to members of the Administrators group.
Lock pages in memory (SeLock MemoryPrivilege)	Advanced	This right allows users to make their allocated physical RAM (random-access memory) unmovable. This means that their data cannot be swapped out to a page file on disk (PAGEFILE.SYS). While there are few direct security implications of this user right, there are significant performance implications. For example, if users are permitted to lock large blocks of physical memory, the system will begin to thrash its disks as it is forced to swap into smaller and smaller quantities of physical memory. By default, no users are granted this right.
Log on as a batch job	Advanced	This user right allows a user to log on using a batch queue facility. It is not supported in the current releases of Windows NT server or workstation. By default, this right is granted only to administrators.
Log on as a service	Advanced	This right allows a user to log on as a service. In Windows NT, services are background processes that run without direct user supervision. Administrators should note that services can be extremely powerful; those that run under the system account have almost full control of the system.

(continued on next page)

User Right	Type of Right	Description
		Few, if any, users should ever need this right. Because of the potential for security risks, we recommend that this right not be assigned to users. By default, no users are granted the log on as a service right.
		When using services, however, it pays to ensure that the user accounts under which services run are limited in scope and privilege. We strongly recommend that administrators keep a close watch on the user accounts used by third-party services.
Log on locally	Standard	This user right allows users to log onto a Windows NT system interactively at the console. By default, this right is granted to Administrators and Backup Operators on both Windows NT workstations and servers.
		In addition, it is granted to Server Operators, Account Operators, and Print Operators on NT servers and to Power Users, Users, and Guests on NT workstations.
Manage auditing and security log (SeSecurity Privilege)	Standard	This user right allows users to identify the types of user access which should be audited. In addition, this right grants the privilege of viewing and clearing the security log. Note that when the security log is cleared, an unremovable entry is placed in the new log.
		This right does not, however, give full authority to set the systemwide auditing policy.
		By default, members of the Administrators group are granted this right. However, this right is not required for members of the Administrators group to view and clear the security audit event log.

(continued on next page)

User Right	Type of Right	Description
Modify firmware environment (`SeSystem Environment Privilege`)	Advanced	This user right allows the user to modify the system environment variables. These variables affect the executables which are executed when users call a particular filename. Therefore, this right is quite powerful, in that an attacker could use the right to change the system path to point to a trojan horse program. As a result, this user right should be strictly limited to those users with a specific need for it. By default, this right is granted only to members of the Administrators group.
Profile single process (`SeProfSingle Process`)	Advanced	This user right allows users to use Windows NT's performance monitoring tools in order to monitor the performance of a single process. By default, this right is granted to Administrators on Windows NT workstations and servers and Power Users on Windows NT workstations.
Profile system performance (`SeSystemProfile Privilege`)	Advanced	This user right allows users to monitor the performance of an entire Windows NT system using NT's monitoring tools. By default, this right is granted to members of the Administrators group.
Replace a process-level token (`SeAssignPrimary TokenPrivilege`)	Advanced	This right enables the user to replace the security access token used by a process with another. Windows NT for provides mechanisms regulating this process through the OS; as a result, users should never have to access this right directly. Administrators should be aware that granting this right to a user may seriously compromise the security of the entire Windows NT system. *We strongly recommend that this right not be assigned to any user.* By default, this right is not assigned to any user or group.

(continued on next page)

User Right	Type of Right	Description
Restore files and directories	Standard	This right is a companion right to the *back up files and directories* right. It is perhaps slightly more sensitive than the backup right, but still must be protected. We recommend that only a small number of users who require this functionality be granted this right. By default, the *restore files and directories* right is granted to Administrators and Backup Operators.
Shut down the system (SeShutdown Privilege)	Standard	This user right allows the user to shut down the system from the system con sole. By default, this right is granted to Administrators, Backup Operators, Everyone, Power Users, and Users. *We strongly recommend that on Windows NT servers, this right be restricted to Administrators and Backup Operators.* On Windows NT workstations, this right might also be extended to Power Users. In either case, we recommend that this right be removed from the Everyone and the Users groups.
Take ownership of files or other objects (SeTakeOwnership Privilege)	Standard	This permission gives users the right to take control of any object in the system. These objects may include files, directories, printers, processes, and threads. As a result, this is one of the most powerful user rights which may be granted. *We strongly recommend that this user right never be given to any user outside of the administrators group.* Although the exercise of this right may be audited, granting this right is akin to handing over all system rights to a user. By default, only members of the administrators group on both NT workstations and servers are permitted this right.

Assigning User Rights

Note that the preceding table lists both standard and advanced user rights. Both can be assigned using the User Manager (or User Manager for Domains). In order to assign specific rights to a user, first launch the User Manager. Then, from within the User Manager, select the *User Rights* option from the *Policies* menu. This option enables the administrator to assign either standard or advanced user rights, depending on the value of the checkbox at the bottom of the dialog box, as seen in Fig. 2.6.

Figure 2.6
Assigning user rights.

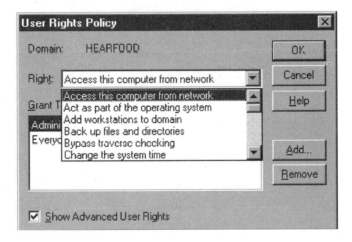

Note that the standard user rights are always displayed in this dialog box; clicking the checkbox marked "Show advanced user rights" will add the advanced user rights to the list.

In order to change the assignments of user rights for a user, you must first select the user right you wish to assign. Thus, user rights are assigned by first selecting the right, then identifying the users who should be granted or denied that right. Administrators should note that this process is counterintuitive and is, in fact, the reverse of the rest of the user management procedures. In assigning groups membership, for example, Windows NT allows you to select a user, then specify the groups of which the user is a member.

Of course, performing the user rights procedure in this way does have a side benefit: it's tough to quickly grant all rights to a given user. Therefore, administrators are less tempted to do so, and those attempting to intrude on the system will not be able to do so quickly. Let's consider an example in which we wish to assign the advanced user right Change System Time to user SuzanneU.

Once the User Rights Policy dialog box is displayed, click the checkbox at the bottom of the box to display the advanced user rights. Then, select the Change System Time option from the pull-down listbox. The lower portion of the dialog box then displays the users who have been granted this right. In order to add SuzanneU, we should then click the button marked *Add....* This brings up the Add Users and Groups dialog box. From within this dialog box, we may select users and groups who should be assigned the Change System Time user right.

In many cases, we will want to assign system rights to groups of users, to allow for easier administration of large systems. In this case, however, we wish only to grant the right to SuzanneU. Therefore, we must first press the button marked *Show Users*. This will add the list of valid usernames to the top scrollbox. Then, we can select SuzanneU from that list and click the *Add* button in the middle of the dialog box.

This will add SuzanneU to the list of users (displayed at the bottom of the dialog box) who have been granted the Change System Time advanced user right. Finally, click *OK* in the User Rights Policy dialog box, and the change is complete.

User Security Risks

This section presents some of the outstanding risks to user security. Although some of these risks have been noted above, this section provides a deeper understanding of the potential security risks associated with various policy settings and user rights.

Passwords

By default, the standard identification for a Windows NT user includes a username and associated password. Unfortunately, passwords are notoriously insecure. Some of the problems encountered with passwords are as follows:

Poor password selection. Users tend to choose passwords which are easily guessable. Often, users select passwords which relate to their family, pets, birthdays, or other such easily obtained information. As you might expect, Windows NT is incapable of solving this problem.

Weak (English-language) password selection. Unfortunately, many users choose passwords which are English words. These passwords are vulnerable to a dictionary-based attack in which an attacker supplies an entire dictionary of words to try as passwords. Although this attack may be foiled by an account lockout system policy, not all administrators implement this policy. We strongly recommend that administrators implement this policy as described below.

In order to help understand the risks associated with using English-language passwords, Appendix B, *Passcrack for Windows NT,* shows an example of a password cracking program for NT. Using the Windows NT Win32 API set, it is possible to crack NT passwords in a brute-force (or dictionary-based) attack. The only way to fully prevent this attack process is to maintain a strong auditing policy which will both alert you to the attack in process, and, hopefully, shut it down.

Password length. Unless forced to use passwords of significant length (7 + characters), most users tend to choose short passwords. We strongly recommend that administrators implement password length controls as described above. In addition, the use of both text and numeric passwords significantly reduces the risks associated with brute-force attacks. Although Windows NT is not capable of requiring the use of both numbers and letters in their passwords, we recommend that organizations make this a matter of policy and strongly encourage their users to do so.

Password aging. Unless forced to do so, most users will never change their passwords. This increases the likelihood of potential compromise due to any of the factors noted earlier. We recommend that all administrators utilize the functionality provided by Windows NT to force users to change their passwords on a regular basis. Moreover, users should be forced to use different passwords each time (within reason).

We recommend that users be forced to change their passwords at least every 45 days and not more than once per day. Also, they should be forced to use at least six to eight different passwords over time. The rationale for not permitting passwords to be changed more than once per day is simple—given the opportunity, some users will change their password many times quickly in order to return to a password which they prefer. This would eliminate the benefits of password aging.

As was noted in Chapter 1, *Security Architecture,* Windows NT does provide for the possibility of authentication using mechanisms other than a simple password. Indeed, for high-security Windows NT implementations, we recommend that users investigate the possibilities of using alternate authentication technologies.

Backup/Restore Authority

By default, Windows NT has no account which has access to all files in the system. While members of the Administrators group do have the ability to take ownership of any file, then grant themselves rights to the file, this activity may be audited. Other operating systems, such as Novell's NetWare, have accounts which have default access to all files (e.g., Supervisor).

Windows NT does, however, contain a series of accounts which may gain control of files without their owners' knowledge or permission. These accounts are those which are permitted to perform file backup and restore operations. This ability represents one of the most significant—and often overlooked—security risks in Windows NT.

Users who are granted the Backup/Restore user rights are permitted to open any file for backup purposes. Of course, the user need not really be backing up the file. Once the file is open for read access, the user may redirect the information at will. Therefore, no file in the system—regardless of its NTFS-based ACL protection—is safe from the Backup/Restore users.

By default, only three sets of users are granted these rights. On Windows NT servers and workstations, the members of the Administrators group and the Backup Operators group are granted this right. On Windows NT servers functioning as domain controllers, users in the Server Operators group are also granted the Backup/Restore right. The only specific user account granted this right is the Administrator.

Because regular backups are a required element of a production Windows NT system, there is little that administrators can do to fully close this potential security breach. There are, however, some commonsense strategies to limit the potential for misuse.

For example, administrators should grant the Backup/Restore rights to as few accounts as possible. Each of these accounts should belong to a completely trusted member of the administrative staff; without trust among administrators, there is no possibility of creating a secure Windows NT system.

In addition, administrators should be careful to ensure that whenever the Backup/Restore rights are exercised, the activity is noted in the system security log. *Unfortunately, Windows NT does not log Backup/Restore activities by default.* In order to turn on Auditing, launch the Registry Editor and change the following key:

```
HKEY_LOCAL_MACHINE\System\CurrentControlSet\Control\Lsa\
FullPrivilegeAuditing
```

Setting this key to a value of 1 will enable auditing of the Backup/Restore privilege. For more information on the Registry and setting Registry keys, refer to Chapter 5, *The Registry*.

Of course, actually performing backups and restores of files is not the only system function which might require access to all files in the NT files system. For example, consider the problems associated with scanning an NTFS volume for viruses.

In order to scan for viruses, the virus scanner must open each and every executable file in the file system. This requires at least read access (and write access as well, if the program attempts to disinfect infected files) to each file. As was noted above, however, there is no user in the system who has default ownership of all files. Because the NTFS allows hierarchical security through the common Windows NT ACL/ACEs, users and administrators are limited to the rights which have been granted to them.

Therefore, most antivirus scanners which are integrated with Windows NT will require the Backup/Restore right in order to properly do their job. Withholding this right from them will reduce the potential for a security breach. At the same time, however, it will drastically reduce their effectiveness, as all users will be required to scan the files that they own. Contrast this to a single user with Backup/Restore privilege having the ability to scan and disinfect all files in the system at once.

Guest Accounts

On installation, Windows NT creates a relatively unprivileged guest account. Although it has far fewer rights than do, say, members of the Users group, the guest account can still prove a significant security hole. Thankfully, Microsoft has changed the default system settings in NT version 4.0, and the Guest user is disabled by default.

NetWare Note

How does backup of an NT server differ from that of a NetWare server?

A NetWare user with administrative privileges (also known as *supervisor equivalence*) has full access to all the file systems and all the data within files. If the backup application runs on the console of the NetWare server, no login is required to copy file data to a local tape drive. If the application runs on a client machine, the logged-in user must have rights explicitly assigned for each file and directory, or must have Administrator or supervisor equivalence.

NT requires that a user be logged in, whether the tape drive is on the server, or on a client machine. Additionally, the user running the backup utility must be owner of all the files on the system (a practical impossibility) or must be a member of the Backup Operators group.

Administrators should note, however, that there are at least two potential major security problems with the default guest account if it is enabled:

File shares.   By default, all new file shares created under Windows NT assign Full Control rights (read, write, modify, delete, etc.) to the Everyone group. This means that anyone who can gain access to the system is able to have full control over the shared files. This includes users who log in using the Guest account, which has no default password assigned to it. Although all users who create file shares should be careful to reassign rights immediately after creating the share, experience tells us that many users forget to do so. By not changing the permissions, these users risk leaving their data unprotected—even from strangers using the unprotected Guest account.

Registry.   The registry contains all the relevant configuration data about the Windows NT server or workstation on which it resides. As a result, it contains information that is vulnerable to both disclosure and corruption. Unfortunately, Windows NT versions 3.1 and earlier are incapable of easily protecting the entire registry from either disclosure or corruption. The only way to do so is key by key—a process that would take weeks to complete properly.

By default, many of the registry keys are both readable and writeable by members of the Everyone group. The guest account is a member of this group, and has no default password. Thus, the possibility exists of a user logging into the guest account, then overwriting critical portions of the registry, either purposely or accidentally.

Managing File and Printer Security

He that has a secret should not only hide it, but hide that he has it to hide.

—*Thomas Carlyle*

When most people think about security in an operating system, what they're really thinking about is file system security. The security restrictions which an operating system places on who can access which file—and hence, which information—are the most obvious, and arguably the most important, to users.

Windows NT *can be* configured to provide significant file security. The system defaults, however, are notoriously insecure. Remember, however, that this insecurity is hardly unique to NT—indeed, nearly all competing operating systems have the identical flaw.

So why don't system vendors like Microsoft change the defaults to provide more security out of the box? Because security—unlike performance and ease of use—doesn't sell many products. Creating more security by default has the appearance of limiting system functionality. As a result, system administrators are bound to properly configure NT security for themselves.

Much of the information presented in the following paragraphs relates to the issue of security with which most users are concerned: *access control*. Some of it, however, relates to the related fields of data integrity and availability. Although these requirements often take a back seat to access control (or confidentiality), they are at least as important for most systems. We recommend that administrators pay careful attention to the fault-tolerance and recoverability capabilities of the various Windows NT file systems and disk management options.

File Systems

In the past, Windows NT supported three distinct file systems for writable disks. Each has its unique advantages and disadvantages, but only one can be considered remotely secure under Windows NT. Note that the most current version of Windows NT (4.x) supports only two of the three previous choices. Although new installations of Windows NT cannot use the HPFS file system, it is discussed below for those users who are still using versions 3.x. Each of the other two file systems is covered in greater detail.

Regardless of which file system is chosen, Windows NT provides translation among them. That is, any file which exists within one file system may be copied to another file system via NT. The process of translating a file from one file system to another is transparent to the user. Note, however, that conversion of one file system to another in its entirety is another matter altogether. For more information on this topic, consult the *Converting to NTFS* section later in this chapter.

File Access Table (FAT)

The FAT (file access table) file system is a holdover from MS-DOS. By default, all MS-DOS computers (and their variants) use a standard version of the FAT system to store files. Windows 95, for example, uses FAT as its only file system. In addition, the default file system for floppy diskettes on nearly all Intel-based microcomputer operating systems (including NT) is FAT.

Standard FAT provides severely limited fault-tolerance and restoration options. This lack of fault tolerance stems from its roots in the early days of the microcomputer industry. Moreover, there are significant restrictions on the maximum file sizes and directory structures which may be created using the FAT system.

Finally, FAT by default supports only the 8 + 3 character filename convention. As MS-DOS users well know, this restriction often leads to unintelligible filenames.

Administrators should be aware that the FAT implementation in Windows NT does provide limited relief from some of these restrictions. For example, the default settings for FAT under NT provide a way to use longer, more descriptive filenames. Unless explicitly configured otherwise, all Windows NT FAT volumes support filenames of up to 255 characters—more than enough for most users to effectively describe their files.

In some instances, however, the use of these long filenames can be troublesome. For example, consider the case of a volume used for both Windows NT and for MS-DOS. Under Windows NT, long filenames look as they should—Windows NT provides all the "translation" that is necessary to keep the filename intact up to 255 characters. Under MS-DOS, however, the file looks suspiciously different. Because MS-DOS makes no allowances for filenames greater than 8 + 3 characters, it must assign strange-looking names to the files. Often, it is quite difficult to distinguish among a large number of such files.

Moreover, while FAT supports only limited means to recover from system faults, there are a tremendous number of excellent third-party disk-repair tools which are able to repair damage to FAT volumes. The vast majority of these tools support only the 8 + 3 filename convention; other filenames are often viewed as damaged files and treated accordingly.

In sum, there are some compelling reasons not to want to make use of Windows NT's long-filename support in the FAT file system. This option is controlled by the registry key:

```
HKEY_LOCAL_MACHINE\System\CurrentControlSet\Control\FileSystem\
Win 31FileSystem
```

Setting this key with a value of 1 will limit the FAT file system to the standard 8 + 3 filename convention. The default value of 0 will allow 255-character extended filenames.

Perhaps most significantly for our purposes, the FAT file system does not support Windows NT-based access control lists. As a result, administrators cannot assign either file- or directory-level security restrictions. This restriction undermines much of the security provided by Windows NT and voids the possibility of achieving C2 compliance.

This security restriction, combined with the limited availability and recoverability functionality provided by FAT, leads us to strongly recommend against the use of FAT. Although FAT is required in some instances, we recommend that it be used only in limited circumstances—and then, in conjunction with another file system.

For example, some dual-boot Windows NT and MS-DOS systems require FAT in order to provide a common volume for each to use. Windows 95, for example, does not support any file system other than FAT. In this case, we recommend using a single FAT volume in addition to an NTFS (see below) volume for secure file storage. Only files which need not be secured should be placed on the FAT volume.

Note also the fact that not all FAT partitions are created equal. This is especially true for FAT partitions which utilize proprietary disk compression technologies such as that found in STAC Electronic's Stacker and Microsoft's own DriveSpace compression software. Most disk compression software requires a device driver to integrate with the operating system in order to translate the compressed information into standard data. At this time, most disk compression formats are unsupported under Windows NT. Therefore, dual-boot systems using the FAT file system must not be compressed unless a compression driver is available for Windows NT.

High-Performance File System (HPFS)

The HPFS was first introduced with Microsoft and IBM's OS/2 operating system. The HPFS was intended to reduce the restrictions so evident in the FAT file system, including the 8 + 3 filenames, and the limitations of file and directory structures. As was mentioned earlier, HPFS is not supported under versions 4.x of Windows NT.

HPFS was designed from the beginning to effectively support the storage of large numbers of files while still retaining both speed and efficiency. In its default implementation, it also supports far more system recoverability and security functionality than does the FAT system.

As we noted above, the FAT implementation in Windows NT is effectively a *superset* of the default MS-DOS implementation; that is, it provides all the functionality of the original with a few minor additions (such as extended filename support). Unlike the FAT implementation, however, the HPFS implementation in Windows NT 3.x is a *subset* of the default OS/2 implementation.

From a security perspective, this distinction is quite important. Under OS/2, the HPFS implementation provides for secure file system access via OS/2 ACLs stored within the file system. Windows NT, however, ignores these ACLs when accessing HPFS volumes. *As a result, neither file- nor directory-level security is provided on HPFS volumes under Windows NT.*

In addition, the OS/2 implementation of HPFS provides for real-time recovery of system faults such as bad sectors (hot fix) and provides its own internal read/write cache support. Under Windows NT, the hot-fix capability is not supported. Moreover, the internal read/write cache support is ignored in favor of the Windows NT Cache Manager.

Even with all these restrictions, the HPFS is still more efficient for large volumes than is FAT. Because HPFS utilizes an efficient binary tree structure, its efficiency benefits scale well to volume sizes of about 2 Gbytes. FAT, on the other hand, is far less efficient and is not recommended for volumes sizes above 1 Gbyte.

With such a limited implementation of HPFS, many have questioned why it was present in versions 3.x at all. The rationale was that it provided backward compatibility (at least as far as reading and writing files) with OS/2 systems. This feature was considered to be extremely important during the early development of NT. More recently, of course, there have been relatively few systems utilizing OS/2 HPFS, making these backward compatibility features of little value.

We strongly recommend against the use of HPFS in Windows NT systems, and indeed, systems upgraded to version 4.x cannot support it at all. In limited cases where version 3.x is being used to support HPFS, we recommend the use of an HPFS volume only in addition to an NTFS (see below) volume to provide a secure file repository. Only files which need not be secured should be placed on the HPFS volume.

NT File System (NTFS)

The NTFS is the preferred file system for all Windows NT volumes. NTFS is the only file system which enables the user to utilize all the security functionality built into Windows NT. In addition, NTFS provides significant value in terms of both efficiency and recoverability.

The decision to design a new file system for Windows NT was a difficult one. During the original development process, there was significant discussion concerning whether the inclusion of a third file system was even possible, given the strict time constraints. Moreover, the complexity associated with the proposed new file system was such that some questioned whether it would ever work properly.

In the end, the file system was implemented in time for the first NT release. Since that time, it has become well respected as the primary choice of most experienced systems administrators.

In time, the NTFS will become outdated. With the next major release of Windows NT, code-named *Cairo,* the file system will change dramatically. Current plans call for the file system to be even more object-oriented in order to fit into the planned enterprisewide directory structure. At least until Cairo arrives, probably in late 1997, NTFS remains the file system of choice.

Perhaps the most important feature of NTFS is its ability to provide crash recovery. Indeed, one primary rationale for creating NTFS was to provide the capability to recover the file system in case of a system crash during intensive file operations. The details of this effort require a bit of background.

Early file systems were designed to follow strict rules for both disk reads and disk writes. When a request came to write a file, the request was honored immediately. Similarly, requests to read a file were immediately followed by a disk seek and file read. These file systems were termed "careful-," or "immediate-," "write" file systems.

Over time, however, operating system designers came to recognize that there was more potential efficiency to be gained by adding caches of memory for both reading and writing. Because memory access is far faster than disk access, operating systems utilize them to make repetitive file operations faster. In addition, write caches allow the system to write bytes to the disk when the system is idle, rather than immediately on receipt.

This operation, called a "lazy write," yields efficiency in that disk writes are performed when it is efficient to do so—not necessarily immediately on request. The drawback, of course, is that if the system crashes before the lazy write takes place, that data is lost forever. Such a system crash might be software-related (an operating system crash), or hardware-related (a power failure). Even worse, the act of partially writing some of the data might cause the file system to become corrupted, leading to a loss of the entire volume of data.

NTFS provides the best of both immediate- and lazy-write file systems. Although it is not quite as efficient as immediate-write systems (such as the FAT system under MS-DOS), it makes up for it in terms of increased system reliability. It works by providing a three-step process for disk writes:

First, the data to be written is logged in a separate transaction log. This transaction log contains all the information required to undo (reverse) the change to the file system.

Next, the file system completes the file write in its entirety.

Finally, the file system updates the transaction log to indicate success.

In the case of a system failure before the data has been fully written successfully, NTFS can recover the file system by undoing the change that was in progress. This leaves the file system in a state which is nearly guaranteed not to be corrupted.

Note that the management of the transaction logs is completely transparent to the user. In the case of a system failure, recovery happens automatically the next time the NTFS volume is mounted.

Hot Fixing

Of course, not all system failures occur as the result of a system crash. NTFS must also handle the possibility that some sectors of the physical disk might fail to retain data effectively during normal system operations. These sectors of the disk, called "bad sectors," are present on every piece of magnetic media. Although they usually account for a minuscule portion of the whole, they must be managed effectively so as to minimize their potential impact on the system.

NTFS handles the bad sector through a process known as "hot fix" (or sometimes called "sector sparing"). During normal system operation, NTFS constantly monitors the process of reading and writing data to and from the disk. If (or when!) errors occur in reading from or writing to the disk, NTFS is able to move the data from the sectors causing an error into other known good sectors. Once the process of moving data is complete, NTFS marks the sectors in question as "bad." This marking prevents the reuse of these sectors in the future. In this manner, NTFS provides real-time fault tolerance for bad disk sectors.

File System Recommendations

In addition to the robust recovery, NTFS also provides other significant advantages over both HPFS and FAT. First, it provides greater expandability; for instance, NTFS volumes can grow larger, in terms of both gross size and directory structure, than can either of the other two file systems (up to 16 exabytes). Second, NTFS can remain efficient for volume sizes larger than either HPFS or FAT. Perhaps most importantly, NTFS provides full Windows NT ACL support for file and directory security.

We strongly recommend that administrators utilize the NTFS whenever possible. Without NTFS, much of the information provided elsewhere in this book regarding file security is of little use.

Fortunately, administrators who have formatted their disks using either HPFS or FAT need not reformat their disks in order to convert to NTFS. Windows NT provides a one-way transformation for each of these file systems to NTFS. Note that once converted, there is no reverse conversion supported. To switch from NTFS to either of the other file systems, an administrator must back up the data, reformat the volume(s), and then restore the data from backups.

Converting to NTFS

Converting a volume from FAT to NTFS can be performed quite easily using the CONVERT program. By default, this program resides in the

%SYSTEM_ROOT%\System32 directory. Note that the conversion requires the user to be logged into Windows NT as a member of the Administrators group.

To convert a drive from FAT to NTFS, use the command

```
CONVERT drive: /FS:NTFS
```

Administrators should also be aware that the CONVERT utility will not operate on the currently used drive. Therefore, if there is only a single volume available, the system will schedule the conversion to take place on the next system boot. Once this command is issued, the conversion will occur automatically the next time the system is restarted.

Conversion from HPFS to NTFS is only slightly more complicated. Because HPFS can store security ACL information within the directory structure, the conversion process must account for these ACLs and integrate them into the new NTFS structure.

First, administrators should utilize the OS/2 utility BACKACC to back up the ACL information contained within the HPFS file system and then use the same command shown above to convert (or schedule the conversion) of the disk formation from HPFS to NTFS. Finally, the ACLs that were backed up from HPFS must be restored to NTFS. This is performed using the ACLCONV utility. By default, this utility resides in the %SYSTEM_ROOT%\System32 directory. To restore the ACLs, use the following command:

```
ACLCONV /DATA:filename from BACACC </LOG:log filename>
```

This command will convert the ACLs into NTFS format to the greatest extent possible. By default, the ACLCONV program will search across domains to find matching users. Be aware, however, that there are likely to be some circumstances in which ACLs do not match up exactly; these will need to be fixed by the administrator on a case-by-case basis.

Supporting Removable Media

Much of the preceding discussion centers around the use of fixed mass-storage media. While removable hard disks are becoming popular and may be formatted using any of the above file systems, they are far less popular than standard fixed media.

More standard removable media, such as floppy disks and compact disks, may rely on either the FAT file system or other, more customized file systems. Chief among these is the CD file system, or CDFS. The CDFS is supported only on read-only media, and provides an efficient means for reading data from read-only volumes.

From a security perspective, removable media present a significant potential problem. First, removable media rarely support the Windows NT-based security ACLs. Therefore, information which resides on most removable volumes is not subject to security protection from the operating system. Second, removable media are just that—removable. This might allow a potential intruder to walk off with significant amounts of proprietary data.

One solution to the dilemma posed by removable media is to deny their use. Through the registry, an administrator may control whether both floppy and CD-ROM disk drives are allocated at the time of system boot. Although this will not affect the use of some removable storage, such as Bernoulli or Syquest disks, some of these more sophisticated devices *can* be protected using the NTFS file system. When doing so, however, administrators should be careful to shut down the system before removing the volumes, because of the lazy-write properties explained above.

In order to limit access to the floppy drive(s), administrators have two choices. The first is to use the FloppyLock service program provided as part of the Windows NT resource kit. This service can be started and stopped by the administrator as required. When started, it prevents access to the floppy disk drives.

Alternatively, administrators may set the value of the registry key:

```
>HKEY_LOCAL_MACHINE\Software\Microsoft\WindowsNT\CurrentVersion\
Winlogon\ AllocateFloppies
```

Setting this key with a value of 1 will enable the use of floppy disk drives. Setting a value of 0 will disable the use of floppy disk drives. Note that this key is read-only on user logon. Therefore, changing this key will not affect users currently logged into the system. Only users that log in after the key has been set will be affected. To ensure that making this change affects all users, administrators might wish to reboot the system after making this change.

To restrict access to CD-ROM drives, administrators may set the value of the registry key:

```
HKEY_LOCAL_MACHINE\Software\Microsoft\WindowsNT\CurrentVersion\
Winlogon\ AllocateCDRoms
```

Setting this key with a value of 1 will enable the use of CD-ROM drives. A value of 0 will disable access to all CD-ROM drives. As with the `AllocateFloppies` key, changes affect only those users who log into the system after the change has been implemented. Users currently logged on to the system will have full access to CD-ROM devices until the next time they log into the system. As a result, we recommend that the system be rebooted following this change to ensure that the change affects all users.

Directory Replication

One of Windows NT's most unique features is its ability to replicate standard files among servers and workstations on a periodic basis. This feature enables administrators to maintain identical copies of shared data on multiple servers with little or no administrative effort.

Distributing data among servers provides an efficient means to share the loads associated with large numbers of users accessing the same data from the same servers. Moreover, administrators can configure Windows NT to replicate configuration files for applications across the network, thereby limiting the effort required to change application configurations on multiple servers.

At the same time, however, the replication function provides an interesting security dilemma. Although the act of replicating data among servers and workstations is appealing, administrators should consider the security implications. Each computer that will function as either an import (receiving data) or an export (sending data) replication partner must be configured securely. Note that the replication service pays no attention to the files which it replicates—and therefore makes it relatively easy for an administrator to inadvertently replicate the wrong files. Moreover, directory replication presents the troubling possibility that a system intruder might obtain data from an infiltrated system long after having logged out of the system.

Setting Up Directory Replication

The first step in setting up directory replication is to create a new user account under which the replication service will run. This account will need to have sufficient privilege to perform the replication operations.

To create the account, first launch the User Manager or User Manager for Domains on the computer that will be used as the export server. Then, create an account with the following properties:

Username.   This can be any valid user name. Note that Replicator is not a valid user name, as it is the name of a user group.

Membership.   The account must be a member of the Backup Operators, Users (or Domain Users), and Replicators groups.

Time restrictions.   None, assuming that you want full control over the time and date of replications.

Password expiration.   Most system administrators set the Replicator account password expiration to "never," allowing them to set up the account and forget about it. More secure systems administrators set this to a reasonable length of time, then change it when required. Note that the system will not prompt you when it is time to change the password; rather, the replication will fail.

For more detailed information on setting up user accounts, refer to Chap. 2, *Managing User Security.*

Next, create an identical account on the import server. Note that the account name and the password on the remote system must exactly match the value entered for the export server.

Then, configure the Replicator service on both the import and export servers. There are several ways to do so. First, you may load the Server Manager, which by default resides in the *Administrative Tools* group under the Start menu. Within Server Manager, select the first server, then select the *Services* option on the Computer menu.

Alternatively, load *Control Panel,* which by default resides within the Start menu. To launch Control Panel, select the *Start, Settings,* and *Control Panel* options. Then, double-click on the Services icon within Control Panel.

The Services dialog box is shown in Fig. 3.1.

From within this dialog box, scroll down until the Directory Replicator service is highlighted. Then, press the *Startup* button, which will bring up the service startup and account options.

From within this dialog box, set the startup type to *Automatic.* This tells Windows NT to launch the Directory Replicator service whenever necessary. In the lower portion of the dialog box, select the option *Log on*

Figure 3.1
Services dialog box.

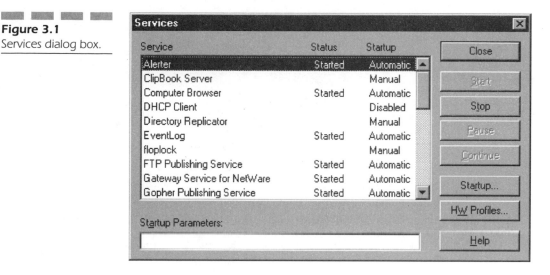

Figure 3.2
Directory replicator
services.

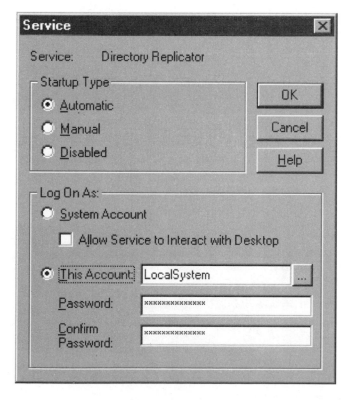

as This Account. Then, enter the name of the account which you created in the User Manager. Alternatively, select the *Browse* button next to the entry field and select the account from the list provided. Finally, enter the proper password in both the *Password* and *Confirm Password* entry fields. Then press *OK*.

Windows NT will then indicate that the account name that you entered has been granted the *Log on as a Service* right. This enables the Replicator account to start up, log into the system as a service using the password you provided, and perform the replication functions. When replication is finished, it will log out of the system to ensure ongoing security. Finally, perform the same operations on the import server. This will allow the two servers' replication services to communicate when the need arises.

The last stage in the process is to configure both the import and export servers to send and receive the proper data. System administrators should be extremely certain of the data they wish to replicate; once data are replicated, it cannot be taken back.

To configure the Export Server, first launch the Server Manager (or Server Manager for Domains) as described above. From within the Server Manager, select the export server, then double-click on it to show its properties. Alternatively, select the server, then select the *Properties* option from the *Computer* menu.

This brings up a dialog box, which appears as follows:

Figure 3.3
Server manager properties.

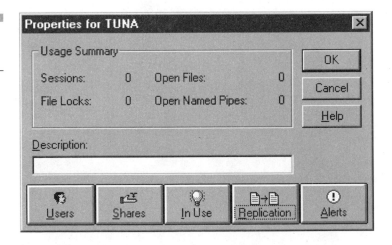

From this dialog box, select the *Replication* option to bring up the Directory Replication dialog box:

Figure 3.4
Directory replication
main dialog box.

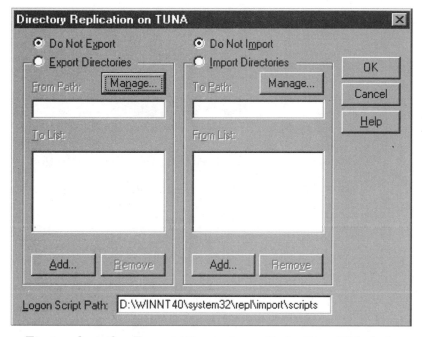

First, select the *Export Directories* radio button. This brings up the default export directory choice of `%SYSTEMROOT%\System32\ Repl\Export`. We recommend that administrators use this directory for replication exports, placing their data to be replicated within subdirectories underneath this directory. Note that administrators can configure the source directories for replication by clicking on the *Manage...* button within this dialog box. Clicking the *Manage...* button brings up the following dialog box:

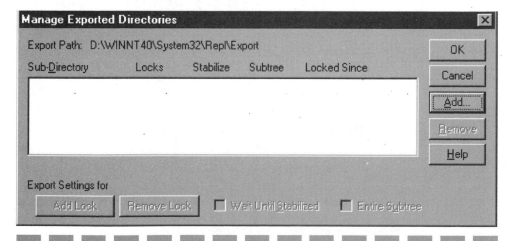

Figure 3.5   Manage export directories dialog box.

The first column in the dialog box indicates the subdirectories which may be replicated. Additional subdirectories may be added by clicking the *Add...* button. Subdirectories may be removed by clicking on the *Remove* button.

The next column indicates the "locks" which have been placed on the subdirectory. In Windows NT, locks indicate that a subdirectory may not be replicated at a given time. Note that multiple locks may be placed on a single subdirectory. Often, system administrators place locks on subdirectories to temporarily prevent their replication.

The next column indicates whether the directory needs to be stabilized prior to replication. *Stabilization* means that the files within the directory must remain static for at least 2 minutes. A "Yes" value indicates that the Replicator will wait for two minutes of static data. A "No" value indicates that the Replicator will replicate all data as soon as changes occur.

The fourth column indicates whether subdirectories of the named directory should be replicated. If you wish to replicate subdirectories, click the checkbox at the bottom of the dialog box. Then, click the *OK* button to return to the Directory Replication dialog box.

The bottom left portion of the Directory Replication dialog box permits the administrator to add and remove computers which will receive the exports from the replication server. Note that you must specify the NetBIOS name for the receiving computer. Clicking the *OK* button will exit and save the export server configuration options.

The last step is to configure the import server. To do so, bring up the Directory Replication dialog box in the manner described above. Then, using the right side of the dialog box, indicate that you wish to import directories. Once again, select the replication partners, then choose the directory you wish to replicate. Clicking *OK* will save and exit the dialog box and begin the replication process.

Windows NT and Viruses

Over the past several years, computer viruses have garnered an inordinate amount of popular press attention. Although the dangers posed by viruses are not necessarily greater than those posed by hackers or other system invaders, there is something apparently intriguing about a purely software-based attack.

Like all other operating systems, Windows NT is vulnerable to viruses. Arguably, however, it is less vulnerable than some other platforms, such as Windows 3.1 or the Macintosh. This section describes Windows NT's vulnerability to viruses and the steps administrators can take to limit their exposure.

Definition of a Computer Virus

Although a precise English-language definition of a computer virus has eluded virus researchers for nearly a decade, most experts agree that a virus is a program with two main characteristics:

1. It is able to make copies of itself (replicate).
2. It requires a "host" file in which to reside.

Note that a related type of malicious program, a "worm," meets criterion 1 but not criterion 2. Trojan horse programs, on the other hand, need meet neither criteria.

Viruses are said to "infect" their host files by modifying their executable code. Note that viruses can effectively infect only those files which contain executable code—simple data is never executed directly by the processor, and hence cannot support the propagation of a virus.

Infectible Targets and Viruses "in the Wild"

As of mid-1996, the number of computer viruses which have been written numbers somewhere close to 10,000. It is impossible to make an exact estimate of the number of viruses, as the number changes daily.

Even with thousands of known viruses, however, only a small number of viruses are ever found outside a virus researcher's lab. Each month, Joe Wells (formerly of Symantec) publishes a list of viruses known to be "in the wild." Viruses in the wild are those which have been found by normal users in the course of their everyday activities. Of the 10,000 or so known viruses, only about 200 are known to be actively in the wild. Therefore, the risk to any given computer is centered around this subset of the virus population.

The majority of the known viruses have been written to infect Intel-based personal computers. The rationale for this is twofold: (1) it is the most prevalent platform in the world, thereby providing the greatest possible infectible audience; and (2) by token of its popularity, many virus authors have access to Intel-based platforms, and are thereby able to program their creations.

On Intel-based platforms, most viruses infect executable files residing on floppy and hard disks and/or the boot sectors of floppy disks and/or the boot sectors or master boot sectors of hard disks. Each of these infections requires a slightly different approach, and each may be prevented by a tailored response to the threat.

The majority of the 10 most common viruses in the world are known as either *boot sector* or *master boot sector* infectors. These viruses are able to infect the boot programs which exist on floppy and hard disks. Note that even nonbootable floppies may be infected. With boot sector infectors, viruses are carried among different systems via floppy disk, and are transferred to systems when a system is booted using an infected floppy disk.

Although few users intentionally boot their systems from floppy disks, many accidentally leave floppies in their disk drives when they restart their computers. On the next boot, the executable code residing on the boot sector of the floppy disk will be executed—this is where the virus resides.

More recently, a new type of virus has become extremely prevalent. This virus, the Macro virus, infects data files from programs which contain robust macro languages and associated interpreters. It is possible to write a program using many of these macro languages which has all of the characteristics of a virus. The most common of these viruses is the so-called Winword. Concept virus, which infects Microsoft Word document files on all platforms which support Microsoft Word—including Windows NT.

Thus, Windows NT is vulnerable to virus infection on three fronts:

- Executable files in any of the file systems
- Boot sectors and master boot sectors
- Data files with associated macro-language interpreters

Each of these potential infections represents a potential security breach in Windows NT. Once a virus executes, it may merely continue to replicate, destroy data, or modify the system such that it is more vulnerable to other attacks. Therefore, it is essential that steps be taken to prevent virus infection.

Today, there are no known viruses which are written specifically to attack Windows NT. The majority are written to infect DOS executable files, while there are a handful of viruses which are intended to attack Windows 3.x executables. Unfortunately, Windows NT is at risk from all of these viruses, as it maintains compatibility with both previous executable formats.

NT VDMs

Windows NT DOS emulation is provided by an architecture called the *Virtual DOS Machine* (VDM). An NT server or workstation can create an unlimited number of VDMs in a single Win32 session. Each of these VDMs provides the following features:

- MS-DOS 5.0 Application Support
- Over 625 kbytes of Free Memory
- XMS/EMM LIM Support
- Completely Pageable Memory
- DMPI 0.9 Support (the same as Windows 3.1)
- Transparent Access to File Systems and Network Drives

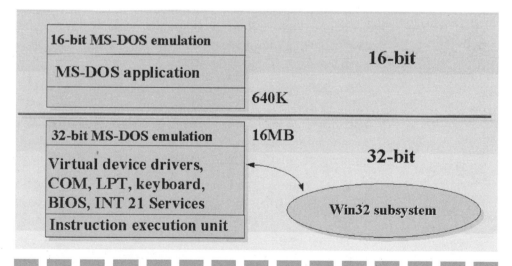

Figure 3.6 VDM structure.

Thus, NT provides credible DOS application support. At the same time, the emulation provided by Windows NT is not perfect, nor is it intended to be. As a result, some of the "tricks" used by virus authors will cause their viruses not to execute properly under Windows NT.

For the most part, DOS executable file infectors will execute properly under Windows NT, but they will be subject to the access control restrictions placed on their owner (see below). Most will execute only within a DOS window, and will be unable to properly infect Windows NT executables.

In most cases, DOS viruses will inadvertently damage Windows NT executables on attempted infection. This attribute is both good and bad; while some files will be damaged by viruses which do not appreciate their complexity, the same files will be unable to continue the spread of the virus. Therefore, the virus will be stopped much more quickly, although at the cost of some corrupted files.

NT WOW and Boot Viruses

Windows 3.x emulation is provided through a process called *WOW*, or Win16 on Win32. The WOW architecture provides for emulation of the standard MS-DOS function calls in addition to the Windows 3.1 kernel and GDI stubs. In much the same manner as VDMs, WOW provides credible—albeit not perfect—backward emulation.

Boot viruses, on the other hand, are to a limited extent operating system–independent; that is, they load from the disk before the operating system loads, thereby controlling the hardware directly without interference from the operating system.

At the same time, this means that they may be vulnerable to the operating system once the system boot takes place. Under Windows NT, most boot infectors will refuse to infect additional floppy disks once the OS load is complete. Therefore, while the system may be infected, it is unlikely to continue spreading the infection to other machines.

Finally, there is at least one virus known to be written specifically for Windows 95. This virus, Boza, is of relatively little interest to the population as a whole. The only significant feature of it is that it functions as a Win32 application—and therefore represents the first of a new breed of potential viruses.

Viruses and Hierarchical Access Control

As is described elsewhere in this book, Windows NT provides hierarchical access control for files which reside in NTFS-based file systems. This means that an administrator (or file owner) can limit another user's access to specific files on the basis of their security rights.

Note that viruses are executable programs like any other—as a result, they run with the privileges of their owner. In Windows NT, this means that any program which is launched intentionally or unintentionally by a user is subject to the restrictions of that user's security access token. The Windows NT security model ensures that any program launched by a user (or any program launched by that program) will be subject to the original subject's access restrictions.

In order to infect an executable program, the user must therefore have "write" rights to that file. One simple way to limit the potential spread of file-infecting viruses, then, is to restrict executable programs to "read" and "execute" access for most users. Of course, in a complicated system this is easier said than done. With potentially thousands of executable files in a Windows NT system, it is difficult (if not impossible) for an administrator to configure the rights to all files properly at all times.

As far back as 1984, Fred Cohen and others showed that even this security model is not necessarily immune to computer virus infiltration. Even when files are protected in the "proper" way, there is still the potential for file infection. In most cases in Windows NT, at least one user has write rights to many of the executables in the file system. By default, members of the Administrators group have write rights to a significant number of executable files within the system. This user may then infect executable files stored within the system and pass the infection along to other users who then access those executable files.

In the general case, virus infection within a system providing hierarchical access control proceeds as shown in Fig. 3.7.

Initially, a user with limited rights might infect file 1 with a file-infecting virus. Another user, with slightly greater access rights, might read file 1, infect her computer, then write to file 2 and infect it with the virus. In turn, a third user with even greater rights might read file 1 or 2, infect his system, then proceed to infect file 3. Over time, an infection can spread to every file in the system.

The solution to this problem, unfortunately, is policy-based, rather than technology-based. Administrators should try to ensure that executable files are not writable by standard users. Moreover, administrators should not perform nonadministrative daily tasks with a fully privileged account. Rather, administrators should maintain two accounts, one

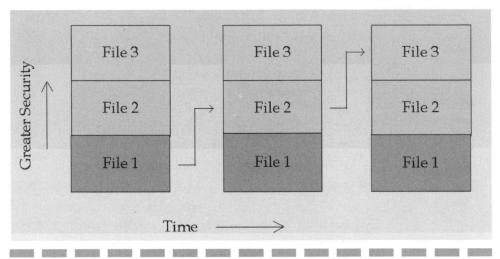

Figure 3.7 *Virus spread in hierarchical access control.*

as a member of the Administrators group with all the associated rights, and another with more limited access rights for chores which do not require high levels of system access. This will help prevent the possibility of accidentally infecting protected files.

These recommendations apply equally to Windows NT servers and workstations. Human nature, however, shows that users of Windows NT workstations are far less likely to maintain hierarchical access control over files in their workstations. Rather, experience shows that most NT workstations are assigned to a single user—and that users often assign themselves an account in the Administrator's group. As a result, that user is far more likely to infect large numbers of files within their system. Administrators should warn users about the risks associated with this behavior.

Hierarchical access control also poses some difficulty for antivirus products. Most users tend to use antivirus scanners, which search the disk for known viruses within executable files. To scan a given file for the presence of a virus, however, the user must have rights to read from that file. In a system with hierarchical access control, that may not always be the case.

Within Windows NT, for example, there is no user who has default rights to all files in the system. Administrators can read only those files to which they have access—although they have the power to take ownership of other files, they cannot read them without taking ownership, then granting themselves rights. This leads to difficulties in searching for viruses as well as in disinfecting viruses once they are found.

Fortunately, there is a solution. Other sections of this book describe the potential security hole associated with the users who are members of the Backup Operators group. These users may read any file in the system for backup—or any other—purpose. While this hole poses a difficult security risk, it makes antivirus scanning much easier. Many of the current antivirus products for Windows NT are designed to run under a Backup Operator–class account. Doing so allows them to exploit the backup/restore security weakness in order to scan the entire file system for the presence of viruses. We strongly recommend that these Backup Operator accounts be limited both in number and in scope.

The NT Boot Process and Boot Viruses

In order to understand how boot viruses work within the context of Windows NT, it is instructional to understand the Windows NT boot process. Indeed, understanding the boot process is essential to understanding the potential virus risks unique to Windows NT.

The boot process proceeds as follows:

Figure 3.8
NT boot process.

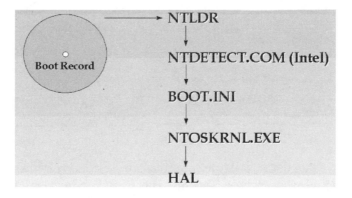

Once the hardware has completed its Power-on Self-Test (POST) and transfers control to the master boot sector of the hard disk, the NT Loader (NTLDR) program is loaded. This program is responsible for mapping memory into the flat, 32-bit model recognized by Windows NT. In addition, it loads mini–file system drivers for each of the three default file systems: HPFS, NTFS, and FAT (or just NTFS and FAT under NT 4.x). On Intel-based systems, the NTLDR program then calls the NTDETECT program.

Note that on ARC (Advanced RISC Computing) platforms, the system provides hardware configuration information directly to Windows NT.

The NTDETECT program is responsible for building a list of the installed hardware components. In doing so, it updates the Registry, indicating the current hardware configuration. Note that the Registry contains two separate sections: one which is termed "volatile," as it is not maintained between boots; and one termed "involatile," as it maintains its information indefinitely. The NTDETECT program updates the volatile section of the registry.

Once the NTDETECT program (or the ARC data-capture routine) is complete, the system refers to the BOOT.INI program to proceed with the boot process. BOOT.INI contains the menu of operating systems from which the user may select. Note that the BOOT.INI file must reside in the root directory of the partition from which NTLDR was loaded.

Figure 3.9
Sample BOOT.INI file.

```
[boot loader]
timeout = 30
default = multi(0)disk(0)rdisk(0)partition(1)\WINDOWS
[operating systems]
multi(0)disk(0)rdisk(0)partition(1)\WINDOWS = "Windows
NT Server Version 4.00"
multi(0)disk(0)rdisk(0)partition(1)\WINDOWS = "Windows
NT Server Version 4.00 [VGA mode]" /basevideo /sos
C:\ = "Windows 95"
```

The BOOT.INI file contains two sections: a Boot Loader section and an Operating System section. The Boot Loader section is the first section, containing information regarding the default operating system and the time limit during which a user may select an operating system to load. Note that this time period may be set to 0; this forces the system to boot from the default operating system, regardless of any other choices in the menu. Some administrators may wish to choose this option to help prevent users from booting an alternate operating system.

The next section of BOOT.INI describes the location of each operating system on the disk(s). Each operating system loaded on the system will have an associated entry in the operating system section.

Following an OS selection, the system will load the Windows NT kernel itself, contained in a file called NTOSKRNL.EXE. This file, in turn, loads the hardware abstraction layer (HAL) to abstract the differences in the multiple hardware platforms on which NT may run. Once the HAL has loaded, the system consults the System Hive in order to load the various subsystems, services, and device drivers that must be loaded before a user may log on.

Many boot-block-infecting viruses will have no effect on Windows NT; they will load before the operating system, but will be disabled in memory by the NT operating system. Others, however, may do significant damage to the file structures stored on Windows NT volumes. The distinction between these two possible outcomes is extremely dependent on both the virus and the configuration of the system.

Unfortunately, most antivirus programs do not recognize NTFS partitions without loading Windows NT. Therefore, recovering from a boot infection may be complicated. On the other hand, NTFS maintains multiple copies of its boot-block information, yielding a greater chance of success in the disinfection process.

Several boot-block infecting viruses will manifest themselves with a similar Windows NT error. If, when booting a Windows NT system, you see the error.

```
Stop 0x0000007B
Inaccessible_boot_device
```

be aware that there is a significant chance that the system is infected with a boot-block-infecting virus. Because of the complexity associated with removing boot-block infections on Windows NT volumes, we recommend that users utilize current antivirus products in order to remove this type of infection.

More and more antivirus products are shipping today with the capability to deal with viruses in Windows NT. We strongly recommend that users obtain a best-of-breed antivirus program and use it regularly. Current ratings for antivirus software and hardware may be obtained from the National Computer Security Association at (717) 258-1816 in the United States, or HTTP://WWW.NCSA.COM on the World Wide Web.

Potential Windows NT-Based Virus Attacks

This section describes some of the virus attacks that are unique to the Windows NT platform. Although many of these attacks have yet to be confirmed in the wild, there is a strong likelihood that they will be seen at some point in the future.

BOOTSECT.DOS.   The BOOTSECT file resides on the same volume as the NTLDR. This file is an exact copy of the boot sector which will be loaded in the event that a user selects an operating system other than NT on system startup. Note that this file is called BOOTSECT.DOS regardless of the actual operating system boot sector contained within it; it may be DOS, OS/2, or another operating system entirely.

When an alternate operating system is selected, this file is loaded directly into memory and executed. As a result, it offers an inviting target to virus authors. If the BOOTSECT file resides on a FAT or HPFS partition with no hierarchical access control, there is no restriction on a virus infecting the file, then waiting until the next time an alternate operating system is loaded. At that time, the virus will be loaded into memory and have full control over the system.

VIRUSES AS SERVICES.   Within Windows NT, services remain resident regardless of which user(s) are logged into the system. In doing so, they retain the rights (via a copy of the access token) of the user who first launched them. Therefore, they, too, offer an inviting target to virus authors. Consider the possibility of a virus which infects a service executable. Once the executable is infected, the infecting user may log out of the system while the virus remains resident. In theory, this would allow the virus to continue infecting other files long after the original user logged out.

BOOT.INI.   As described above, the BOOT.INI program has a section which describes the location of all operating systems on the disk. Because BOOT.INI is a simple text file, any user with write rights to it may modify it at any time. If, for example, the BOOT.INI file resides on a FAT or HPFS partition, any user (or process created by that user) may modify it at any time. Thus, acting under the auspices (and security token) of a user, a virus might modify the BOOT.INI program such that a menu choice leads to an operating system—or virus code—of the virus author's choice. Once the virus code executes, it might then pass control back to the legitimately selected operating system. Given the speed with which this might happen, users would be hard pressed to notice the infection process.

AT SERVICE.   In Windows NT, the AT service functions much like the CRON daemon in UNIX. It permits a user to issue a command-line execution request at a given time in the future. This time can be scheduled on a single-occurrence basis or on a regular basis (one a week, etc.). The AT service does not run by default; it must first be enabled by an administrator.

Note that the AT service has implications for both virus infection and antivirus protection. For example, an administrator might use the AT service to schedule a nightly virus scan. On the other hand, a virus author might use the AT service to schedule some action (infection, file damage or access, etc.) at some point in the future, long after the virus might have seemed to disappear.

DEVICE DRIVERS.   Device drivers in Windows NT are often loaded before the user is permitted to log in. This presents an interesting opportunity for virus authors, who might be tempted to write their viruses such that they are launched from the System Hive at system boot time. This would enable their virus to ensure that it is executed, regardless of which user is logged into the system. Moreover, like services, device drivers continue their execution even as various users log into and out of the system.

Virus Summary

Viruses present a small but difficult problem for Windows NT system administrators. Although viruses represent only a small portion of the great number of potential system attacks, they are among the most difficult to prevent. We recommend the following:

1. *Use write rights effectively where possible.*   Although setting write rights properly will not guarantee that your system cannot be infected, they will go a long way toward reducing risk.

2. *Don't use a fully privileged administrator account to perform tasks which don't require excessive rights.*   Instead, use an account with fewer write rights to executables. Recommend that NT workstation users do the same.

3. *Use the FlopLock service or the NT registry settings to eliminate floppy disk access.*   Unless there is an explicit reason for requir-

ing floppy disk access, consider using method 1 or 2 described above for limiting floppy disk access.

Protecting the Boot Process

As is mentioned throughout this book, the boot process represents one of the largest potential security holes in the Windows NT architecture. Unfortunately, there is little that can be done to help eliminate this risk—indeed, the risk is associated more with the very architecture of the Windows NT hardware platforms than with the operating system itself.

One way to provide minimal protection is to use the NTFS file system, although this will not provide absolute security in the face of physical access from a system intruder. However, note that some users dual-boot their Windows NT systems with another operating system, such as Windows 95 or Windows 3.1. When this is the case, the Windows NT boot loader will present the user with a boot menu. Moreover, this boot loader will also be loaded if there is no alternate operating system, but if there is another boot choice, such as a different screen resolution.

Windows NT can, however, be forced to boot directly, without pausing for input from the user. In order to force a default Windows NT boot, load the Control Panel and the System applet. This applet allows you to set the default wait time for the boot menu. By setting this value to 0, an administrator can ensure that the Windows NT default selection will boot without pausing for user input.

Managing Files Securely

Managing files in a secure manner is one of the most important—and most difficult—jobs of a system administrator. In order to understand the process of securing files, we must first understand Windows NT's flexibility in this area. Also, we must assume that files which are to be protected are residing on an NTFS partition; no other file systems are permitted to have file- or directory-based access control.

For any given file in the NTFS file system, the administrator (and owner) can set the following custom access rights listed in the following table.

Permission	Description
Read (R)	The specified user/group may read from the file.
Write (W)	The specified user/group may write to the file.
Execute (X)	The specified user/group may execute the file (if executable).
Delete (D)	The specified user/group may delete the file.
Change Permission (P)	The specified user/group may change the permissions on the file.
Take Ownership (O)	The specified user/group may take ownership of the file.

Note that these rights may be assigned to individual users, groups of users, or any combination of either. In order to make administration easier, however, Windows NT provides generic sets of rights for commonly used access profiles. Consider the generic rights listed in the following table (where *user/group* denotes an individual user or a group of users).

Generic Rights	Description
No Access	The specified user/group has no access to the file. If this generic right is assigned to a given user/group, it supersedes any other inherited rights to the file.
Read	The specified user/group may both read the contents of the file and execute it (if in executable format). (RX)
Change	The specified user/group may read from the file, write to the file, execute the file (if in executable format), and delete the file. (RWXD)
Full Control	The specified user/group has all rights to the file. (All)
Special Access...	The specified user/group has a custom (not generic) set of rights to the file.

Most administrators utilize the generic rights whenever possible. Under some circumstances, however, administrators are required to set special permissions. Consider the common access rights and their associated generic permissions listed in the following table.

Permission Set	Generic Rights Required
Change file attributes	Change or Full Control
Change data within the file	Change or Full Control
Change the file's permissions	Full Control
Delete a file	Change or Full Control
Display file attributes	Read, Change, or Full Control
Display file data	Read, Change, or Full Control
Display file's owner/permissions	Read, Change, or Full Control
Execute the file	Read, Change, or Full Control
Take ownership of the file	Full Control

Each of these rights may be assigned to an individual file. Of course, most administrators find it tedious—if not impossible—to assign access rights to each and every file in the system individually. To simplify this task, Windows NT provides directory-based rights as well.

The specific access rights which may be granted to directories are the same as those which may be assigned to individual files: Read, Write, Execute, Delete, Change Permissions, and Take Ownership. The generic assignments which may be made using these rights, however, are slightly different. In other words, the implications of these rights on a directory—as opposed to an individual file—are not identical to files.

Consider the generic directory access rights listed in the following table.

Generic Rights	Description
No Access	The specified user/group has no rights to any files in the directory.
List	The specified user/group may list the files and subdirectory names within this directory, and may change directories to it. By default, this also means that the user may list the files in the subdirectories.
Read	The specified user/group can read and execute files within the directory.

(continued on next page)

Generic Rights	Description
Add	The specified user/group may create new files within the directory. The user/group may not, however, read files in the directory.
Add & Read	The specified user/group may create new files within the directory and may read and execute files within the directory.
Change	The specified user/group may create new files, read files, and execute files within the directory. Moreover, the user/group may modify existing files in the directory.
Full Control	The specified user/group has full control over all files in the directory, including the ability to read, change, create, take ownership of, and execute files within the directory.
Special Access	The specified user/group has a custom (not generic) set of rights to the files in the directory.

As with file permissions, most administrators will utilize generic rights, rather than specify specific rights for each directory. Consider, however, the specific rights and their implications for commonly assigned user tasks listed in the following table.

Permission Set	Generic Rights Required
Add files and subdirectories	Add, Add & Read, Change, or Full Control
Change directory attributes	Add, Add & Read, Change, or Full Control
Change directory permissions	Add & Read or Full Control
Change to subdirectories	Any Rights
Delete directory	Change or Full Control
Display directory attributes	Any Rights
Display directory owner and permissions	List, Read, Add & Read, Change, or Full Control
Take ownership of directory	Full Control

Now that we understand the individual rights which may be assigned to files and directories, we can begin to understand how to utilize these rights to provide effective security.

Calculating Effective Rights

In abstract form, the file and directory rights shown above represent a simple approach to assigning security rights. When used in a complicated Windows NT system, however, the picture is not always so rosy. In fact, determining which users have which access to which resources is one of the most difficult problems facing Windows NT administrators.

To understand why this is the case, consider the possibilities. For any given file, any user may be granted any of the specific or generic user rights and may also be assigned rights to other files in the same directory through either file-based or directory-based rights. Moreover, this user may have membership in multiple groups, each of which may have different—and possibly conflicting—permissions for either that file or that directory as a whole. In such a case, the calculation of effective user rights is difficult at best.

In order to understand how Windows NT calculates user rights, we must understand the three fundamental assumptions on which rights calculations are based:

- *Permissions are additive.* When users are assigned specific or generic rights to both files and directories from multiple sources (i.e., membership in different groups), their effective rights are additive; that is, all the rights assigned are added together to achieve the user's effective security. Therefore, the effective rights of a user who has both Change and Full Control rights to a file are Full Control. This is because Full Control is a superset of Change, or stated another way: Change + Full Control = Full Control.

- *NT assumes nothing.* Unless explicitly specified, all users have no access rights whatsoever to any given file or directory. Therefore, there is no requirement to assign the No Access right to every user to whom administrators wish to deny access.

- *By default, explicit denials are calculated first.* It is possible that the various rights granted to a user through group membership might be in direct conflict with one another. Consider the possibility of a user who is a member of two groups: Accounting and Personnel. Because Personnel files are sensitive, the system administrator has assigned Full Control rights to the Personnel group and has explicitly assigned the No Access right to the Accounting group. Tom, who is a member of both groups, now has security rights which are indeterminate. Under Windows NT, explicit denials are, in most cases, processed first. Therefore, Tom would be denied access to the Personnel files.

In addition to these assumptions, Windows NT provides for default inheritance of file access rights. This means that access rights need not be assigned to every directory or every file in those directories. Rather, rights may be assigned to a directory higher in the NTFS tree structure and flow downward appropriately.

By default, when a user creates a new subdirectory, Windows NT assigns new security rights to that subdirectory. Note that this happens without the user's approval (or, even, his knowledge) in many cases. The rights assigned are exactly the same as those in the parent directory. This process is called *right inheritance.*

The user, of course, is free to accept the inheritance of rights or may change them at whim. Administrators should be aware that inherited rights are quite useful in some circumstances and quite insecure in others. In either case, inherited rights are considered by some to be dangerous over time.

Consider an example in which an administrator wishes to allow several users access to an application. The application, much as is the custom today, resides within a directory which contains several subdirectories of related files. By assigning the proper group of users the Read right to that directory, each of those users will be able to read and execute files both in the directory itself and in all the subdirectories below. Moreover, to change the rights in the future, the administrator need change only the rights assigned to the directory itself—the rights to the subdirectories will be inherited once again.

Consider, however, another case. Many administrators place their shared applications within subdirectories under a single directory. In such a case, the administrator might be tempted to assign user rights to the parent directory itself, rather than to each application subdirectory. Unfortunately, this would mean that administrators would lose granularity in their security scheme. No longer could they assign specific rights to

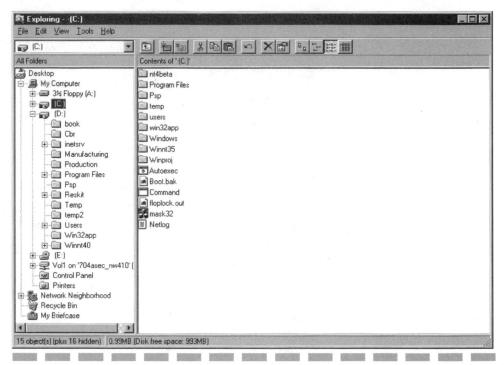

Figure 3.10 The NT 4.0 Explorer.

a given application—rather, all application directories would retain the rights assigned to the parent directory. In this case, we recommend that administrators use inherited rights only on application subdirectories in order to retain individual application-level control.

Many new Windows NT system administrators use inherited rights extensively. Note, however, that extensive use of inherited rights may cause trouble down the road. Because of the complicated directory structures associated with many Windows NT implementations, administrators often lose track of their inherited rights. Unless administrators are extremely careful in the placement of new subdirectories and modifications to the rights of parent directories, it is quite possible to accidentally configure the file and directory rights improperly.

Protecting NT System Files

Some files, of course, require more protection than others. The Windows NT system files fall into this category. We believe it is instructive to understand the default access rights assigned by Windows NT Server on system setup, as indicated in the following table.

Directory	Default Permissions
`Root (\)`	Full Control: Administrators
	Change: Server Operators, Everyone
`%SYSTEM_ROOT%\System32`	Full Control: Administrators, Creator/Owner
	Change: Server Operators, Everyone
`%SYSTEM_ROOT%`	Full Control: Administrators, Creator/Owner
	Change: Everyone, Server Operators
`%SYSTEM_ROOT%\Profiles`	Full Control: Everyone
`%SYSTEM_ROOT%\Profiles\ All Users`	Full Control: Administrators
	Read (RX): Everyone
`%SYSTEM_ROOT%\System`	Full Control: Administrators, Creator/Owner
	Change: Everyone, Server Operators
`%SYSTEM_ROOT%\Config`	Full Control: Everyone
`\Win32App`	Full Control: Administrators, Server Operators, Creator/Owners
	Read (RX): Everyone
`\Program Files`	Full Control: Everyone
`\Temp`	Full Control: Administrators, Creator/Owner
	Change: Everyone, Server Operators
`\Users`	Special (RXWD): Account Operators, Administrators
	Read (RX): Everyone

Consider an example of calculating effective user rights. Users Ivan, Omar, and Geoffery are members of the Manufacturing group. In addition, Omar is a member of the Engineering group, while Geoffery is a member of the Production group. Ivan is a member of the Management group. The group assignments for the `C:\Manufacturing` directory are as follows:

- The Manufacturing group is assigned Change rights
- The Engineering and Production groups are assigned Read rights
- The Management group is denied access

Within the `C:\Manufacturing` directory, both Omar and Geoffery may read, execute, create, or delete files. Ivan, on the other hand, may not have any access whatsoever to the directory, because of his membership in the management group.

Consider the rights assigned when Omar creates a new file in the `C:\Manufacturing` directory. As the file's owner, he is automatically assigned Creator/Owner rights, which enable him to have Full Control over the file. At his discretion, he may provide alternate access to any user or group. By default, however, the new file maintains the same rights as do all the other files in the directory.

Suppose that Omar wishes to allow access only to Geoffery and Ivan. As the owner of the file, he may assign the rights to that file to any user. Therefore, he may assign specific rights to the file which allow access to Geoffery and Ivan.

Remember, however, that Ivan is denied access to the file by token of his membership in the Management group. To assign Ivan rights to the file, Omar must place a copy of the file in another directory to which Ivan may read, then assign the appropriate access rights.

Next, consider what might happen if Omar then copies his newly created file into the `C:\Production` directory. When a user requests that a file be copied, Windows NT actually views the copy process in two steps: copying the information in the file to memory, then creating a new file into which to deposit the data. The new file which is created has the same attributes as any other file which is created by a user.

Therefore, if Omar copies his file into the `C:\Production` directory, Windows NT first makes a copy of the file data in memory, then creates a new file in `C:\Production`. This operation assumes that Omar has Change rights to the `C:\Production` directory. For this example, let's assume that Omar, Ivan, and Geoffery each have Change rights to the directory.

When the new file is created, Omar is named as the Creator/Owner, *and the file inherits the access rights associated with the* `C:\Production` *directory*. Note that the security permissions which were part of the file in the `C:\Management` directory are no longer relevant; rather, by copying the file, Omar has effectively reassigned the rights to the newly created file.

Note also the Windows NT makes a distinction between copying and moving files. Moving consists of three separate actions: copying the data to memory, creating a new file and copying the data to it, and deleting the old file. To perform the move function, the user must have rights to create files in the target directory and delete files in the source directory.

Assuming these criteria are met, Windows NT will move the file. *Interestingly, moving a file does not have the same effect on security that copying a file does.* Rather than inheriting the rights associated with the new directory, a file move retains the rights associated with the original file.

Therefore, consider the implications of Omar moving a file from `C:\Manufacturing` to `C:\Production`. Omar has rights to both create files in `C:\Production` and delete files in `C:\Manufacturing`. Windows NT will thus allow the operation to take place. When the file is moved, however, what will the effective rights be?

As was discussed above, the file rights in the `C:\Production` directory will be the same as in the `C:\Manufacturing` directory. Thus, Omar and Geoffery will retain the right to read the file, while Ivan will still not be able to access the file at all.

Assigning File/Directory Rights

Fortunately, the actual assignment of file and directory rights is far easier than calculating which rights to assign. Within Windows NT, there are several ways to assign file and directory access rights. The easiest way is to use the Windows Explorer (in versions 4.x).

First, launch the Explorer by clicking on the Start menu, then select *Programs* and *Windows NT Explorer.* This will bring up a two-sided window which looks like the following:

From within the Explorer, both users and administrators can browse their disks in a logical, hierarchical manner. The left side of the window shows the highest-level hierarchies, including disks and directories. The right side of the window shows lower-level hierarchies, including subdirectories and files.

In Windows NT 4.x, file and directory rights are considered properties of file and directory objects. Therefore, from within the Windows NT Explorer, you can select any file, display its properties, and change its access rights.

Let's consider an example. Suppose we want to change the user rights to a subdirectory called "Shared Stuff," two levels underneath the root in

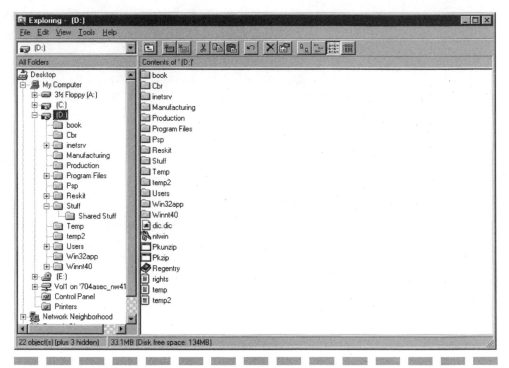

Figure 3.11 Exploring the disk.

the Explorer window above. In this example, we wish to grant Change rights to everyone in the system.

First, within the Windows NT Explorer, we should select the proper disk volume in the left side window. Then, we should double-click on the parent directory of the Shared Stuff directory. In this case, the parent directory is called "Stuff." By double-clicking on "Stuff," the Explorer shows us the subdirectories, including the Shared Stuff directory.

Next, we should right-click the mouse on the Shared Stuff directory. This will bring up a context menu showing us our choices for interacting with the Shared Stuff object. To change the directory access rights, we should select the *Properties* option. This brings up the Shared Stuff properties dialog box. From within this dialog box, we can change the permissions associated with the object.

To do so, select the Security tab at the top of the window. This brings up a dialog box with a button marked *Permissions*. Pressing this button will allow us to set permissions on the directory, as follows:

Figure 3.12
Directory permissions
dialog box.

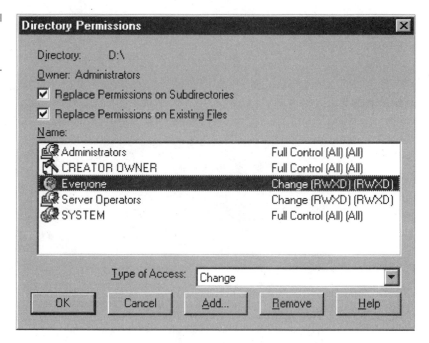

The permissions dialog box first offers us two choices concerning the effects of our changes. The first offers to make the change to subdirectories; the second allows us to change the permissions on existing files. By default, the checkbox to change existing files is marked.

In this case, we want to share all the subdirectories below Shared Stuff, so we'll click the first checkbox marked "Replace Permissions on Subdirectories."

Next, we should select the users to whom we will be assigning rights. In this case, we will be selecting the Everyone group. Note, however, that rights can also be assigned to individual users. In order to assign rights to the Everyone group, we should first click the *Add* button, which will bring up the Add Users dialog box. This dialog box is very similar to that used in assigning user rights from within the User Manager (or User Manager for Domains).

Select the Everyone group and click the *Add* button in the middle of the dialog box. This will add the Everyone group to the list of users shown in the bottom of the dialog box. Then, from the pull-down listbox at the bottom of the dialog box, select the type of access which the Everyone group will be permitted. In this case, let's select *Change*. Then, click *OK* to complete the operation.

NetWare Note

How do NT file rights differ from NetWare rights?

NT Right	NetWare Right	Description
Read	Read	These are the same
Write	Write	These are similar; this permission under NT is more powerful than under NetWare (See Create right below)
Execute	Execute Only	These are similar
	Create	This right is an additional level of granularity that NT does not offer; users may have permission to write to existing files, but not create new files.
Delete	Erase	These are the same
Change Permissions	Access Control	These are similar
Take Ownership		While NetWare supports the concept of file ownership, there is no explicit right associated with taking ownership as Supervisors have all rights to the file
	Modify	This right allows users to change data within a file, but not create new files within a directory
	Supervisory	This allows users full control of the file (it implies all the other user rights)

Command-Line Administration

The Windows NT graphic utilities make it extremely easy to change the permissions on files within an NTFS volume. At the same time, some users, especially those who have extensive experience in UNIX and its

NetWare Note

How do NT file attributes differ from NetWare attributes?

NT Attributes	NetWare Attributes	Description
Read	Read	These are the same
Read Only	Read Only	These are the same
Archive	Archive Needed	These are the same
Compressed	Immediate Compress	These are the same
Hidden	Hidden	These are the same
System	System	These are the same
	Copy Inhibit	Prevents Mac users from copying file
	Don't Compress	Prevents file from ever being compressed
	Don't Suballocate	Prevents block suballocation from occurring on this file
	Rename Inhibit	Prevents users from renaming files or directories
	Sharable	Allows multiple users to access the file simultaneously. This is usually used with the Read Only right.
	Transactional	These files are protected by the NetWare Transaction Tracking System (TTS)
	Purge	When this file is deleted, it will immediately be removed from the disk

variants, prefer to use command-line utilities. In order to accommodate those users, Windows NT provides a command-line utility for assigning and viewing user rights.

The command-line program is called CACLS. By default, the CACLS resides in the %SYSTEMROOT%\System32 directory. The CALCS program has the following options:

```
CACLS <Filename> [/T] [/E] [/C] [/G user : perm] [/R user […]] [/P
user:perm […]] [/D user […]]
```

The switches are used as shown in the following table.

Switch	Description
/T	Used to change the ACLs of specified files within a directory and/or subdirectories.
/E	Used to edit an existing ACL.
/C	Instructs CACLS to continue even after receiving "access denied" errors.
/G user:perm	Used to grant specific access rights: user indicates the user to whom you wish to grant rights; perm indicates the rights which you wish to assign. Allowable permission values are R (for Read), C (for Change), and F (for Full Control).
/R user	Used to revoke privileges: user indicates the user whose rights you wish to revoke. Note that this switch is used in conjunction with the /E switch.
/P user:perm	Used to replace access rights: user indicates the user whose permissions you wish to replace; perm indicates the rights you wish to assign. Allowable permission values are R (for Read), C (for Change), and F (for Full Control).
/D user	Used to deny rights to a user: user indicates the user to whom you wish to deny rights.

Executing CACLS with just a file or directory name will report the rights which are granted to specific users and groups to that file or directory. For example, consider the following example of the \Users\Default directory:

```
D:\users\default>cacls .
D:\users\DEFAULT Everyone:(CI)(special access:)
                 READ_CONTROL
                 SYNCHRONIZE
                 FILE_GENERIC_READ
                 FILE_GENERIC_WRITE
                 FILE_GENERIC_EXECUTE
                 FILE_READ_DATA
                 FILE_WRITE_DATA
                 FILE_APPEND_DATA
                 FILE_READ_EA
                 FILE_WRITE_EA
                 FILE_EXECUTE
                 FILE_READ_ATTRIBUTES
                 FILE_WRITE_ATTRIBUTES
```

```
CREATOR OWNER:(OI)(CI)F
NT AUTHORITY\SYSTEM:(OI)(CI)F
```

Trojan Horse Attacks

Previous sections have shown the default permissions for Windows NT operating system files residing on NTFS partitions. As many readers may have guessed, these permissions are, like many other defaults in Windows NT, defined more for ease of use than for security.

Indeed, the default rights associated with the system utilities in Windows NT present a troubling security hole. Unlike some other holes, however, this is one which can be corrected by proper administration, both on initial system setup and on an ongoing basis.

Consider the potential for an attack using the default access rights and one (pick any one!) of the system utilities. In order to understand this attack, readers should first understand that the assignment of security rights within the operating system is part of the published Win32 API set. Therefore, there is no "security through obscurity" protecting the assignments of either file permissions or user rights.

Using this information, if you are a knowledgeable programmer, you can simply write a program which calls the proper API in order to assign yourself (or anyone else) user rights or file permissions. Of course, the API call will fail if the user's security access token does not have sufficient rights to perform the operation.

Consider the following realistic attack scenario:

Tom is a Windows NT Domain user. As a result, he has few access rights to the Windows NT server which he uses to store his files and retrieve applications. By token of his access to the system, however, he also has Full Control rights to many of the executable files which reside in the %System_Root% and %System_Root%\System32 directories.

Assume also that Tom is a competent Windows NT programmer—and knows all about the Win32 API set. Using his knowledge of the API set and his rights to the %System_Root% directory, Tom is able to write a program which does two things. First, Tom's program grants his user account, TOM, membership in the Administrator's group. Second, his program is designed to call another program of his choosing. For the purposes of this example, let's assume that his program calls another program called notepadd.exe.

To carry out the attack, Tom merely copies the program called `notepad.exe` to a program called `notepadd.exe`. Then, he copies his new program over the original copy of `notepad.exe`. Now, when a user calls the notepad program, Tom's program will be called instead.

When Tom's program executes, it first attempts to grant the user account TOM membership in the Administrator's group, then calls the original notepad program. This process happens so quickly that no user will notice the millisecond delay in starting the notepad program.

Of course, if Tom himself runs the program, it will fail to grant him the user rights he so desires. It will still, however, launch the notepad program. If a user with greater user rights, however, runs the program, Tom might be granted his Administrative membership. And if an Administrator, for example, goes to use the notepad program, Tom will indeed be granted the Administrative rights.

Note that both the failure to gain rights and the granting of rights can be audited by the system. In a busy system, however, Tom might be granted rights and breach the system security long before anyone reads the audit logs to find out about his intrusion. Note also that Tom need not have a user account on the system to carry out this attack. Rather, it is possible to use the Guest account to implement this attack effectively.

To prevent this type of attack, Windows NT administrators can change the default file permissions on existing Windows NT operating system utilities. Note, however, that these permissions can only be used on volumes which utilize the NTFS. Volumes formatted with either FAT or HPFS cannot be protected in this manner. *Therefore, we strongly recommend that all Windows NT operating system files be installed on NTFS volumes.*

Correcting the permission problems with the NT operating system utilities is not as simple an endeavor as might be expected. Some administrators simply revoke users, permissions to write to the `%System_ROOT%` directory and all directories which exist as children of that directory. Unfortunately, this will not be an effective means of closing the potential security hole because of a quirk in the Windows NT application installation conventions.

This is because many (if not most) Windows NT applications install files to the `%System_Root%` and its subdirectories at installation time. These files may include standard executables, dynamic link libraries (DLLs), and other configuration files (e.g., `.INI`). The majority of application installation programs will fail if they are denied the right to write files to the `%System_Root%` directory or its subdirectories.

Therefore, administrators cannot simply revoke users' Write rights to these directories. Rather, files must be managed on an individual basis, both immediately after the operating system installation and over time in order to protect application files which have been added to these directories.

First, we recommend that all executable files within the `%System_Root%` and its subdirectories be individually set with the permissions listed in the following table.

User Right	User Groups
Full Control	Administrators, Creator/Owner Server Operators, SYSTEM
Add & Read	Everyone

Note that this applies to all files which contain code which might be executed by a user (or administrator). Unfortunately, it is not always apparent which files this might include. Obviously, files such as those which have file extensions of `.EXE`, `.COM`, and `.BAT` are included. However, consider the following other file types which might contain executable code:

- `.OCX` (OLE controls)
- `.DRV` (drivers)
- `.INI` (configuration files)
- `.SCR` (screen savers)
- `.CMD` (command files)
- `.CPL` (control panel applets)
- `.MOD` (module files)
- `.SYS` (system files)
- Virtually any other extension whose entry in the registry can be modified

Each of these files might contain either executable code or pointers to files which contain executable code and, therefore, might be targeted by an attacker intent on the type of attack described above. Administrators should be aware, however, that some of these files cannot be protected by revoking Write rights to them. Rather, files such as `.INI` files are often written to during normal program execution, and therefore must remain writable by all users who utilize them.

This means that it is probably impossible (in most Windows NT systems) to fully prevent a Trojan horse–based attack. Administrators who are responsible for highly sensitive Windows NT systems should strictly limit the applications which may be run on their systems. For example, these systems should not permit users to install any applications which require access to the `%System_Root%` directory. Similarly, none of the applications which are used on the system should require Write rights to `.ini` or other files within the `%System_Root%` directory hierarchy. Finally, these systems should not permit users to place arbitrary executable files within shared directory spaces. Rather, all files should be checked for trojan horses before ever being executed by a user with Administrative access.

These latter recommendations also apply to less secure Windows NT systems. Therefore, if a directory contains an application which may be used by multiple users of the system (either from the console or over a network), the executable files within that directory should be protected accordingly.

As is mentioned elsewhere in this book, the registry may also contain pointers to executable files. The registry keys which contain these pointers can be protected using registry permission settings. In reality, however, the complexity of the registry is such that few of these keys are likely to be protected in any given Windows NT system.

This means that any of the registry pointers may therefore contain pointers to executable programs which might have been trojanized by a system attacker. Of course, to modify the registry, a user must have permission to access the registry. Therefore, we strongly recommend that Windows NT systems do not contain accounts which have no (or weak) passwords; this especially includes the Guest Account, which exists by default on Windows NT 3.5X systems. Of course, users on other Windows NT systems within the same network may also be able to edit some portions of the registry of remote systems.

Administrators should be careful to only use Administrator-privileged accounts when truly necessary; in all other circumstances, they should log into their Windows NT systems with less-privileged accounts. In addition, more security conscious Windows NT administrators may consider setting up a private directory to further protect commonly used system utilities.

As was noted above, the registry contains many keys which might contain pointers to trojanized executable code. Chapter 5 contains more data on these locations within the registry. In general, however, the risks include keys which name specific executable files, such as those which name files to run on logon, as well as those that contain executable paths which might be modified to contain additional directories.

Taking Ownership of Files

Within Windows NT, the named owner of a file, by default, has full control over the file. Generally, the owner of a file will be either the Administrator or the creator of the file. As was discussed above, the Take Ownership (P) permission gives any user the right to take ownership of a file or a directory. By default, users who are members of the Administrators group, those who have Full Control permissions, and those who have Special Access permissions including Take Ownership may take ownership.

As has been noted elsewhere in this book, Windows NT has no user with default access to all files. Rather, members of the Administrator's group retain the right to take ownership of any file at any time. We strongly recommend that the exercise of this privilege be audited at all times to ensure that it is not abused by system administrators.

Note that taking ownership of a file or directory is a one-way street. A user who has the Take Ownership privilege may take ownership of the object but cannot assign ownership back to the original user or assign it to any other user. That is, a user cannot give ownership; ownership can only be taken by another user.

As with changing the permissions to a file or directory, Windows NT recognizes ownership as a property of a file or directory object. Therefore, we can select the object and list its ownership property using much the same operation as was demonstrated above for changing file and directory permissions.

An easy way to take ownership of a file (assuming that you have permission), is to first launch the Windows NT Explorer. Then, select the volume, directory, and subdirectory required. Next, select the object you wish to take ownership of. Right-click on this object, bringing up the context menu. Then, select the *Properties* option.

From within the object Properties dialog box, select the *Security* tab. At the bottom of this tab is a button marked *Ownership*. Press this button to bring up the following dialog box:

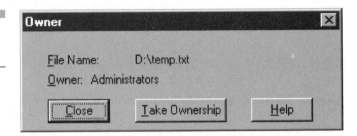

Figure 3.13
Take ownership dialog box.

This dialog box lists the object being examined and the current owner of the object. In addition, there is a button marked *Take Ownership*. Clicking this button will allow you to take ownership of the file (assuming that you have sufficient rights). If the object you have selected is a directory, you will be prompted to indicate whether you wish to take ownership of all the files and directories which exist as children of the selected directory. Selecting the *Yes* option will grant you ownership of all the children of that directory and its subdirectories.

Creating File Shares

Within Windows NT networks, resources are shared with other users by creating *shares*. File shares are used to share the contents of files or directories with other users. They contain all the relevant information about the files which are to be shared, including

- Share name
- Location on the disk
- Users and permissions

One of the most important jobs of a Windows NT system administrator is to ensure that the shares which are created do not violate system policy. Therefore, creating shares requires an understanding of how share access rights interact with the file and directory access rights described above.

Users cannot create shares unless they have access to the files and/or directories they wish to share. This means that one of two facts must be true:

1. The files and/or directories to be shared reside on an HPFS or FAT partition which has no discretionary access control features. In such a case, all files may potentially be accessed and/or shared by any user.

2. The files and/or directories to be shared reside on an NTFS partition within a directory structure to which the share creator has access. A user who does not have access to the share files cannot create the share.

Let's consider an example. Suppose user Clarke wishes to share a Shared Stuff directory. Assume that the directory resides on an NTFS partition and is owned by Clarke.

Shares can be created using the Windows Explorer. To create a share, launch the Explorer by clicking on the Start menu, then selecting *Programs* and *Windows Explorer.* Next, click on a file or a directory—in this case, Shared Stuff—that you wish to share. This will select the shared object.

Then, right-click on the Shared Stuff directory, bringing up the Context menu. From this menu, select the *Sharing...* option. Alternatively, you may select the *Properties* option, then the *Sharing* tab from within the Properties dialog box. Either of these methods will bring up the Sharing dialog box.

The Sharing dialog box has two major options: *Not Shared* and *Shared As:.* By default, all files and directories are not shared. To create a share for the Shared Stuff directory, click the *Shared As* radio button. This will prompt you for a sharename for the directory.

Users and Administrators should try to use descriptive sharenames in order to identify objects when browsing the network. Note that the addition of a $ to the end of a share name will cause that share not to be displayed during the browsing process; this is useful for some file shares which are to be private among a group of users who are aware of the explicit sharename.

In this case, let's name the share "Clarke's Shared Stuff." In addition to the sharename, Windows NT also permits you to place a comment, or a description on the share. This description will be displayed to users as they browse the network using standard Windows NT, Windows 95, or

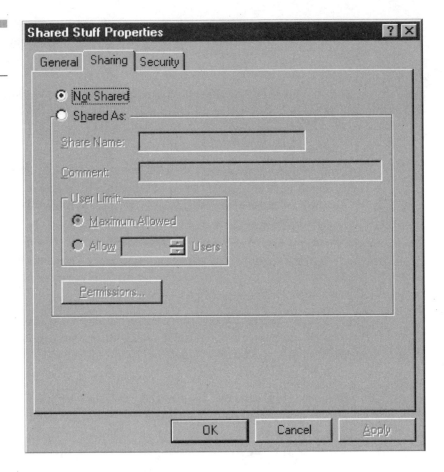

Windows for Workgroups tools. For this example, let's place a comment which reads, "This is Clarke's Stuff."

The next section of the dialog box allows the user sharing the resource to limit the number of users who may access the resource at a given time. For some resources, such as licensed software, this is extremely important. Unfortunately, Windows NT provides no built-in means for providing electronic software metering, other than this function. Therefore, if you wish to share a program to which you own only a single license, you are likely to be obligated to limit the access to the file to a single user. Of course, there is no technical requirement to do so—only your own conscience and your legal liability.

On the other hand, there might—under some circumstances—be a technical requirement to limit access to a certain number of users. Consider a situation in which you, the user, share a popular set of programs or data files from your workstation. Obviously you wish to share the programs or data with other users, but you probably don't wish to significantly degrade the performance of your system in the process. Therefore, you might wish to specifically limit the number of users permitted to use the resource.

Note that on Windows NT workstations, there is an unchangeable limit of 10 connections permitted to a given share. On Windows NT servers, however, the number of connections permitted to any given share is limited only by the number of legal licenses which have been purchased and installed on the server. Effectively, the upper bound on the number of users which may connect to a share on a Windows NT server is limited by the hardware; a single NT Server supports in excess of 4 billion licenses per server!

In our example, let's assume that Clarke's shared directory is on a Windows NT server, and he's not concerned about either licensing requirements or performance degradation. Therefore, we'll leave the share setting at the Maximum Allowed setting in order to permit the maximum legally licensed number of connections.

Finally, we must set the most important part of the share—the permissions associated with accessing it. To set up the share permissions, click on the button marked *Permissions*. This brings up a dialog box much like that seen in previous examples for setting permissions on files and directories. In creating the share, a user or administrator may share the resource with users, groups, or any combination of the two. In addition, each user (or group) authorized to use the share may have discrete permissions to that share.

In this case, let's permit all users to have Read access. Therefore, we'll want to assign Read rights to the Everyone user group. *Note that the default for all new file shares is to assign Full Control access to Everyone.* To change this, select the Everyone group in the lower portion of the dialog box, then select Read access from the pull-down listbox. Finally, click the *OK* button to save and create the share.

As with the directory permissions, Windows NT graphic tools provide an easy way to create and modify permissions on file shares. Some users, however, are more accustomed to using command-line tools. Unfortunately, the Windows NT command-line share tool NET SHARE does not permit modification of user permissions. The NET SHARE command can, however, create new file shares and delete old file shares.

Because of the default permissions for new file shares, however, the use of the NET SHARE command can be quite dangerous. As we have discussed, the default permission settings for new file shares is to grant Full Control rights to the Everyone group. Therefore, any new share created using the NET SHARE command will automatically have Full Control rights granted to everyone. Unlike the graphic Windows NT tools, the NET SHARE command offers no way to modify these defaults. As a result, we strongly recommend that all shares be created using the graphic user tools.

Share Security Considerations

Note that file and/or directory shares may be created only by Administrators and Server Operators on Windows NT servers and administrators and Power Users on Windows NT workstations. Similarly, modifying permissions on shares can be accomplished only by these same user groups.

When assigning rights to shares, administrators should also consider the rights assigned to files and directories through the file system. For files which reside on a FAT or an HPFS partition, the rights assigned as part of the share process form the only security restrictions on those files. Indeed, creating network-based shares is the only way to provide any access control to files which reside on non-NTFS partitions. Be aware, however, that such security cannot be relied on unless users are denied access to logging onto the system directly from the system console.

Note that when a user accesses files from the console, Shares restrictions do not apply; rather, only the file and directory restrictions apply, and under FAT/HPFS, there are no restrictions.

For files which reside on NTFS, the rights which are granted to share users are somewhat related to the rights granted in the file system itself. More specifically, the more restrictive set of rights among the two applies to any user using the file share.

Consider an example of a user Dennis, who has been granted Read rights to the files in the directory C:\Accounting. The administrator then shares the C:\Accounting directory, granting Change rights to the Everyone group. When Dennis attempts to access the share across the network, what will his effective rights be?

As a member of the Everyone group, Dennis should have Change rights to the C:\Accounting share. However, his account has explicitly been granted Read rights within the file system. As the more restrictive set of rights, Windows NT will allow Dennis only Read access to the `C:\Accounting` share. Administrators should be aware of this restriction, as it often causes confusion among new system administrators.

When creating shares on non-NTFS partitions, both administrators and users must be aware of the insecurity of the default settings. In examining the default settings for much of the operating system, it is evident that Windows NT defaults to ease of use for many settings, rather than defaulting to strong security. File shares are an excellent example of these defaults.

By default, Windows NT file shares grant Full Control rights to the Everyone group. This means that any user on a Windows NT network (including Windows 95 and Windows for Workgroups users) may connect to the share and, barring NTFS-based file restrictions, may exercise full control over that share. This control may include intentional or unintentional data modification or destruction.

We strongly recommend that all users modify the share settings on their newly created shares immediately after they are created. After creating new shares, the first order of business should always be to limit the Everyone group's access to that resource.

Note that the use of NTFS partitions does provide some protection against this default setting. As was noted above, users who access shares on an NTFS partition are subject to the more restrictive rights often granted in the NTFS system. Therefore, we also strongly recommend that administrators utilize NTFS partitions whenever possible to limit the potential security risk of creating new file and/or directory shares.

Removing File Shares

One of the most common security risks found on Windows NT systems today is the result of administrative failure. More specifically, many Windows NT system administrators fail to remove file shares after they are no longer needed.

Like the creation of file shares, there are at least two ways to effectively remove a file share:

1. Using the command line NET utility. By using the command line NET SHARE *Sharename* /DELETE, administrators can remove existing shares. For example, if the sharename that you wish to delete is called applications, issue the command line NET SHARE applications /DELETE.

2. Launching the Windows NT explorer as described above and then selecting the directory which is the source of the share you wish to remove. Right-click on the directory, then select *Properties* from the Context menu.

This will bring up the Properties dialog box. From this dialog box, select the *Sharing* tab, then click the radio button marked *Not Shared*. Clicking on the *OK* button will remove the file share and the potential security risk associated with it.

We strongly recommend that all administrators review their file shares on a regular basis and remove those which are no longer required. In order to review the file shares which currently exist on a Windows NT system, first launch the Server Manager.

By default, Server Manager is found within the *Administrative Tools* group inside the *Programs* option of the Start menu. From within Server Manager, select the server whose shares you wish to review. Then, double-click on that server name.

This brings up the Server Properties dialog box. From within this dialog box select the *Shares...* button. This will bring up a list of the current shares on the selected Windows NT system. Note that each share entry contains the sharename as well as its absolute disk reference location. By using the disk reference location, the administrator can make an assessment of the relative security risk associated with each share as well as obtain the share names of those shares which should be removed.

Alternatively, administrators may use the NET SHARE command to view the same information. In order to do so, issue the command line NET SHARE with no parameters. This will list the shares available as well as their disk references. Thus, we strongly recommend that all administrators review these shares on a regular basis and remove those which are no longer required as well as those which pose an unnecessary security risk.

Note that in addition to user- and administrator-created shares, Windows NT also creates some shares for itself. By default, the shares listed in the following table may exist on a Windows NT server.

Sharename	Function
x$, where x is a disk volume letter	This file share is created when volumes are created in Windows NT. In this case, the x stands for the drive letter of the disk volume. Therefore, most Windows NT systems running on Intel-based hardware will have a default share of C$. Note that the share name is not visible under normal circumstances due to the trailing $. By default, only Administrators, Server Operators, and Backup Operators may access these shares remotely.
Admin$	This file share is created on system installation to permit access to the Windows NT home directory (%SYSTEM_ROOT%). It is used primarily for remote system administration. Much like the x$ share, this share may only be accessed remotely by highly privileged users. Note that the sharename is not visible under normal circumstances because of the trailing $.
IPC$	The IPC$ share is similarly used for remote administration of Windows NT systems. It provides the named-pipes support which allows certain programs to communicate with one another. Moreover, this share is also used when viewing the shared resources on a remote Windows NT system. Note that the sharename is not visible under normal circumstances because of the trailing $.
NetLogon	The NetLogon share exists only on Windows NT servers. It is used to provide a home directory for user logons, much like the Login directory in Novell's NetWare.
Print$	The Print$ resource is used to enable users to access shared printers. All remote printer mappings are created using the Print$ share. Note that the sharename is not visible under normal circumstances due to the trailing $.
Repl$	The Repl$ share is found only on Windows NT servers which are acting as replication partners. This share is created when directory replication services are first installed and configured. Note that the sharename is not visible under normal circumstances because of the trailing $.

Windows NT administrators should also be aware that simply removing a directory which contains a file share will not sufficiently remove that file share. If, in the future, another directory is created with the same name, that directory will immediately be subject to the same share settings as was its predecessor. Therefore, we strongly recommend that administrators remove file shares before removing the directories containing the shared files.

Creating Printer Shares

In many cases, Windows NT administrators have little concern about the security of their printer shares. Indeed, in most cases, printer shares need not be bound by significant access restrictions. After all, do most administrators really care about which printers people use?

As it turns out, the answer is sometimes "Yes." Consider a case of a printer loaded with valuable paper, such as blank checks. In this case, an administrator would certainly want to provide significant access control and auditing functionality over that printer.

To demonstrate printer security, let's assume that we wish to create a new printer share for a check printer. First, we must set up and configure the printer. This can be accomplished using the Printer Setup Wizard, which can be found under the *Settings* and *Printers* options of the Start menu. For detailed information on configuring printers, see the Windows NT documentation.

Once the printer is created, select the printer from the Printers dialog box. Then, right-click on the printer and select properties. As with other objects in the Windows NT environment, the security and sharing attributes of printers are considered properties of the printer object.

Selecting the properties of the printer will bring up the dialog box shown in Fig. 3.15.

From within this dialog box, first select the *Sharing* tab. From within this tab, you can identify the printer as one which will be shared with the rest of the Windows NT network. In order to share it, select the *Share As* radio button and enter a sharename. In this case, we're going to be sharing a sensitive printer, so we may wish to hide the sharename of the printer. After all, users who have both the need and the authority to use the printer can be given the explicit sharename; therefore, the sharename need not be accessible to all users browsing the network. For our exam-

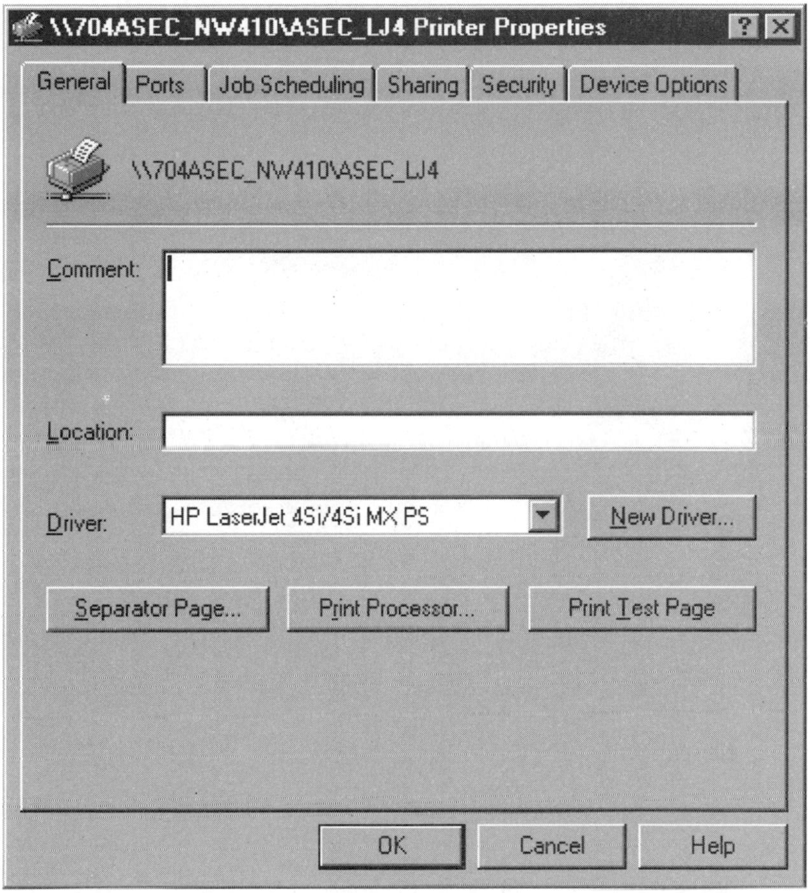

Figure 3.15
Printer properties dialog box.

ple, let's name the printer `Check Printer$`. Note that the trailing `$` will hide the sharename.

Next, select the *Security* tab on the Printer Properties dialog box. From this tab, administrators can set permissions for use of the printer, auditing policies for the printer, and may take ownership of the printer. In our example, we should first set the permissions for use of the printer. Only a few users have both need and authorization to use the printer; those users (in our example) are members of the Check Printing group. Thus, we should assign proper access to the Check Printing group.

Windows NT permits the access rights listed in the following table to be assigned to printers.

Printer Access Right	Description
Full Control	Full Control allows all rights over a printer, including printing, starting and stopping print queues, changing a print job order, changing printer properties, deleting printers, and changing printer permissions. By default, this right is granted to Administrators, Print Operators, and Server Operators.
Print	Print allows users to print documents only to the given printer. It is the lowest level of access which still permits use of the printer. By default, the Everyone group is granted this right to all new printer shares.
Manage	Manage allows users to control document settings and start, stop, or pause specific print jobs. Manage users are not granted the right to print to a printer. By default, this right is granted to the owner or creator of a document.
No Access	No Access specifically denies access to a printer. By default, no user groups are granted this right.

Much like the permissions which may be granted for file and directory access, permissions for printers are *additive,* meaning that users may be granted multiple sets of rights, depending on their membership in various groups. The effective rights which apply to those users are then determined by adding the rights granted by the different groups in which the user has membership. However, much like the file and directory permissions as well, deny permissions are usually processed first. Therefore, if you, the user, are assigned the No Access right to a printer in any group of which you are a member, you will be unable to access the printer at all, regardless of the rights granted to you by membership in other groups.

In our example, we see that the default access rights are not acceptable for our check printer. We should modify them as necessary:

Administrators. By default, Administrators are granted full control. This is acceptable for our check printer.

Creator/Owner. By default, the Creator/Owner is granted Manage access. Because this applies only to specific documents, it is acceptable for our check printer.

Everyone. By default, the Everyone group is granted print access. Obviously, this is not acceptable for our check printer, unless we want everyone to have the ability to give themselves a raise!

Print Operators. By default, the Print Operators group is granted Full Control. While this is acceptable for most printers, a check printer is probably too sensitive to allow this type of control to a large number of print operators. Therefore, we'll remove Print Operators from the permissions list.

Server Operators. By default, the Server Operators group is granted Full Control. Like the Print Operators group, this is probably too large a group to permit access to the check printer and still maintain effective security. Therefore, we'll remove Server Operators from the permissions list.

Thus, our permissions listed in the Printer Permissions dialog box should be as follows:

Figure 3.16
Assigning rights to printer.

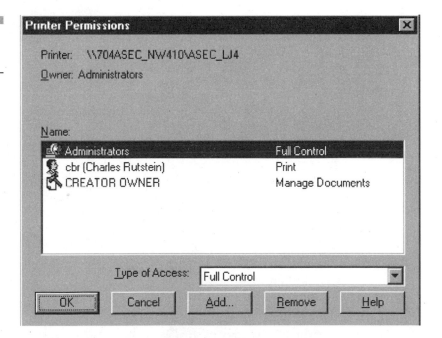

To save these settings, click the *OK* button.

Finally, we'll want to audit the use of our check printer. To do so, select the *auditing* button on the *Security* tab of the printer properties dialog box. This will bring up the Printer Auditing dialog box:

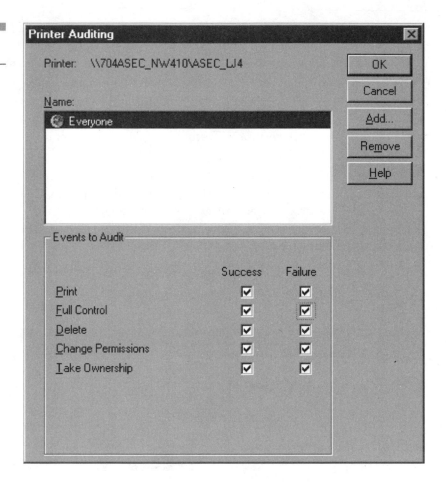

Because the check printer is so sensitive, we're probably going to want to place the greatest amount of auditing possible on its use. Therefore, we should first click the *Add...* button to indicate a group or user we wish to audit. Because of the sensitivity of the printer, we'll create audit events whenever a member of the Everyone group (i.e., all users in the system) use the printer. Select the Everyone group and press the *Add* button, then the *OK* button.

Now, we can select the printer events that we want to audit. The choices are shown in the following table.

Print Event	Description
Change Permissions	A Change Permissions audit event is generated whenever a user changes the permissions associated with a printer.
Delete	A Delete audit event is generated whenever a printer is deleted.
Full Control	A Full Control audit event is generated whenever a user changes a print job's settings, starts, or stops; rearranges the order of print jobs; or modifies the current printer properties.
Print	A Print audit event is generated whenever a user prints a document.
Take Ownership	A Take Ownership event is generated whenever a user takes ownership of the printer object.

Note that each of these events can be audited for both success and failure. In most cases, administrators will want to audit at least the failure of these events. In some cases, such as with our check printer, we'll also want to audit the success of each of these events. Therefore, in the Printer Auditing dialog box, we should select all of the checkboxes in the lower portion of the dialog box.

Then, we can select the *OK* button twice to save our settings and create the new printer share.

Printer Spool Files

Under Windows NT, all print jobs are automatically spooled to disk before printing. This frees end-user applications from having to manage their interactions with comparably slow printers. It also, however, introduces a potential security risk on some Windows NT systems.

By default, print jobs will spool into a designated directory (usually Spool) under the `%System_Root%\System32` directory. On NTFS volumes, this directory has default protections which permits all users at least Read access. Users who need to create print spool files must have permission to create new files in this directory.

Of course, Windows NT implementations which utilize FAT volumes are unable to provide any protection for spool files. Under these circumstances, spool files will be available for all users, regardless of the creator/owner.

Based upon these requirements, users should be cautious about the sensitivity of print jobs which traverse the spool directory on their way to a printer. Users who require significant security for their print jobs should be assigned personal printers directly attached to their workstations, rather than printing via a network-based spool file.

Moreover, administrators should be careful to assign spool directories to volumes which are not vulnerable to denial-of-service attacks. For example, a malicious user might spool an excessively large number of files to the spool directory in order to potentially crash a server. To prevent this problem, ensure that spool files are on volumes which are not vulnerable to these types of attack.

Crypto API

In version 4.0 of Windows NT, Microsoft introduced several new additions to the standard Win32 API set. One of these additions—the Crypto API—has direct use for securing Windows NT systems.

The Crypto API was designed to isolate both programmers and users from the complexity of data encryption and digital signature management. In the process, the Crypto API can help programmers to eliminate the need for users to manage key generation and exchange. In short, the Crypto API brings encryption to the masses.

Note, however, that the Crypto API is just that: an API set. Without an associated program to call the API functions, it provides no benefit. Moreover, the API set requires the addition of a Cryptographic Service Provider (CSP) in order to perform the actual encryption functions.

Although the Crypto API was just beginning to be used at the time of writing, we expect significant numbers of vendors to provide both CSPs and encryption applications using those CSPs. We believe that within the next year (1997), administrators will be able to choose from among a number of applications to encrypt their native NT file systems in order to provide additional security to those files.

Potential Security Weaknesses

As we have shown, Windows NT provides significant file system security, in terms of confidentiality, integrity, and availability of data. When properly configured, Windows NT administrators can effectively limit access and manage control over large numbers of files with relative ease. Moreover, they can plan for unforeseen system failures such as disk failures by implementing software-based RAID configurations (for more information on this topic, see Chapter 7, *System Integrity and Availability*).

There are, however, some potential areas of weakness. Although these weaknesses are discussed elsewhere in the text, we mention them here to provide a reminder to system administrators to be ever vigilant about their configurations:

LACK OF ENCRYPTION/BOOT PROTECTION. According to industry sources, over 90 percent of all Windows NT installations are run on Intel-based hardware. Unfortunately, most Intel-based hardware lacks any formal boot protection; anyone with physical access to a system may reboot that system from any given bootable device, including a floppy disk drive. Once the system has been booted using an alternate operating system (or another copy of Windows NT), the system is an open book—anyone may peruse any of the data residing in the file system.

The only effective way to counter this attack is to combine good physical security with the use of strong encryption. Unfortunately, Windows NT does not currently provide full file system encryption, although it is likely to be able to encrypt files on a limited basis using the Crypto API in the future. Administrators should be careful about the physical placement of their Windows NT servers and use encryption where possible.

The primary factor barring a boot-based attack today is the limited availability of NTFS drivers for other operating systems. However, there is currently an NTFS driver under development for Linux, a public-domain version of UNIX, and a DOS-based TSR (terminate and stay resident) available which is able to read NTFS partitions. In addition, NTFS drivers might be available in the future from developers of a wide range of future operating systems. Unauthorized access via these drivers will continue to be a problem until Microsoft builds strong encryption into the file system, perhaps in the Cairo release of Windows NT.

We should note, however, that this potential security weakness is not limited to Windows NT. Rather, any computer system which can be booted from an alternate device by an interactive user is potentially at risk from the same type of attack.

BACKUP/RESTORE RIGHTS. As has been discussed elsewhere in this book, members of the Backup/Restore group have full access to all files in the file system, whether it is HPFS, NTFS, or FAT. Therefore, accounts in this group must be closely contained.

DISK SPACE QUOTAS. Surprisingly, Windows NT lacks one of the basic features of other file and print server operating systems: the ability to assign disk space quotas to users. The current releases of Windows NT make no provision for limiting the amount of disk space users may use within their home directories. This means that a user might be able to launch a denial-of-service attack against an NT system by filling the file system until there is no space remaining. There are, however, several third-party utilities available which can provide disk space quotas. We recommend that administrators utilize these tools until such capability is built into the operating system.

DEFAULT RIGHTS TO FILE SHARES. Windows NT is designed to provide easy connectivity out of the box, although not necessarily secure connectivity. As a result, the default permissions for all new file shares are to give Full Control rights to the Everyone group. This means that all users will have full control of any file in any share until steps are taken by the share operator to reduce the potential risk. We strongly recommend that users modify the permissions on all file shares immediately after they are created.

LACK OF DISCRETIONARY ACCESS CONTROL ON FAT/HPFS. Windows NT can provide significant file security, but only if the NTFS file system is used. Although the use of the FAT file system may provide some convenience in terms of backward compatibility, we strongly recommend that users always utilize the NTFS file system, for both its security and its recoverability functions.

CHAPTER 4

Security Logging and Auditing

Few men have virtue to withstand the highest bidder.
George Washington

Perhaps one of the most overlooked foundations of information security is the importance of security logging and auditing. Although not as "sexy" as advanced authentication techniques or exploiting advanced system vulnerabilities, logging and auditing are essential to building a secure Windows NT—or other—computer system.

Unlike much of the other security measures that are discussed throughout this book, security logging and auditing tools are able to function both proactively and reactively. Proactively, they represent the watchful eye of the system administrator. If users understand that their security violations are being logged and reviewed by the administrator, they're far less likely to purposely try to reach beyond the bounds of their privileges.

In the case of a real system intrusion, security logs function reactively to help the administrator paint a clearer picture of how the attack was possible, what information or resources might have been compromised, and, perhaps, what steps to take in the future to prevent a recurrence.

Protecting Security Logs

In all cases, security logs are of value only if two criteria are met:

1. The system must be able to identify users precisely. Fortunately, Windows NT is able to authenticate users and track their activities with great precision. Using an object model, NT tracks all users, use of resources, including spawned processes and processes spawned by processes. Of course, this model works only when users log into Windows NT using their own unique user accounts. If users share accounts, it is impossible to provide a precise logging capability. Therefore, we strongly recommend that all users—including administrators—use their own unique user accounts. Administrators should resist the temptation to log into the system under the Administrator account; rather, they should use a unique user account with membership in the Administrator's group. The Administrator account should be reserved for emergencies.

2. The security logs are protected from tampering from attackers. Experience has shown that most successful hackers are extremely aware of security logs. As a result, their first activities after penetrating a system often include disabling or modifying security logging in order to hide their activities. In addition, most successful hackers try to destroy the evidence of their penetration. They do so by deleting or corrupting the security logs. In Windows NT, the default security log file is named SecEvent.Evt. It is stored in the `%SystemRoot%\System32\Config` directory. Only two user groups are granted default access to this file; both Administrators and the System account have Full Control rights.

In Windows NT, only a small number of user accounts are granted the ability to modify audit policy and view or clear the audit logs. By default, only the Administrators group has the right to clear the audit logs. For this reason (and many others!) accounts within this group should be granted only to a few trustworthy administrators.

Event Logging

Within Windows NT, all logging for both system and security functions are integrated together into a centralized logging facility. Moreover, applications that are written according to approved NT design criteria should be able to send their log data to this facility as well. As a result, NT provides a more useful central logging mechanism than do many other competing operating systems.

To access the logs, administrators should launch the Event Viewer from within Program Manager:

Date	Time	Source	Category	Event	User	Computer
4/22/96	2:00:36 PM	Security	Privilege Use	578	Administrator	TUNA
4/22/96	2:00:34 PM	Security	Privilege Use	578	Administrator	TUNA
4/22/96	2:00:17 PM	Security	Logon/Logoff	529	SYSTEM	TUNA
4/22/96	2:00:06 PM	Security	Privilege Use	578	Guest	TUNA
4/22/96	2:00:01 PM	Security	Privilege Use	578	Guest	TUNA
4/22/96	1:59:35 PM	Security	Privilege Use	578	IUSR_TUNA	TUNA
4/22/96	1:57:59 PM	Security	Privilege Use	578	IUSR_TUNA	TUNA
4/22/96	1:56:36 PM	Security	Privilege Use	578	IUSR_TUNA	TUNA
4/22/96	1:44:39 PM	Security	Privilege Use	578	Guest	TUNA
4/22/96	1:43:18 PM	Security	Privilege Use	578	IUSR_TUNA	TUNA
4/22/96	11:50:44 AM	Security	Logon/Logoff	529	SYSTEM	TUNA
4/22/96	11:33:21 AM	Security	Logon/Logoff	537	SYSTEM	TUNA
4/22/96	11:33:14 AM	Security	Privilege Use	578	Administrator	TUNA
4/22/96	11:31:06 AM	Security	Privilege Use	578	Administrator	TUNA
4/22/96	11:30:28 AM	Security	System Event	517	SYSTEM	TUNA

Figure 4.1 Event viewer.

From the log menu, users may select the logs they wish to view. Within each of the logs, similar types of events are logged. Moreover, administrators may often select whether events are to be logged when certain system criteria are met due to a successful or an unsuccessful user activity. The high-level categories of events which can be logged are listed in the following table.

Security Event Category	Description
Account Management	Account Management events include changes to user and group accounts, including creation, deletion, modification, and group membership changes. Note that more detail on some of these events may be recorded as Object Access events.
Detailed Tracking	Detailed tracking events provide (as the name suggests) low-level tracking of things such as program activation and indirect object accesses (such as when an object uses its inherited security token to access another object).
Logon/Logoff	Logon/Logoff events are created for each logon or logoff attempt. Administrators may decide whether to audit successes or failures; *we strongly recommend that both successes and failures be recorded*. Further information recorded by the event log includes the type of logon attempted: interactive, network, or service.
Object Access	Object Access events are among the most common of events found in the event log. They are created when a user attempts to access an object within the Windows NT system or across a Windows NT network. Auditing the success of this operation will yield tremendous security logs and, as a result, is not recommended. *We strongly recommend auditing failures on object access.* Although some of the high-level activity captured by the Object Access events are also captured by other types of events, Object Access events are perhaps the most useful in providing a detailed picture of user activity.
Policy Change	Policy change events are captured whenever a change is made to the security policy database. Because of the sensitive nature and far-reaching effects of all changes to the security policy database, all attempted policy changes (both successful and unsuccessful) should be logged.
Privileged Use	Privileged Use events are generated when users exercise the rights that have been granted to them, as well as some data regarding the assignment of specific user rights. Failed attempts which generate Privileged Use events should be logged.

Security Event Category	Description
System Event	System Events are generated when the system detects something which may affect the security of the entire Windows NT system or audit log. This includes the nonremovable event generated when an administrator clears the security log.

Event Log Sizing

From within the Event Viewer, administrators may also set the maximum sizes for the three types of Windows NT logs. From the Log menu, administrators may select the *Log Settings* option. This brings up a dialog box which allows the administrator to set the overall log size:

Figure 4.2
Event log settings

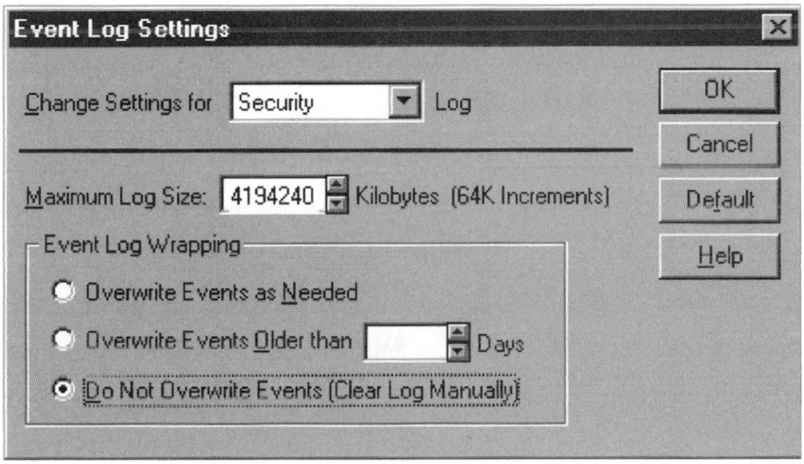

For each of the three logs, administrators may set a maximum size for the log. Regardless of other settings selected, the log will never grow beyond this maximum amount. The maximum size setting requires a log size which is a multiple of 64 kbytes; if another value is entered, it will be rounded up to the nearest 64 kbytes. The maximum permitted log size is 4,194,240 kbytes.

Once the log reaches this maximum size, there are several possibilities, each configurable by the administrator. The first choice is to overwrite events in the security log *"As Necessary."* This means that when the event log grows to its maximum size, the log will overwrite events in the log, beginning with the oldest events, in order to maintain the logging process. If this setting is chosen, the system will never run out of auditing space (assuming that there is sufficient disk space for the maximum log file size).

The second choice is to "Overwrite Events Older Than...." This option permits the system to overwrite entries in the log, but only when they are older than the number of days set in this field. The maximum number of days which may be set in this field is 365 (1 year). Note that the use of this setting may cause an audit failure. Because audited events do not have an even daily distribution, it is entirely possible that the log could grow to its maximum size, then not be able to overwrite events in the log because they are not yet of sufficient age.

The final choice is to never overwrite events in the log. This choice requires the services of a committed system administrator, as the event log will continue to grow until it is cleared manually by an administrator. If the maximum size of the log is reached, no events will be overwritten and an audit failure will result.

In the case of an audit failure, one of two events will occur, depending upon the value of the registry key:

```
HKEY_LOCAL_MACHINE\System\CurrentControlSet\Control\Lsa\
CrashOnAuditFail
```

If this key is set with a value of 1, the system will perform an immediate shutdown once an audit failure is detected. This is the setting which we strongly recommend and which is required for C2 compliance. A key value of 0 for this key will allow the system to proceed, regardless of audit failures. Administrators should be aware that this circumstance may lead to a breakdown of the auditing process and should not be allowed to occur.

For audit log sizing, we recommend that the security audit log be set to the maximum potential size of 4,194,240 kbytes. Disk space is quite inexpensive, and the value provided by detailed logs is significant. With respect to event log reuse, we recommend that administrators choose the third option: to never overwrite the logs. While this choice requires that administrators remain attentive to the size of the logs in order to prevent audit failures and system shutdowns, we believe that the administrative time required is both minimal and worthwhile.

When the administrator does reset the security log, a system event is automatically added to the new security log. This event, which is not removable by any user in the system, indicates the time, date, and user-name of the user who resets the log. This event is an important one in that it indicates a benchmark for evaluating whether the log might have been compromised since the last review. Administrators should take care to note the time and date when they reset the log; these should be compared to the first log entry the next time the logs are examined.

Setting Audit Policy

On the whole, audit policies represent a truism in information systems: garbage in, garbage out. The only way to ensure that you obtain useful information from your audit logs—and you'll need this information if there is an intrusion—is to ensure that you're auditing the correct activities.

One approach is to simply audit every activity of which NT is capable. Unfortunately, while your audit logs will not be lacking any detail, they also won't be terribly easy to parse and understand. Certain audit settings cause huge increases in the number of events which will be written to the audit logs. Often, a log which has too many entries in it will be nearly as useless as one with only a few; it's just too difficult to separate the wheat from the chaff.

In times past, audit logs were often limited by the availability of disk space. Today, disk space is cheap and plentiful. This allows us to do far more extensive security logging than ever before. At the same time, however, administrators should be attuned to the issue of audit log space and capacity. An audit log which runs out of space is not recording potential violations—and may well shut down the system. Administrators should be careful to provide significant quantities of available disk space on the volumes where their audit logs are kept. Also, older audit logs should be archived and removed from the system; they should not be immediately discarded.

Windows NT permits several options for determining the maximum size of event log files. The maximum potential size of each of the three major event logs—System, Security, and Application—may be individually controlled.

The issue, then, is striking the proper balance between auditing those activities which are important and discarding those which aren't. This section will make recommendations regarding audit policies and procedures; as an administrator, however, you are responsible for determining the right settings for your particular environment.

In Windows NT, there are three primary ways to set audit policy. From within the User Manager, administrators can set systemwide policy for high-level auditing functions. Moreover, enabling auditing from within the User Manager is a prerequisite for enabling other auditing functions.

More specific auditing of registry activities are possible from within the Registry Editor, and more specific auditing of file and directory activities is available in the File Manager.

Audit Policies: Users

To enable systemwide auditing, administrators should first launch the User Manager (or User Manager for Domains). From the Policies menu, select the *Audit* option. This brings up a dialog box which lists the high-level auditable events and allows the administrator to select among them:

Figure 4.3
Audit policy.

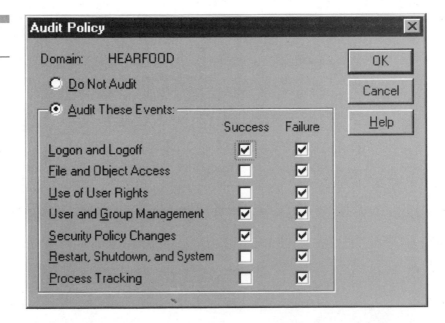

For each type of event which Windows NT is capable of auditing, the administrator may choose whether to audit the *success* or *failure* of that event. Success indicates that a user attempted to use the privilege or attempt the activity in question and was successful in that endeavor. Failure indicates the opposite—that an operation was attempted but was thwarted by the system security.

The auditable events are listed in the following table.

Events	Description
Logon and Logoff	These events cover both users' local inter- active logons and network logons.
File and Object Access	These events cover access to standard objects, including file, directory, and print- er objects.
Use of User Rights	These events cover nearly all the user events not covered by other events. This includes use of all user rights except those related to logon/logoff.
User and Group Management	These events cover creation, modification, and deletion of users and groups. This may include changing group membership, modi- fying account details, and updating user passwords.
Security Policy Changes	These events cover any and all changes to audit policies, assignment of user rights, and establishment and removal of Win- dows NT Domain trust relationships.
Restart, Shutdown, and System	These events cover restarts and shutdowns of the system.
Process Tracking	These events cover most indirect use of system rights—this includes indirect object access (i.e., a process acting on an object) and program and process starts and stops.

Audit Policies: Files

In most cases, Windows NT administrators will want to provide some auditing capability for important files within the file system. Indeed, we strongly recommend that file system auditing be enabled for all Windows NT systems.

Note, however, that the file system auditing can be used only in conjunction with the NTFS file system, and not with FAT or HPFS. Therefore, we once again recommend the use of only NTFS volumes in Windows NT systems which require secure file access.

The auditable events within the file system are listed in the following table.

Event	Description
Read	Permits an administrator to monitor when users read from a specified file
Write	Permits an administrator to monitor when users write data (overwrite or append) to a specified file
Execute	Permits an administrator to monitor when users execute a specified executable file
Delete	Permits an administrator to monitor when users delete a given file
Change Permissions	Permits an administrator to monitor when users change the file access permissions on a given file
Take Ownership	Permits an administrator to monitor when users take ownership of a specified file

To set these auditing permissions on a given file, first launch the Windows NT Explorer. By default, the Windows NT explorer may be found in the *Programs* option under the *Start* menu.

From within the Explorer, select the file, directory, or volume which you would like to audit. Note that auditing may be enabled within parent directories in order to encompass all child directories.

Next, right-click on the file, directory, or volume, then select Properties from the Context menu. This will bring up the following dialog box:

Figure 4.4
Folder properties.

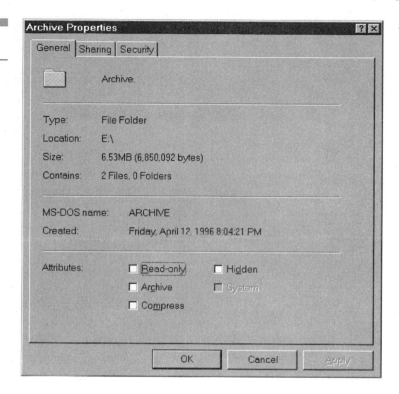

From within the dialog box, select the *Security* tab and the *Auditing* button.

This dialog box permits the administrator to configure the auditing features which will be enabled or disabled for the named file(s). For most systems, we recommend that administrators audit failure events for all the file access types shown in the dialog box. Moreover, we recommend that administrators enable success auditing for the Take Ownership, Change Permissions, and Delete file access events.

Finally, select whether the new auditing settings should be used to replace existing auditing settings and whether the same setting should apply to child directories. Note that using the latter option on the root directory of a volume will enable the specified auditing for all files within that volume.

Figure 4.5
Directory auditing.

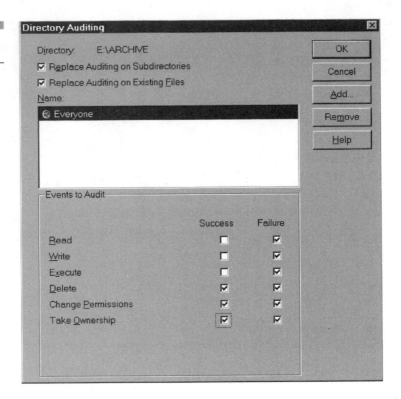

Audit Policies: Registry

The value of the information residing in the registry necessitates some additional auditing functionality. From within the Registry Editor, administrators may select the *Security* menu, then the *Auditing* option.

As with the other auditing functionality elsewhere in Windows NT, administrators can audit both successful and unsuccessful exercise of user rights. Moreover, each key may be independently audited; this leads to tremendous flexibility, but may also lead to complicated configurations. We recommend that administrators set auditing options on each of the four master keys and let the auditing options propagate downward through the trees. Propagation downward may be configured through the auditing dialog box in the Registry Editor. The events which may be audited are listed in the following table.

Event	Description
Query Value	This event allows an administrator to audit the success or failure of any request to read the value of a key. Auditing the success of this function will yield large numbers of event log entries.
Set Value	This event allows an administrator to audit the success or failure of a request to set the value of a key. We recommend that failure auditing (if not success, as well) be implemented for this key.
Create Subkey	The event allows an administrator to audit the creation of new subkeys. We recommend auditing both success and failure of this event.
Enumerate Subkeys	This event allows an administrator to audit a user request to list the subkeys of a given key. Auditing this event is likely to generate large numbers of event log entries.
Notify	This event allows an administrator to audit a user request to open a key with Notify access.
Create Link	This event allows an administrator to audit a user request to create a symbolic link to a named registry key.
Delete	This event indicates the exercise of a right to delete a registry key. We strongly recommend that this event be audited for both success and failure.
Write DAC	This event allows an administrator to audit a user request to modify the permissions associated with a named registry key. We recommend that this event be audited for both success and failure.
Read Control	This event allows an administrator to audit a user request to read the security data associated with a registry key. We recommend that this event be audited for failure.

Auditing Base Objects

In addition to auditing each of the three major system areas described above (users, files, registry), Windows NT is also capable of performing auditing of lower-level system resources. In most cases, these system resources are not directly available to interactive or network users; rather, they are objects which are accessible only through the Win32 API. These objects generally have little security value, but may be useful for those users developing device drivers or other low-level code.

In order to audit the use of these so-called base objects, first set the system audit policy (in User Manager) to audit the success or failure of object accesses. Then, set the following registry key:

```
HKEY_LOCAL_MACHINE\System\CurrentControlSet\Control\Lsa\AuditBase
Objects
```

to a value of 1. Note that the system must be restarted for this change to take effect.

Reviewing the Event Logs

Of course, simply capturing data in the event logs is no guarantee that you'll catch a system intruder. Only by reviewing the logs on a regular basis and understanding the data within will the logs be of any value.

In a complex Windows NT system, the logs will grow at a rapid rate; therefore, reviewing the security logs can be a burdensome chore. We recommend the old mantra "work smart, not hard." NT provides some well-designed filtering features intended to make the administrator's job easier. These filtering rules should be used to help sort through the volumes of data which may be present in security logs.

Filtering Rules

The Event Viewer allows filtering on the basis of several criteria, including the following:

Dates.   The Event Viewer may filter events between two given sets of dates and times. Therefore, administrators may easily pick out one small segment in time to examine in closer detail. By default, the event viewer will display all events in the log, regardless of their date of entry.

Types.   The Event Viewer may filter events on the basis of their type and relative seriousness. The types range from Information (the least important) to Error (the most important). In addition, two security types, Success Audit and Failure Audit, may be filtered independently.

Source. The source indicates which system process or resource generated the log event.

Category. The category is determined by the program which issues the event alert. Examples of categories for security alerts include Logon/Logoff, Privilege Use, and System Event.

User. The User field allows the administrator to select the events in the log which were generated by a single user. This is useful when attempting to determine whether a single user account has been compromised.

Computer. The Computer field allows the administrator to filter the log results and display only the activities of a single computer. This is particularly useful in an NT network in which large numbers of computers might be generating centralized events in the log.

Event ID. Each event which appears in the log has a specific ID associated with it. For more information on these IDs, consult the Windows NT Resource Kit or this volume, App. C (*Security-Related Event IDs*).

Judicious use of these filtering rules will allow an administrator to identify those events in the log that are significant and reject those which are not. In addition, administrators should always check the first entry in the security log, as this event will indicate the time and date when the log was last reset. Administrators should note the time and date when they reset the log, then compare it with the first entry in the log when they next review it.

The Registry

Don't ever take a fence down until you know the reason why it was put up.

G. K. Chesterton

In prior versions of Windows, system configuration data was maintained in a relatively complex and unwieldy series of configuration files. While functional, these files (mostly .ini files) represented a kludge approach to system configuration. Moreover, they were not functionally in sync with Microsoft's intention to provide full point-and-click configuration for their newest operating systems.

With the introduction of Windows NT, Microsoft integrated much of this system configuration functionality into a centralized database called the *Registry*. It contains configuration information for nearly everything associated with the operating system, including

- Hardware settings
- Device drivers
- Application configuration details
- Network interface and protocol data
- Environment settings

Note that the vast majority of registry configuration is performed behind the scenes. Although most of the common system administration tools interact quite frequently with the registry, the user often has no knowledge of the interaction. System administration tools, including User Manager, Server Manager, and Disk Manager, enable the user to transparently view, update, add, and remove data from the registry.

Alternatively, system administrators may modify the registry directly. Although the administrator need not know the names of the files which contain the registry, it is helpful to know their location.

By default, the registry files are stored in the `%System_Root%\System32\Config` directory. These files are protected such that only administrators have write access to them, assuming they reside on an NTFS partition. This brings up a good point: when setting up new Windows NT workstations or servers, administrators should ensure that the registry files reside on an NTFS partition. See *Protecting Registry Keys* below for more information on securing registry data.

Editing the Registry

The registry configuration tool for Windows NT is called `REGEDT32.EXE`. By default, this file is found in the `%SYSTEMROOT%\System32` directory. Note that there is no icon created for the Registry Editor by default, thus preventing accidental access to the Registry Editor. Also, bear in mind the fact that limiting access to the Registry Editor will limit the users' ability to edit the registry directly.

Administrators should be aware that interactive use of the registry is a classic double-edged sword. Although the low-level functionality provided is second to none, there exists a strong possibility of system corruption if mistakes are made. As a result, we recommend that users and administrators avoid editing the registry directly except in those circumstances when the changes to be made (and their global implications) are completely understood.

For circumstances in which administrators want to view—but not modify—registry data, we recommend that the Registry Editor be used in read-only mode. In order to enter read-only mode, select the *Read Only* option from within the Options menu. Note that this option remains constant between Registry Editor sessions.

Registry Structure

By default, the Windows NT 3.51 and earlier registry contains four main trees:

HKEY_CLASSES_ROOT. This tree contains configuration data associated with OLE (object linking and embedding) and file/class associations.

HKEY_LOCAL_MACHINE. This tree contains configuration data regarding the local Windows NT machine, including information regarding hardware, software, system configuration, the security account database, and device drivers.

HKEY_CURRENT_USER. This tree contains configuration data regarding user profile information on the currently logged-on user.

HKEY_USERS. This tree contains configuration data regarding the profiles for all users of the local machine. By default, this tree will have two major subkeys—the DEFAULT subkey and an SID subkey for the currently logged-on user. This is a quick way to view the SID of the current user.

The Windows NT 4.0 registry contains an additional registry tree called HKEY_CURRENT_CONFIG.

Consider the following view of the Registry Editor:

Figure 5.1
Registry editor.

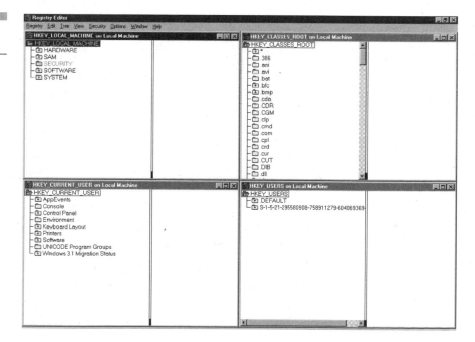

Each of the four main trees is represented with a single window. Within each window, individual keys are represented in a hierarchical storage paradigm not unlike that found within the Windows Explorer. Each key has a unique name, a set of allowed data types, and a specific value.

At a lower level, much of the data contained in the registry is stored in a series of files termed *Hives*. The major system Hives are stored as shown in the following table.

Key	Hive Filename
HKEY_LOCAL_MACHINE\SAM	%SYSTEM_ROOT%\SYSTEM32\CONFIG\ SAM (and SAM.LOG)
HKEY_LOCAL_MACHINE\SECURITY	%SYSTEM_ROOT%\SYSTEM32\CONFIG\ SECURITY (and SECURITY.LOG)
HKEY_LOCAL_MACHINE\SOFTWARE	%SYSTEM_ROOT%\SYSTEM32\CONFIG\ SOFTWARE (and SOFTWARE.LOG)
HKEY_LOCAL_MACHINE\SYSTEM	%SYSTEM_ROOT%\SYSTEM32\CONFIG\ SYSTEM (and SYSTEM.LOG)
HKEY_USERS\DEFAULT	%SYSTEM_ROOT%\SYSTEM32\CONFIG\ DEFAULT (and DEFAULT.LOG)

In addition to the four main trees described above, Windows NT 4.0 adds an additional tree to the registry called HKEY_CURRENT_CONFIG. This tree is used to store additional configuration settings regarding the configuration of local hardware. Note that this tree is not found in versions of Windows NT prior to 4.0.

Registry Security

The need to secure the registry data should be obvious to most system administrators. A potential intruder who is able to manipulate the registry entries will have the ability to change crucial configuration information, including user and password policies, logging policies, and service policies.

On the other hand, certain changes can be made to the registry data to make Windows NT more secure. Although these changes are referenced and recommended throughout this book, this section provides a single-source reference to all of the recommended registry changes.

In addition to the obvious security implications of changing the system policies noted above, there are some even more subtle changes that can be made to the registry which can cause significant security problems. Consider the problems associated with arbitrary users having the ability to change settings such as the system path.

With such access rights, a malicious user could introduce any selected piece of malicious code into the system at whim. This malicious code could be a Trojan horse, designed to change user or file system rights, or could be a virus with similar functionality. These and other threats can be countered only by effective registry security.

Finally, note that the threat to the registry is not limited to a local attack. Users and administrators should be aware that the Windows NT registry is remotely accessible across an NT network using the Registry Editor. As a result, users may potentially attack the registry on any remote computer on which they have an account. Alternatively, this may include remote computers with guest accounts that are enabled. Note that these warnings apply to both remote Windows NT servers and workstations.

Protecting Registry Keys

By default, Windows NT allows members of the Everyone group substantial access to the registry keys. Fortunately, Microsoft has built some ACL-based security into the registry itself. Any given key can be restricted as indicated in the following table.

Permission	Implications
Read	Allows explicitly named users to read the values of the key, but disallows attempts to change its value. Most administrators should audit this permission by default.
Full Control	Allows explicitly named users full control over the key. This may include the rights to read, modify, delete, or take ownership of it.
Special Access	Allows explicitly named users to have specific rights to the key. See the next table (below) for special permissions.

The special permission setting allows the use of permissions with more precise control. The available permissions are listed in the following table.

Permission	Implications
Query	Allows users to read the value of a key
Set Value	Allows users to set or modify the value of a key
Create Subkey	Allows users to create a new subkey under the named key
Enumerate Subkey	Allows users to list the subkeys of a named key
Notify	Allows users to open a key with notify access
Create Link	Allows users to create a link from a named key to another named key
Delete	Allows users to delete a key
Write DAC	Allows users to modify the ACL for a named key
Write Owner	Allows users to take ownership of a key
Read Control	Allows users to read the security data associated with a key

It is apparent from the two preceding tables that there is significant flexibility available to NT administrators in setting security attributes for various registry keys. Administrators should also note that it is possible to assign security permissions to specific keys, then allow those security permissions to propagate downward to all respective subkeys.

Realistic Registry Security

Some users ask why the registry must be shared at all. After all, if there is such potential for security risks, why risk sharing the registry?

Unfortunately, in this case a simple solution isn't possible. In fact, users are likely to have quite valid reasons for needing to access some portions of the registry—especially those which apply to application settings. Nor can we simply make the entire tree of keys Read Only for all users except the administrator. Doing so causes errors when programs with legitimate need to write to the registry are unable to do so. Therefore, access to the registry must be assigned carefully, with attention given to each and every key.

Realistically, however, the complexity associated with maintaining effective controls over each key is beyond both the experience and time constraints of most administrators. Microsoft has noted that the default registry key permissions are based on a system requiring "standard-level security" while providing a high level of usability. Microsoft does recommend that users who require greater security make some changes to the default permission structure. Please refer to the section on Microsoft-recommended changes below.

Thus, the only way to effectively secure all the registry keys is to examine each and every one, figure out its potential security implications, then set the permissions accordingly. From a more pragmatic standpoint, however, there is little that can be done, other than to follow Microsoft's registry security recommendations.

Key Ownership

In keeping with the overall security architecture of Windows NT, no user in the system has default ownership of all keys. Rather, individual keys may be owned by different users and accessed through the access rights discussed above.

Normally, however, the administrator should be the owner of all keys. Administrators have the default right to take ownership of registry keys at any time. To do so, administrators may select the *Owner* option on the Security menu within the Registry Editor. Then, clicking the *Take Ownership* button will transfer the ownership to the current user.

When taking ownership of keys, however, administrators should bear in mind the fact that taking ownership of keys will likely mean that users will be unable to uninstall applications which they have installed and which have included themselves in the registry. Over time, the net result may be excessive "garbage" in the registry.

Our Recommended Registry Changes

As was noted above, Microsoft makes some specific recommendations regarding registry modifications. For these recommendations, refer to the section on Microsoft-recommended changes below. In addition to the Microsoft recommendations, the changes that we recommend making to the registry settings are listed below.

AUDITING OF BACKUP RIGHTS. As is noted elsewhere, the right to perform backups (identified by users in the Backup Operators group) is one of the most powerful rights which administrators can be assigned. Using the backup rights, Backup Operators may gain access to any file in the system. We recommend that administrators log all use of this right. In order to do so, set the following key:

```
HKEY_LOCAL_MACHINE\System\CurrentControlSet\Control\
Lsa\FullPrivilegeAuditing
```

This setting will allow for auditing of backup operations.

SYSTEM SHUTDOWN ON AUDITING FAILURE. We recommend that system audit logs be set to never overwrite themselves. This prevents users from filling the audit logs with spurious events in order to disguise their real purpose. Setting the registry flag

```
HKEY_LOCAL_MACHINE\System\CurrentControlSet\Control\Lsa\
CrashOnAuditFail
```

will cause the system to halt on an error writing to the audit logs. This error may be caused by an audit log which is full (or out of disk space) or a lack of memory to allocate to the logging task. Note that this key may also be set using the Microsoft C2 configuration utility within the Windows NT 3.51 resource kit.

AUTOMATIC LOGON. Some administrators choose to use Windows NT computers for very specialized and limited tasks, such as use as a print server. In order to make system reboots transparent, they often wish to force an automatic system logon on boot. We disagree with this notion; we strongly believe that Windows NT computers should require a valid logon ID and password to be manually entered on each system boot. To ensure that this is the case, turn off the following key:

```
HKEY_LOCAL_MACHINE\Software\Microsoft\WindowsNT\CurrentVersion\
Win Logon\AutoAdminLogon
```

Setting a value of 0 for this key will require an ID and password to be entered.

Note that the use of this key for automatic logons also requires that the two related keys, `\DefaultPassword` and `\DefaultUserName,` also be present and contain valid entries. For optimal security, we recommend that the `AutoAdminLogon` key be set to 0 and the `DefaultPassword` and `DefaultUserName` keys be removed from the system.

SHUTDOWN WITHOUT LOGON.   By default, Windows NT workstations display a *Shutdown* button on the Logon dialog box. This enables a user to shut down the workstation without logging into the system. If the computer is not physically secure, this setting is of little security value. If the system is physically secure, however, you may wish to disable this button.

Similarly, Windows NT servers may or may not display the *Shutdown* button on the logon screen. In order to remove the *Shutdown* button from the Logon dialog box, turn off the following key:

```
HKEY_LOCAL_MACHINE\Software\Microsoft\WindowsNT\CurrentVersion\
Win Logon\ShutdownWithoutLogon
```

Setting a value of 0 for this key will disable the *Shutdown* button. Note that this key may also be set using the Microsoft C2 configuration utility within the Windows NT 3.51 resource kit.

DISPLAY LAST LOGGED-ON USER.   By default, the username of the last user logged into the system is displayed in the Logon dialog box. This could, however, be a security risk in that the username of a valid user might be leaked to an intruder. Although such an intruder would still have to determine the corresponding password, it would be more secure to hide the name of the last user. In order to do so, we recommend setting the following registry key:

```
HKEY_LOCAL_MACHINE\Software\Microsoft\WindowsNT\CurrentVersion\
Win Logon\DontDisplayLastUserName
```

Setting a value of 1 for this key will not permit the system to display the last username. Note that this key may also be set using the Microsoft C2 configuration utility within the Windows NT 3.51 resource kit.

CUSTOM LOGON MESSAGE.   Many organizations place legal liability disclaimers on their logon screens warning of the private nature of their systems. This may help in the possible conviction of identified system intruders. We recommend using such a logon message in Windows NT. Doing so requires setting two related keys. Each is located in

```
HKEY_LOCAL_MACHINE\Software\Microsoft\WindowsNT\CurrentVersion\
Winlogon
```

The first value contains the caption text for the dialog box which will be presented to the user. The second contains the text which will appear within the dialog box. The two values are `LegalNoticeCaption:` and `LegalNoticeText:`. Note that each of these values may also be set using the Microsoft C2 configuration utility within the Windows NT 3.51 resource kit.

CUSTOM LOGON SCREEN. By default, the logon screen contains the Windows NT logo. Some organizations may wish to place a company logo or legal liability information onto the logon screen in order to make clear the ownership of the system. Others may wish to camouflage the ownership and operating system to the greatest extent possible. Either is possible by setting the following key:

```
HKEY_USERS\Default\Control Panel\Desktop
```

This key should point to a valid `.BMP` (bitmap) file which will be displayed on the logon screen.

SCHEDULE SERVICE. The Schedule Service (using the AT command) is very similar to the UNIX cron service. It permits an administrator to schedule a batch process (identified by a given command line) to be executed at some point in the future. By default, the Scheduler service runs with the permissions of the operating system's System account, and is therefore extremely powerful. We recommend that organizations which do not have a strong need for the Scheduler service disable it. In order to do so, select the service from the Services dialog box, then select Disable. This will stop the service from running.

For those organizations which do require the use of the AT command, we recommend that only members of the Administrators group be permitted to submit AT jobs. This is the default setting, although some system administrators may have changed the defaults. To ensure that only members of the Administrators group may submit AT jobs, ensure that the registry key

```
HKEY_LOCAL_MACHINE\System\CurrentControlSet\Control\LSA\
SubmitControl\
```

has a value of 0. A value of 1 for this registry key will allow System Operators to also submit AT jobs. We strongly recommend that this key be set to a value of 0.

FLOPPY DRIVE ALLOCATION.   By default, Windows NT allocates all local removable and nonremovable disks on system boot. This means that all hard disks, floppy disks, CD-ROM drives, and so on will be available to users of the system. In some cases, however, it is not advisable to allow the use of removable media, such as floppy disks. Examples of this situation include systems which are not placed in physically secure locations. To disable the allocation of floppy drives at startup and logon time, set the key

```
HKEY_LOCAL_MACHINE\Software\Microsoft\WindowsNT\CurrentVersion\
WinLogon\AllocateFloppies
```

to a value of 1. Setting the key to a value of 0 (or removing the key from the tree entirely) will allow all floppy disks to be allocated at logon time.

Note that this change will not take effect until the current user has logged out of the system and logs back in. Therefore, we recommend that when this change is made, the system be shut down and restarted at the first possible opportunity. This will ensure that all users will be restricted from accessing floppy disk drives.

CD-ROM ALLOCATION.   Much as is the case with floppy disks, CD-ROM drives may pose a potential security problem. Administrators can disable the allocation of CD-ROM drives by setting the following registry key:

```
HKEY_LOCAL_MACHINE\Software\Microsoft\WindowsNT\CurrentVersion\
WinLogon\AllocateCDROMS
```

Setting this key with a value of 1 will disable the allocation of CD-ROM drives at logon time. Setting the key with a value of 0 (or removing the key from the tree entirely) will result in CD-ROM drives being allocated.

As with the floppy allocation, this change will not take effect until currently logged-on users have logged out and logged back into the system.

Therefore, we recommend rebooting the system after making this change to ensure that all users are affected by the change.

EXTENDED FILENAMES.   By default, the FAT file system under Windows NT supports extended (greater than 8 + 3) filenames. In addition, while the FAT system supports only limited means to recover from system faults, there are a tremendous number of excellent third-party disk-repair tools which are able to repair damage to FAT volumes. The vast majority of these tools, however, support only the 8 + 3 filename convention; other filenames may be viewed as damaged files and treated accordingly.

Therefore, administrators who make use of the FAT file system and wish to use third-party disk utilities may not wish to make use of Windows NT's long-filename support in the FAT file system. This option is controlled by the registry key

```
HKEY_LOCAL_MACHINE\System\CurrentControlSet\Control\FileSystem\
Win 31FileSystem
```

Setting this key with a value of 1 will limit the FAT file system to the standard 8 + 3 filename convention. The default value of 0 will permit the use of 255-character extended filenames.

HIDDEN SERVER NAMES.   In most cases, it's probably safe enough to allow users of a Windows NT network to browse the network at will. After all, Windows NT was designed to permit and deny access to specific resources according to well-defined access control lists and user IDs.

In some cases, however, administrators might not want users to interactively browse some parts of the network. For example, some administrators might wish to hide servers which are either not yet fully operational or have extremely sensitive content. In the latter case, an administrator might simply hide the name of the sensitive resource by appending a $ to the end of the sharename. But what if the entire server contained highly sensitive information?

Windows NT provides a means to address this problem. The registry key

```
HKEY_LOCAL_MACHINE\System\CurrentControlSet\Services\LanmanServer\
Parameters\Hidden
```

determines whether the server name itself will be displayed in the browsing windows of client workstations. Setting this key to a value of 0 will allow the name to be displayed. Setting this key to a value of 1 will hide the server name from browsing workstations. Note that both the browser and server service need to be restarted before this change will take effect.

REMOTE REGISTRY ACCESS. Unfortunately, Windows NT 3.x lacks the ability to easily prevent remote users from accessing registry keys. Under these versions of the operating system, each part of the tree must be manually locked using registry ACLs.

With Windows NT 4.0, however, Microsoft has added a way to disable remote access to the registry to all users except administrators. By setting the key

```
HKEY_LOCAL_MACHINE\System\CurrentControlSet\Control\
SecurePipeServers\WinReg
```

administrators can ensure that only administrators have remote access to the registry. We strongly recommend that administrators set this key with a value of 1. Note that it exists by default on Windows NT Servers— it can, however, be added to Windows NT workstations.

Sensitive Registry Keys

In addition to the keys mentioned above, there are some other keys which may, if used improperly, present a significant security risk. While there are too many to mention here, those described below present some of the greatest potential risk.

WINLOGON. The *WinLogon* key contains the values which control the logon and startup of Windows NT. Several of these keys (`AutoAdminLogon`, `DontDisplayLastUserName`, `LegalNoticeText`, etc.) were mentioned above. Others, however, have more complicated implications. Consider the following keys:

- `\System`. This value contains the filenames of executables to be run by the WinLogon process at the time of system initialization. Executables which are run at this time are run in the system—not the user—context. By default, this value is used to launch `lsass.exe` (the Local Security Authority executable). Note that the addition of a Trojan horse to this key value could have significant implications for system security. The default protections on this key (and all others listed in this section) permit Administrators, Creator/Owners, and the System account to have Full Control. Members of the Everyone group are granted Read access. We strongly recommend that this key be audited and monitored on a regular basis.

- `\UserInit.` Similar to the System value, the `UserInit` value is used to store the filenames of executables which will be executed at the time of logon. Unlike the System value, however, executables which are named in the `UserInit` value are run in the user—not the system—context. As a result, this key is perhaps less sensitive than the System key, but may provide similar vulnerabilities in terms of Trojan horse attacks. We strongly recommend that this key be audited and monitored on a regular basis.

- `\ParseAutoexec.` This key indicates whether the `Autoexec.Bat` file will be parsed on user logon. When this key is set with a value of 1, the `Autoexec` file will be parsed; a value of 0 will cause it not to be parsed. Note that neither setting has an effect on the parsing of `Autoexec.NT` or `Config.NT`. Much like the two previous keys, the improper use of this key may lead to exposure to a Trojan horse attack. For example, consider the implications of parsing the `autoexec.bat` file when it resides on a FAT volume or on an improperly protected NTFS volume. In either case, any user could make an addition to the system path in the file to be executed on system logon. Unless there is a specific requirement to parse the `autoexec` file, we strongly recommend that this key be set with a value of 0.

ENVIRONMENT CONTROL. The *Environment Control* key contains the values which control significant environment settings, including the Windows NT file path and the location and filename of the command interpreter. These key values are found under the following key:

```
HKEY_LOCAL_MACHINE\System\CurrentControlSet\Control\Session Manag-
er\Environment
```

- `\ComSpec.` This value indicates both the path and the filename of the Windows NT command interpreter. The command interpreter, similar to `Command.Com` in MS-DOS, is used to interpret the Windows NT command-line interface. This key might be modified by a system intruder to name a different—and possibly trojanized—command interpreter. Fortunately, the default security for this value (and others in this section) permits Administrators, Creator/Owners, and the System account to have Full Control. Members of the Everyone group are granted only Read access. We strongly recommend that this key be audited and monitored on a regular basis.

■ \Path. This value indicates the system file path for the Windows NT system. The directories listed in this path statement will be searched in order to find executables which a user wishes to run. This key is sensitive because a system intruder might modify the path so as to put an additional directory entry before the legitimate directories in the path. This would mean that the executables in the intruder's directory would be searched first—before the legitimate directories. The intruder could therefore effectively replace an application program with a trojanized version—all without touching the original file. Therefore, we strongly recommend that this key be audited and monitored on a regular basis.

ALERT NOTIFICATION. Many administrators rely upon the Windows NT Alerter service to alert them to potentially serious problems with their NT servers and workstations. For example, the Alerter service can be used to notify administrators of low-disk-space conditions, of problematic network connections, and of high resource utilization. Moreover, they can be configured to warn about security or other access issues, printing difficulties, and power loss (when the UPS service is active).

As a result, the Alerter service may make an inviting target for potential system intruders. Although tampering with the Alerter service will have no impact on the ability of the system to audit these events, it may affect the speed at which potentially serious events are noticed. Therefore, the registry keys which control these events might be used in denial of service attacks or for hiding the short-term activities of an intruder.

The Alerter service itself is controlled by the following key:

```
HKEY_LOCAL_MACHINE\System\CurrentControlSet\Control\Services\
Alerter
```

Note that the values for this key (and its subkeys) can be most effectively set using the Server Manager and the Performance Monitor. To protect these keys against tampering, however, we recommend that administrators set security ACLs on them appropriate to their security needs. For many administrators, this will include denying both Delete and Set Value rights to the Alerter main key.

Microsoft Recommended Registry Permissions

As was noted above, the default permissions for registry keys in Windows NT are for a system with standard security requirements. Many Windows NT users, however, want to provide a greater degree of security. In order to do so, there are some simple registry key changes that should be made. Microsoft recommends that the following key permissions be changed such that the Everyone group is granted only Query Value, Enumerate Subkeys, Notify, and Read Control access:

```
HKEY_LOCAL_MACHINE on Local Machine
    \Software\Microsoft\RPC (and subkeys)
    \Software\Microsoft\Windows NT\CurrentVersion
    \Software\Microsoft\Windows NT\CurrentVersion\Profile List
    \Software\Microsoft\Windows NT\CurrentVersion\AeDebug
    \Software\Microsoft\Windows NT\CurrentVersion\Compatibility
    \Software\Microsoft\Windows NT\CurrentVersion\Drivers
    \Software\Microsoft\Windows NT\CurrentVersion\Embedding
    \Software\Microsoft\Windows NT\CurrentVersion\Fonts
    \Software\Microsoft\Windows NT\CurrentVersion\FontSubstitutes
    \Software\Microsoft\Windows NT\CurrentVersion\GRE_Initialize
    \Software\Microsoft\Windows NT\CurrentVersion\MCI
    \Software\Microsoft\Windows NT\CurrentVersion\MCI Extensions
    \Software\Microsoft\Windows NT\CurrentVersion\Port (and subkeys)
    \Software\Microsoft\Windows NT\CurrentVersion\WOW (and subkeys)
    \Software\Microsoft\WindowsNT\CurrentVersion\Windows3.1Migra-
       tionStatus (and subkeys)
HKEY_CLASSES_ROOT on Local Machine
    \HKEY_CLASS_ROOT (and subkeys)
```

Auditing Registry Data

Because of the complexity of the registry, we expect that most administrators will require assistance from auditing tools to make sense of registry editing. At the time of writing, however, few products are able to assist administrators with effective auditing of the registry data.

Although many of the more popular NetWare-based auditing tools are being ported to Windows NT, few are yet available. At this time, SOMAR software (http://www.somarsoft.com) produces two related products to assist with auditing Windows NT. Both products are intended to allow the administrator to dump configuration information within NT into a format that is more useful.

DUMPACL allows the user to dump ACL data from NT to assess how much access individual users have to given system resources, including registry keys. It does so in a manner that is far more useful than simply using the Registry Editor alone. DUMPREG is a companion program which allows the user to dump the contents of the registry into a more readable format.

Enabling Registry Auditing

Logging of changes to registry data is possible using only the functionality built into Windows NT. We strongly recommend that administrators enable logging of registry changes.

In order to do so, administrators should first launch the User Manager. From within user manager, select the Policy menu, then the *Auditing* option. From within the Audit dialog box, enable *Auditing,* then enable *Auditing* for File & Object Access. At minimum, administrators should audit the failure of these events—auditing success is acceptable, but be aware that this will generate extensive log files.

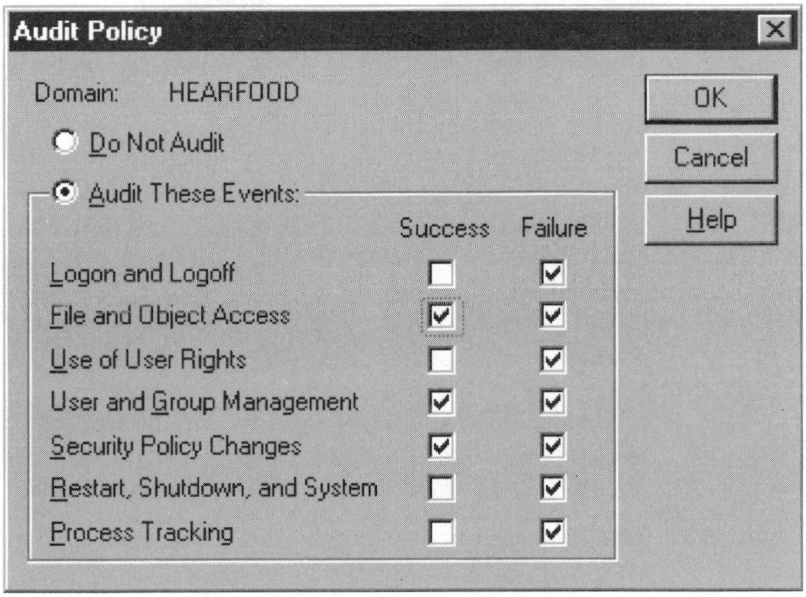

Figure 5.2
Registry auditing.

Next, launch the Registry Editor. Then, select the key (or tree) to be audited. We recommend that all the major trees be audited. Select the Security menu, then select the *Auditing* option.

Click the box labeled "Audit Permission on Existing Subkeys." This will enable your auditing settings to propagate downward to all subkeys; most administrators will want to audit all subkeys at all times. Finally, add users to be audited (most administrators will want to audit Everyone) and select the auditing criteria. Our recommendations are as follows:

Figure 5.3

Auditing a key.

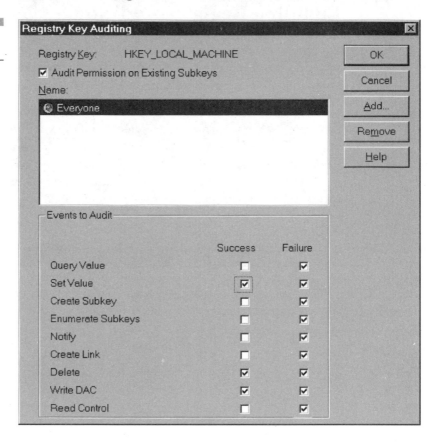

As this diagram shows, we recommend that members of the Everyone group (i.e., all users of the system) be audited for the failure of the following events in each of the four major trees (including all subkeys):

- Query Value
- Set Value
- Create Subkey
- Delete
- Write DAC
- Read Control

For most systems, we do not recommend that administrators audit the success of these events. Doing so will generate large numbers of audit events. These audit events must then be sorted through and the logs reset on a more regular basis.

Note that auditing the failure of the events listed above will enable the administrator to gain insight into both failed and successful attacks as well as alerting the administrator in the case of applications run amok.

Registry Internals and Using the Registry Editor

In order to understand how to edit the registry effectively, it first helps to have an understanding of the registry structure. Above, we described the structure of the high-level registry components—namely, each of the four main registry trees. However, we did not discuss the different types of keys which may be attached to those trees. By default, there are six types of registry keys, listed in the following table.

Key Type	Description
REG_Binary	The REG_Binary type is used for storing pure binary data.
REG_DWORD	The REG_DWORD type is a double word (4 bytes). The Registry Editor may view this type in several formats, including decimal, hex(adecimal), and binary.
REG_EXPAND_SZ	The REG_EXPAND_SZ type is used to store string variables.
REG_FULL_RESOURCE_DESCRIPTOR	The REG_FULL_RESOURCE_DESCRIPTOR type is used to store hardware configuration data.
REG_MULTI_SZ	The REG_MULTI_SZ type is used to store several string values in a single key.
REG_SZ	The REG_SZ type is used to store a standard string variable. Most of the values which relate to Windows NT security are of type REG_SZ.

As was mentioned above, the Registry Editor may be launched by issuing the command line `REGEDT32`. Note that there is another version of the Registry Editor which is designed for 16-bit systems called `REGEDT`.

Let's take an example of editing a registry key. Assume that we want to change the value of the registry key:

```
HKEY_LOCAL_MACHINE\Software\Microsoft\WindowsNT\CurrentVersion\Win
Logon\DontDisplayLastUserName
```

By default, this key does not exist within the Windows NT registry. Therefore, we must first find the appropriate location, then create a key with the proper name and of the proper type, then add the desired value.

First, we should look in the `HKEY_LOCAL_MACHINE` subtree. This subtree will be found in one of the four windows within the Registry Editor. From within this window, we should then select the first key following the subtree name. In this case, the next key in the chain listed above is *Software*. Thus, we should double-click on the *Software* key in the `HKEY_LOCAL_MACHINE` window.

Following this same approach, click on the names of each of the following subkeys in the key chain. In this case, we would click on the following keys in order:

- *Microsoft*
- *Windows NT*
- *CurrentVersion*
- *WinLogon*

By default, there is no key under the *WinLogon* key named `DontDisplayLastUserName`. Therefore, we must add the key. In order to do so, we should first select the *Add Value* option from under the Edit menu. This brings up a dialog box which looks like this:

Figure 5.4
Adding a key.

Add Value	☒
Value Name:	
Data Type:	REG_SZ ▼
	OK Cancel **H**elp

Note that to add a new key, you selected the *Add Value* option. For many users, this is counterintuitive. The option most users select—incorrectly—is the *Add Key* option. Rather than creating a new key, this menu item is actually used to create a new subkey. Administrators should be aware of the differences in the menu items.

In the Edit field of this dialog box, type the name of the key you wish to add. In this case, the key name is `DontDisplayLastUserName`. Then, from the pull-down listbox, select the class of the new key. The allowable class values are listed in the chart on the previous page.

For the majority of the keys which are mentioned in this chapter, the class `REG_SZ` is appropriate. In this case, select the `REG_SZ` in the second field of the dialog box. Then click the *OK* button. This will create the new key and bring up the String Editor.

The String Editor is used to place values in string-related registry classes. In this case, you will want to enter either a 1 or a 0, depending on your configuration policy. As was noted above, a 1 in this key will erase the username of the last user logged into the system, denying an intruder access to a legitimate user ID. A value of 0 will display the username of the last user to successfully log into the system.

Once you have entered the proper value, press the *OK* button. This will save the new registry key, along with its associated key class and key value. You should then see the new key appear immediately in the right side of the `HKEY_LOCAL_MACHINE` window.

Locating Registry Keys

Another useful utility for system administrators is the registry Find utility. I know that I've personally used this utility countless times; it seems that I'm constantly thinking of registry keys that I need to change, but I can never remember quite where they reside in the rather complicated registry tree structure. The Find utility bails me out every time.

More specifically, the Find utility is useful for locating a key when the administrator knows the key name (or part of the key name) or the value (or part of the value) but is unsure of its location in the registry tree. To use the find utility, select the *Find Key...* option from the View menu. This brings up the Find dialog box:

Figure 5.5
Finding a key

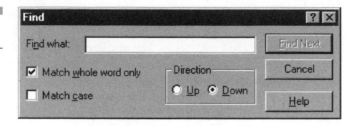

In the Edit field of this dialog box, select the key or value text for which you wish to search. Then, select whether you're searching for an entire word or just a part of a word. Note that searching for an entire word is much faster, but will only find words you've entered correctly in their entirety. Then, select whether you're searching in a case-sensitive mode and which direction in the tree you'd like to search (from your current position). Click on the *Find Next* button, and the search begins.

The Find utility will stop when it reaches a value which matches the one you entered. If it's not the value you're looking for, click the *Find Next* button again until you find what you want. One caution—when searching for a value, the Find utility doesn't stop to check for mouse clicks within its window. This means that if you enter a search and wish to stop it, you must wait until either a value is found or a message box appears indicating that the value cannot be found.

Designing Secure NT Networks

No one can build his security upon the nobleness of another person.

—Willa Cather, 1912

Windows NT provides a stable platform for nearly any application a user might wish to run. Its real value, however, comes in its strong networking components.

Of course, connecting a Windows NT system to a network creates an entirely new set of challenges for maintaining system security. No longer must all attacks take place at the physical console—as a result, the pool of potential attackers grows enormously. Moreover, the scope of attacks also grows such that the complexity of ensuring that a system is secure becomes far more difficult.

This chapter describes the process by which Windows NT administrators may design and construct well-secured Windows NT networks. It is split into two major sections—the first discusses the design and implementation of Windows NT–native networks.; the second discusses a topic which is at the forefront of popular interest in Windows NT: the use of Windows NT Server as an Internet server. Note that later chapters contain more information on the secure use of Windows NT as an Internet host while using Microsoft's Internet Information Server or similar third-party products.

Building and Securing Windows NT Networks

Windows NT, unlike nearly all the Microsoft operating systems which came before it, was designed with robust networking components at its core. Right out of the box, Windows NT Workstation and NT Server support all the most popular networking protocols in use today: TCP/IP, IPX, NetBeui, DLC, and others. At the same time, it supports native connectivity to the most popular network operating systems in use today, including Novell's NetWare and Banyan's Vines.

Windows NT Workstation and Windows NT Server: So, What's the Difference?

Many Windows NT users and administrators are confused about the differences between Windows NT Workstation and Windows NT Server. Much of the blame for the confusion rests with Microsoft—little public attention has been paid to the differences between the two operating systems.

In reality, there is very little difference between the two operating systems. Each shares a core set of functionality, and each rests on nearly identical operating system kernels. They are, however, tuned to provide different types of performance and have some slightly different options associated with them.

Windows NT Workstation, for example, has been optimized to provide superior performance for interactive applications. Contrast this with Windows NT Server, which is tuned for the best possible network performance.

More specifically, Windows NT Server will never swap the operating system out to disk—Windows NT workstations may do so when necessary.

In addition, there are some slight differences in the capabilities of the two operating systems. Windows NT Server, for example, contains additional services which the Windows NT Workstation product does not. Among these are servers such as WINS (Windows Internet Name Service) for NetBIOS name resolution, and DHCP (Dynamic Host Configuration Protocol) for the dynamic assignment of TCP/IP addresses to client computers.

Windows NT and the Domain Structure

In general, Windows NT supports two types of organizational groupings: workgroups and domains. *Workgroups* are simply groups of Windows NT systems which are associated with one another only because they do not share domain membership.

Within workgroups, each system functions as its own master—there is no central authority to manage users, groups, or other administrative information. With regard to security, each system in the workgroup maintains its own security policy and security account database.

As a result, Windows NT workgroups are really suitable only for small groups of systems which don't require significant centralized administration. From a security perspective, NT workgroups are problematic, as they cannot be administered from a central location. This means that many of the system security settings, including security policies, audit policies, and user management, must take place at each node in the network individually. In short, the result is often an unmanageable collection of different systems with little coordination among them.

Domains, on the other hand, were designed to solve many of these problems. Domains consist of Windows NT workstations and servers which share a common security policy and security account database. In the domain model, network authentication takes place at a Windows NT server acting as a domain controller.

Domains consist of three integral elements: primary domain controllers, backup domain controllers, and domain members. *Primary domain controllers* (PDCs) maintain the centralized security account databases and maintain the account and system security policies. *Backup domain controllers* (BDCs) are available to replace failed PDCs in the event of a system failure.

This means that the PDC is not *necessarily* a single point of failure in the network. However, note that the presence of a BDC is optional—although highly recommended. Domain member computers are those systems running Windows NT (or Windows for Workgroups or Windows 95) which act as members of the domain.

Trust Relationships

At this point, the reader should understand the differences between domains and workgroups from a security perspective—namely, that domains provide far better management and security tools to a network administrator. But what happens when organizations combine multiple workgroups and/or domains together?

With respect to workgroups, the answer is "very little." Multiple workgroups may coexist within the same network with relative ease. This is due to the fact that there is no centralized control either within or among workgroups. Therefore, there is no problem combining multiple workgroups within a single network. Be aware, however, that doing so will likely cause confusion among user communities.

Combining domains, however, is not nearly so simple. Unlike workgroups, domains require significant planning in order to achieve success. In addition, because of the centralized control and authority associated with the domain model, domains will not interact with one another by default. When two domains coexist within a single network, there is no default sharing of data or permissions. Rather, they exist as two islands unto themselves.

In some circumstances, this might be seen as a feature—we can certainly imagine a circumstance in which we would not like users from one department to access information in another department. Therefore, we might create a domain structure which consists of several domains, each of which exists as a separate unit from all others.

Consider the following diagram, in which each department has its own domain.

None of the domains has any logical connection with any other. As a result, all domain administrators set their own personal account policies, create and delete their own user accounts, and retain responsibility for all other system administration tasks. Note, however, that a given Windows NT system can be a member of only a single domain at any given time.

▬ ▬▬ ▬▬ ▬
Figure 6.1
Separate domains.

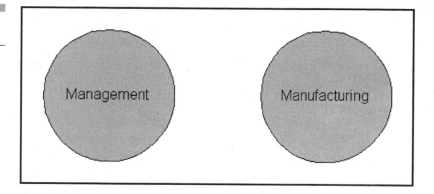

As you might imagine, this configuration—while possible—is hardly desirable for many organizations. Why? Because few organizations maintain dedicated support staff at the departmental level.

Instead, most organizations have a centralized staff of network administrators who are tasked with supporting an entire organization. Indeed, this latter organizational structure seems to better utilize the resources of the organization.

Therefore, there is likely to be a requirement for domains to share information among one another. The method that Windows NT provides for this functionality is called a *domain trust relationship*. Trust relationships allow users in one domain to access resources in another—provided that they meet the authentication criteria set out by the system administrators.

In the Windows NT vocabulary, a trust relationship consists of a *trusting* domain and a *trusted* domain. In this relationship, the users in a trusted domain may potentially access resources which reside in the trusting domain. Note, however, that trust relationships are dependent on the system configuration choices made by the administrators of both domains.

In the following diagram, the manufacturing domain trusts the management domain; that is, the users in the management domain may, subject to other configuration settings, access resources which reside within the manufacturing domain:

Note that this relationship exists in only one direction—simply because the manufacturing domain trusts the management domain doesn't mean that the reverse is true.

Figure 6.2
One-way trust.

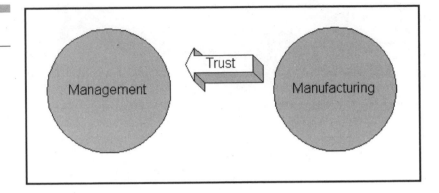

This type of relationship is termed a *one-way trust relationship*. With-in Windows NT, all trust relationships are, in fact, one-way trust rela-tionships. It is also possible, however, to use two one-way trust relation-ships to build a *two-way trust relationship*. Very simply, two-way trust relationships exist when two domains, A and B, each trust one another and are, in turn, trusted by the other.

Figure 6.3
Two-way trust.

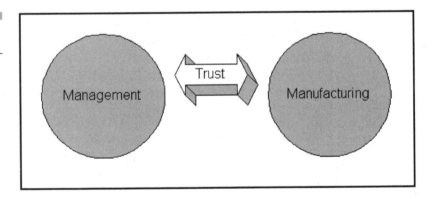

In this above diagram, the manufacturing and management domains have a two-way trust relationship. This relationship potentially allows users in either domain to access resources which reside in the other.

Thus, system administrators may regulate access to resources across domain boundaries by using trust relationships. *Administrators should be aware, however, that trust relationships are not transitive.* In other words, trust relationships cannot be leveraged by any domain other than the two which are parties to the trust relationship.

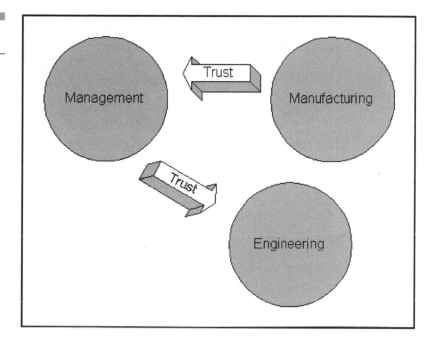

Figure 6.4
Trust is nontransitive.

Consider an example in which the manufacturing domain trusts the management domain, and the management domain trusts the engineering domain. In such a scenario, there is no effective domain trust relationship between the manufacturing domain and the engineering domain. The existence of trust relationships between the manufacturing and management domains and between the management and engineering domains has no impact on the overall relationship between engineering and manufacturing.

PASS-THROUGH AUTHENTICATION.   In the preceding paragraphs we saw how a Windows NT domain trust relationship can be used to provide access to resources in remote domains. However, the question of how security is provided among domains still remains.

In general, Windows NT servers acting as domain controllers will try to authenticate all user access requests against their own local security account database. Failing in this, however, domain controllers will attempt to authenticate all requests with the domain controllers in other trusted domains.

In the following diagram, user Suzanne maintains a user account in the management domain.

Figure 6.5
Pass-through
authentication.

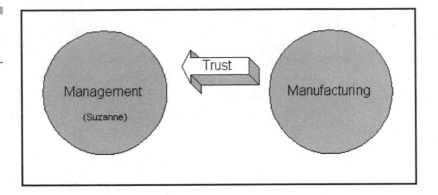

As the trust arrow indicates, the management domain is trusted by the manufacturing domain. What happens when Suzanne attempts to log into a Windows NT system in the manufacturing domain?

In this case, the domain controller in the manufacturing domain is unable to authenticate Suzanne's account. Therefore, it passes the request on to its trusted servers, including the domain controller in the management domain. The domain controller in the management domain is able to use its security account database to authenticate Suzanne's account.

After verifying Suzanne's account, the domain controller passes a message back to the manufacturing domain, indicating that Suzanne is a valid user. This authentication method is termed *pass-through authentication.*

CREATING TRUST RELATIONSHIPS. NT administrators should be aware that the creation of a trust relationship should not be treated lightly. Rather, administrators should recognize the implications of trust relationships on their local resources. When administrators create a trust relationship in which their own domain trusts another domain, the users in the remote domain are immediately granted significant rights to the administrators' domain.

For example, users from the foreign domain may log into the administrators' domain from local workstations. Moreover, the creation of the trust relationship allows users from foreign domains to be granted explicit rights to resources within the administrators' domain.

Unfortunately, we are unable to make blanket recommendations regarding the creation of trust relationships. Indeed, too many of the implications are based on the exact configuration of a given organization's network. We can, however, offer the advice that unless administrators are fully willing to offer rights to users outside their own domain, they should never create outbound trust relationships.

Administrators should also note that trust relationships can be created only with the permission of both servers in the relationship; that is, the administrator of a given domain cannot establish a trust relationship with another domain without the express consent of the administrator of the foreign domain. This means that administrators need not be concerned about the creation of trust relationships without their knowledge.

In short, trust relationships may pose significant risk. Although the granting of a trust relationship need not grant any specific rights to the foreign domain, it does expose any existing security holes in the local domain to a larger potential audience. In some circumstances, however, trust relationships can be quite useful (see below).

To create a trust relationship, administrators should first identify the two domains which will participate in the domain trust relationship, and identify which role(s) each will play. In the case of a two-way trust relationship, each system plays two roles: that of trustor and trustee.

Note that the order in which trust relationships should be established is a matter of some debate. Although Microsoft recommends that the trustee side of the relationship be established first, there is no requirement to do so. In fact, there is some reason to believe that it is easier to create the trustor side of the relationship first.

Consider the following procedure for creating a trust relationship by utilizing the method prescribed by Microsoft. First, administrators should go to the system which will function as the trusted domain and launch the User Manager for Domains. By default, the User Manager for Domains resides in the *Administrative Tools* group of the *Programs* option in the Start menu. From within the user manager, select the *Trust Relationships* option from within the Policies menu. This brings up the Trust Relationships dialog box.

The Trust Relationships dialog box shows all of the current and pending trust relationships. The top box shows those trust relationships in which the local server is the trusting domain; the lower box shows those domains in which the local server is the trusted domain.

Next, the administrator should click the *Add...* box at the bottom of the dialog box. This brings up another dialog box in which the administrator

Figure 6.6
Trust relationships
dialog box.

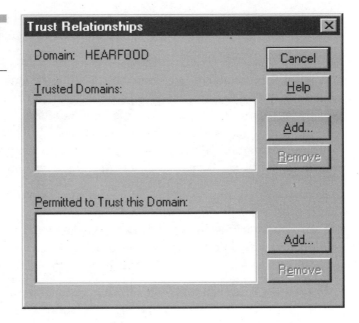

can name the trusting domain and select a password to be used for establishing the trust relationship. Note that any password can be used for this relationship—it need not be related to the password for any specific user account.

Clicking the *OK* button will save this information and complete one side of the relationship. Then, the administrator of the trusting domain should follow nearly the same procedure and launch the User Manager for Domains.

From within the User Manager, the administrator should bring up the Trust Relationships dialog box as described above. Then, click the *Add...* button next to the top box. Add the name of the foreign domain that this domain should trust. Then, enter the same password that was entered on the previous server. Finally, click *OK* to save the information and attempt to establish the trust relationship.

Note, however, that our experience shows no requirement to create a trust relationship in this order. Indeed, our experience indicates that a trust relationship may be created in the opposite order—*and, without requiring the administrators to agree on a password*. As of version 3.5x, trust relationships created in the order opposite that shown above could use any password at all on both sides of the relationship. Unfortunately, this points to a flaw in the underlying authentication method for creating trust relationships. But because of the other requirements for creating a trust relationship—including membership in the Administrators group—we consider this flaw to pose only limited risk.

REVOKING TRUST RELATIONSHIPS. As with creating a trust relationship, revoking a trust relationship requires that the relationship be modified on both ends: the trusting and the trusted sides. Both can be performed by bringing up the Trust Relationships dialog box shown above, then highlighting the relationship in question and clicking the *Remove* button. Note that for two-way trust relationships, each side of each of the two relationships must be terminated.

Microsoft recommends that when revoking trust relationships, the trusted side of the relationship be terminated first. Once again, however, our experience shows that there is no requirement to do so. Rather, it appears that administrators may terminate either side of the relationship in either order and yield the same effect.

Designing a Domain Strategy

Many organizations utilize multiple domains and manage trust relationships among them. Unfortunately, this often leads to a complex web of domains, interconnected with trust relationships in a manner that is difficult—if not impossible—to understand all at once.

When establishing security, complexity breeds insecurity; that is, the greater the complexity of any given system, the greater the likelihood of introducing inadvertent security holes. A complex web of domains and trust relationships is a perfect example of this complexity.

In order to reduce potential complexity, we strongly recommend that organizations plan their domain architectures well ahead of time. Moreover, we recommend that organizations utilize one of the well-understood models for domain architecture, as this limits the potential for mistakes.

To this end, Microsoft recognizes four major models for domain architecture. Each has advantages and disadvantages in terms of administration and efficiency; each also has its own benefits and risks in terms of security policy. The four recognized models (single domain, master domain, multiple master domain, and universal trust) are documented below.

SINGLE DOMAIN. In the single-domain model, all activity within an organization takes place within a single master domain. All user accounts are created within the single domain, and all user groups are local to the domain.

This model has as its advantages the fact that there are no trust relationships to manage and there is no cross-domain account administration to be managed. This leads to a crystal-clear security architecture—all users and groups are immediately apparent, with no concerns regarding cross-domain access.

The problem with the single-domain model, of course, is its limited scalability. A single domain can realistically hold about 10,000 user accounts. Practical experience, however, shows that few organizations will ever wish to grow a single domain to that size. Rather, organizations of that size often wish to use some of the advantages of multiple domains to provide additional security (albeit at the cost of additional complexity).

Figure 6.7
Single domain model.

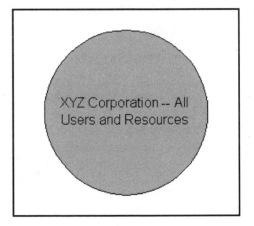

XYZ Corporation -- All Users and Resources

MASTER DOMAIN. The master-domain model has a single master domain in which all user accounts and global groups are created. This master domain is trusted by several other departmental or child domains. Note that the relationship between the master domain and the child domains is one-way; the children each trust the master domain, while the master domain trusts no one. None of the children trust each other.

This structure means that there are a limited number of trust relationships to be established, one each per child. Moreover, it means that administrators of the child (or departmental) domains may create local user groups to provide more robust security administration within departments. All user accounts, however, still reside in the master domain. This means that any user may log into the network from any given domain, but that user's rights are still limited to those explicitly granted in the master domain. Moreover, resources which reside in the child domains can be managed locally; this frees the overall system administrator(s) from dealing with department-level administrative tasks.

Much like the single-domain model, the master-domain model has only limited scalability. Because all user accounts reside in a single domain, the master domain is still limited by the 10,000-user practical limitation. Once again, however, few organizations will want to use the master domain model with anything approaching that number of users.

Figure 6.8
Single master domain model.

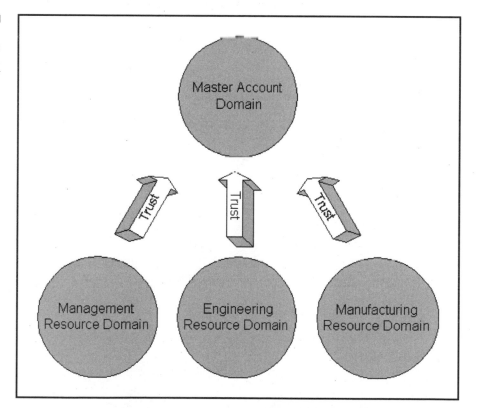

MULTIPLE MASTER DOMAIN. The multiple-master-domain model is much like the master-domain model, except that there are several master domains. In this model, each departmental or child domain establishes a one-way trust relationship with each of the master domains. The master domains, in turn, have two-way trust relationships among themselves. The child domains have no trust relationships with one another.

As with the master-domain model, all user accounts and global groups are created in the master domains. This means that account administration is significantly simplified, and also that users may log into the network from any given domain.

The multiple-master-domain model has the advantage of substantial scalability. Unlike the master-domain or single-domain models, the multiple-master-domain model allows for multiple domains to contain user accounts. Under this model, the number of user accounts may grow well beyond the realistic 10,000 user limitation placed on a single domain.

Keep in mind, however, the fact that the number of trust relationships associated with the multiple-master-domain model is significantly more than with the two preceding options. Each time a new master domain is added, new trust relationships must be established with all other master domains (two-way) and all the child domains (one-way). Each time a new child domain is added, new trust relationships must be established with all the master domains (one-way). This process may yield a large number of trust relationships which must be managed and verified.

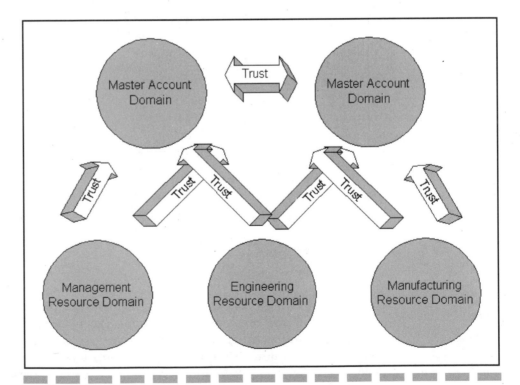

Figure 6.9 Multiple master domain model.

UNIVERSAL TRUST. The universal trust model is designed for companies or organizations with limited central administration staff. Under the universal trust model, all the participating domains act in conjunction with one another to provide both authentication and resource services.

Note that in the universal trust model, user and group accounts may exist in any domain; there is no restriction placed on where they may reside. Of course, this means that there is also no central administration possible. All the user and group accounts must be managed within the context of their individual domains.

In addition, administrators should be aware that the universal trust model, while among the most simple to understand in terms of security complexity, can also be extremely difficult to manage. Because each domain has a two-way trust relationship with all other domains, the number of trust relationships to be maintained can be enormous.

For any given organization, the implementation of the universal trust model will require [$d * (d - 1)$] trust relationships, where d is the number of domains. Therefore, an organization which has six domains would require ⌊6 *(6 − 1)⌋, or 30, trust relationships. Moreover, the addition of a single domain would require the creation of 12 additional trust relationships. While the concept is easy to understand, the mechanics of actually managing these trust relationships may become extremely difficult over time.

Network Authentication Process

Earlier, we discussed the process by which a user is authenticated to a Windows NT system. The process described earlier, however, was more applicable to a Windows NT console logon, rather than a network logon. This section discusses the process by which a user may be authenticated to a Windows NT network.

In general, the process by which a user authenticates to remote computers is similar to the process used for local logons. In both cases, the Local Security Authority (LSA) authenticates the user's credentials against the account database. Once authentication is successful, the LSA creates a security token for the user, allowing access to those resources to which that user has been granted access.

With a network-based logon, the security account database against which the user is authenticated may not be local to the system on which

Figure 6.10
Universal trust model.

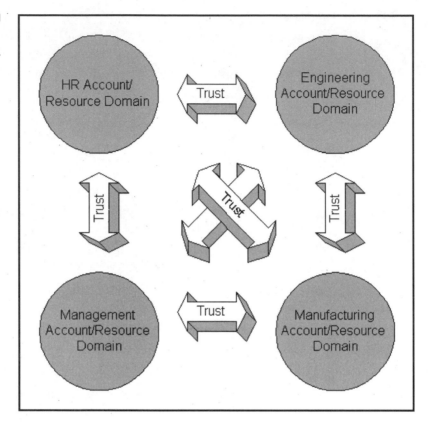

the user is logging. Rather, the security account database is likely to reside on the domain controller(s) of the domain in which the logon occurs.

Within a domain, there must be one (and only one) primary domain controller. This PDC is chiefly responsible for performing authentication tasks within the domain. In addition to the PDC, however, administrators may choose to have multiple backup domain controllers. These BDCs may share in the process of authenticating users against a shared security account database.

The BDCs perform two major functions: first, they act to help reduce the load on the PDC. In a busy domain, such as the master domain in a master-domain model, the PDC can get quite busy performing system authentication tasks. In order to help properly size BDCs, Microsoft offers bare-bones recommendations regarding proper domain controller server sizing.

For example, Microsoft recommends that servers which will handle up to about 3000 users who have at least 32 Mbytes of RAM and a 486/33 processor. Servers with around 10,000 users accounts require a Pentium (or faster) and at least 48 Mbytes of RAM. For systems with over 15,000 user accounts (not recommended!), the RAM required will be at least 2.5 times the size of the SAM.

Second, the BDCs serve to step into the PDC role should the PDC fail. The process of migrating a BDC to a PDC is termed a *promotion*. That is, a BDC is promoted in order to replace a failed PDC. Similarly, a former BDC may be *demoted* once the PDC comes back on line.

Each of the PDCs and BDCs shares a common security accounts database. Therefore, this database must be replicated among these servers such that it remains accurate and up-to-date. The process by which this occurs utilizes a special process called the *NetLogon Service*.

Note, however, that while the PDC and BDCs share a common SAM database, the copy of the SAM resident on the BDCs cannot be modified directly; that is, all changes must be made via the PDC and NetLogon synchronization. Therefore, if a PDC goes off line, administrators may not make changes to the SAM until the PDC comes back on line or a BDC is promoted to PDC status.

NetLogon and DC Synchronization

The NetLogon Service runs on both PDCs and BDCs, and provides background connectivity among them. One of its primary tasks is to provide a way to migrate all changes to the user account database to all other member servers. This synchronization process occurs approximately every 15 min (and is configurable), or may be initiated manually by the administrator.

To synchronize the servers within a domain manually, the administrator should first launch the Server Manager for Domains. By default, the Server Manager resides in the *Administrative Tools* group of the Start menu.

From within the Server Manager, select the PDC from the list of servers. Then, select the *Synchronize Entire Domain* option from the Computer menu. This will start the domain synchronization process.

Note that the manual synchronization process is rarely required. In most cases, Windows NT will synchronize the entire domain properly on its own with no user intervention. Also, note that the manual domain synchronization process may take a significant amount of time.

To synchronize an individual server, follow nearly the same process, but select the server you wish to synchronize with the PDC, and select the *Synchronize with Primary Domain Controller* option from the Computer menu.

The NetLogon process, however, is not limited to replicating data among the PDCs and BDCs within a domain. In fact, the NetLogon service runs on all computers which are members of a domain. On computers which are not acting as PDCs or BDCs, the NetLogon process acts to provide a conduit for authentication queries to the domain controllers.

Of course, to function properly, the NetLogon service must know where the domain controllers reside. Therefore, when Windows NT computers which are members of a domain first boot, the NetLogon process goes through a process known as *discovery*. This process is the one by which domain controllers (either PDCs or BDCs) are located in the local—as well as all trusted—domains. The discovery process consists of a series of datagrams which are transmitted over the network. These datagrams are sent in both broadcast and directed packets.

Assuming that a domain controller can be located, it will be used for all subsequent authentication within its respective domain. Note that this process applies equally to Windows NT workstations which are members of a given domain as well as Windows NT servers functioning as domain controllers. The only fundamental difference between the two is the time spent in discovery—Windows NT systems functioning as domain controllers will try "harder" to locate other domain controllers than will Windows NT workstations.

NetLogon and MSV1_0 Authentication

As was mentioned earlier, Windows NT was designed to use interchangeable authentication packages. The default authentication package is called MSV1_0. This section describes the MSV architecture and process; note that other authentication packages may utilize their own strategies.

The MSV authentication package is split into two main parts, termed simply the *top half* and the *bottom half*. The top half runs on the system to which the user is trying to connect. The bottom half runs on the system which contains the user account. Note that both the top and bottom halves may exist either on the same system or on separate systems. If the MSV top half detects that a pass-through authentication is required, it passes the users, request to the NetLogon process in order to route it to the appropriate remote Windows NT system. The NetLogon service on that remote system then passes the request along to the MSV bottom half.

In the case of local logons, the clear-text password is passed internally to the top half of the MSV package, which converts the password into both appropriate forms: the LAN Manager and the Windows NT native formats. For more information on these formats, consult App. B, *Passcrack for Windows NT*. Then, the encrypted version of the password is handed to either the bottom half of the MSV or to the NetLogon service for remote authentication.

In the case of a network logon, the client system is issued a 16-byte challenge termed a *nonce*. Windows NT systems then form a Windows NT response by encrypting the challenge with the Windows NT password associated with the account in question. This response, in addition to the domain name, user name, and challenge are returned to the remote system for logon.

Secure Channels and Caching

Once discovery is complete, a Windows NT system will attempt to create a secure channel between itself and a remote Windows NT system. Note that this "secure channel" is based on the premise of hidden user accounts; as a result, there is little that an administrator can do to affect the security of it.

The secure channel utilizes three separate types of user accounts, each of which exists within Windows NT systems, although outside the control of the administrator:

- *Server trust accounts*. Server trust accounts have user rights which permit them to obtain copies of the master-domain account database from the domain controller.

- *Workstation trust accounts*. Workstation trust accounts have user rights which permit them to perform pass-through authentication for a Windows NT server within the local domain.

- *InterDomain trust accounts.* InterDomain trusts have user rights which permit them to perform pass-through authentication to another domain.

The secure channels are first initialized when a Windows NT server joins an NT domain. This may happen either manually (via Server Manager) or through the use of a domain administrator account during the setup process. In either case, NT sets up a hidden user account with a constant password (the lowercase name of the server). Once the NetLogon service is started for the first time, the password is immediately changed. After that time, the password is changed once a week. Unfortunately, there is little documentation available regarding the password selection algorithm; therefore, this may be a possible weakness in the architecture.

Each time a secure channel must be reestablished, Windows NT uses its standard challenge-response methodology to ensure a secure connection. More specifically, a Windows NT server requiring a secure channel sends the NT domain controller a message containing a challenge. The challenge is a pseudo-random number based on the current time and the serial number of the NT server. Using this challenge and the known password, the domain controller can calculate a session key. Then, using this session key and the known password, both systems may authenticate one another.

Administrators should also be aware that the Windows NT NetLogon process has a caching function built into it. This means that not all authentication requests need be passed over the network at all times. By default, Windows NT stores the credentials of the last 10 users to log into the system. If one of these users logs in again, the system need not query the domain controller; instead, the authentication request can be processed locally.

The size of this cache can be controlled by the administration. The registry key,

```
\HKEY_LOCAL_MACHINE\Software\Microsoft\WindowsNT\
CurrentVersion\winlogon\CachedLogonCount
```

controls the size of the cache.

Fortunately, the secure channel also includes some additional measures to ensure the security of the system. For example, the API calls which control access to the security databases (I_NetDatabaseSync and I_NetDatabaseDeltas) are valid only when used in conjunction with the secure channel—they cannot be used with normal user accounts. Moreover, the secure channel accounts cannot be used for standard interactive logons.

Windows NT Domains and Protocol Selection

In general, Windows NT supports three types of networking: standard TCP/IP-based Internet connectivity, NetWare NCP-based networking, and the so-called Microsoft Windows networking. Each has its own discrete set of useful functions, and each has its own potential security risks. This section discusses Windows networking; for information on Internet connectivity and security, refer to Chap. 9, *Windows NT Internet Security*.

Windows NT's support for Windows networking provides the services most users normally think of as file-and-print services. This includes sharing access to files through file shares, sharing printers through printer shares, and networkwide browsing using the Network Neighborhood. Indeed, standard Windows networking is perhaps the greatest draw of the Windows NT products; with it, Windows NT provides fully integrated file and printer sharing within a useful and logical user interface.

At root, all Windows networking technology is built on top of the SMB (Server Message Block) application-layer protocol. In this respect, Windows NT shows its heritage as a follow-on to the LAN Manager series of products. SMB provides the base functionality to perform such tasks as opening and closing files, listing directory entries, reading and writing data blocks, providing support for the Universal Naming Convention (UNC), and interacting with the registry.

Unlike some other protocols, SMB has some features which make it reasonably resistant to session hijacking. This is not to say, however, that this type of attack is not possible.

Protocol Selection

At lower levels, Windows NT provides native support for three popular protocols for local and wide area networking. In the past, the default protocol for Windows networking was Microsoft's implementation of

NetBEUI [NetBIOS Extended User Interface, or NetBIOS Frame (NBF)]. In version 3.5 of the operating system, Microsoft added the NWLink IPX/SPX implementation to the default protocol category.

Since version 3.51, however, the default protocol for Windows NT has changed to TCP/IP. TCP/IP is quickly becoming the most popular protocol for both local and wide area networking, because of its efficiency and reliability. TCP/IP is the standard protocol used for Internet access. At the time of Windows NT installation, TCP/IP will be installed by default unless another selection is made.

Each of these protocols provides slightly different support, and hence, has slightly different security implications. Below, we will discuss the potential benefits and risks associated with each protocol. Note, however, that these three are not the only protocols supported—just the three most popular choices.

NetBEUI. The NetBEUI protocol is perhaps the most simple to understand. NetBEUI is designed for small networks with no routers—in fact, NetBEUI is a nonroutable protocol; that is, the information which is contained in the header of a NetBEUI packet is not sufficient to route it effectively. This lack of routability means that networks which utilize the NetBEUI protocol exclusively cannot span router boundaries. However, NetBEUI can be extremely efficient on local area networks with limited numbers of nodes attached.

As a result of the NetBEUI routing limitations, its use within Windows NT networks has some interesting security implications. For example, consider a situation in which an administrator wishes to secure a small local area network within a larger organization. By utilizing the NetBEUI protocol, the administrator could effectively limit access to the LAN to only those users on the local router segment. No other users elsewhere on the enterprise network would be able to see—let alone access—the NetBEUI-based LAN. Of course, the users on the small LAN would then be limited to the use of NetBEUI as their protocol of choice.

NWLink/IPX. The NWLink/IPX protocol suite is an implementation of Novell's IPX/SPX protocol suite, which is itself based on XNS. The NWLink protocol suite was designed originally to provide interconnectivity with Novell NetWare servers and clients.

NWLink/IPX is quite robust in that it provides for efficient data transfer over both local and wide area networks. Unlike NetBEUI,

NWLink/IPX packets are fully routable, based on the information contained in packet headers. Therefore, Windows NT networks which utilize NWLink/IPX have the ability to span router boundaries.

Because it is routable, NWLink/IPX does not have the native security advantages of NetBEUI described above. However, the NWLink/IPX protocol can be put to good security use by pairing it with other protocols. Specifically, NWLink/IPX can be used to provide a "buffer" between networks utilizing NWLink/IPX and, for example, Microsoft's TCP/IP implementation. Although both serve similar functions, the two are completely incompatible—and can be filtered accordingly at router boundaries.

Thus, NWLink/IPX can also be used to create small "island" LANs within larger organizations in much the same way as was demonstrated above for NetBEUI. Consider the possibility of creating a small NWLink/IPX-based network inside of a larger TCP/IP-based network. By filtering IPX packets at the router boundaries, it is possible to create a smaller, more secured local area network.

TCP/IP.   The final major protocol supported by Windows NT is TCP/IP. TCP/IP, like NWLink/IPX, is a protocol suitable for both local and wide area networking, because of its fully routable nature. As a result, Windows NT networks utilizing TCP/IP may span router boundaries.

Once again, TCP/IP-based Windows network do not have the same intrinsic security advantages of NetBEUI-based networks. However, securing TCP/IP-based Windows NT networks is remarkably simple—and quite effective. All Windows NT networking over the TCP/IP protocol takes place over three well-known TCP/IP ports: 137, 138, and 139 (NetBIOS over TCP/IP). Blocking access to these three ports using the filtering capability provided by a router will effectively limit the ability to provide NT networking over that link. Thus, by blocking ports 137 to 139, administrators can quite easily deny access to their network over TCP/IP links.

Consider the possibilities associated with connecting an internal network running TCP/IP with the largest TCP/IP network of all: the Internet. By blocking TCP/IP traffic on ports 137 to 139 on the link between the internal network and its Internet service provider, the administrator of the network can eliminate the risk of Windows NT networking data being exposed to the Internet. Of course, this doesn't come close to completely eliminating the risks of connecting a Windows NT network to the Internet, but it does limit the Windows NT networking risks. For more information on using Windows NT as a secure Internet server, see Chap. 9, *Windows NT Internet Security*.

Network Snooping

We should also note that each of these protocols has another potential security problem associated with it. This problem centers around the fact that none of the protocols provides a native encryption capability. Therefore, any user who can capture packets on a Windows NT network could, conceivably, capture sensitive data as it traverses the physical wires.

Of course, encryption can be provided to limit this exposure. In fact, encryption may be provided at either higher levels in the protocol hierarchy (application layer), or at lower levels (physical network layer). In either case, the ability of a user to "snoop" on the physical network is reduced.

By default, there is no native application or physical network-layer encryption for Windows NT. There is, however, application-level encryption available for Windows NT systems connected to one another via the Remote-Access Service (RAS). For more information on RAS, please refer to Chap. 8, *Remote-Access Service (RAS) Security*.

Fortunately, Windows NT does, by default, provide native encryption for passwords as they traverse the network. This effectively limits the ability of potential intruders to capture usernames and passwords, but does nothing to prevent potential intruders from capturing other potentially sensitive data.

The most effective means of protecting this sensitive data is encryption. In addition to encryption, however, there are some other steps which network administrators may take to help limit their exposure to potential snooping attacks.

For example, administrators should ensure that their environments have good physical security, both in user offices and especially in wiring closets. The reasoning behind this is simple; many organizations utilize Ethernet, which is a broadcast transmission medium. This means that all packets on any given segment are transmitted to every station on the segment. This fact, in turn, means that any user who gains physical access to the segment can capture all packets which traverse that segment.

In addition to good physical security, we recommend that Ethernet-based organizations with high data security requirements utilize either "secure" network hubs and/or Ethernet switches. Secure Ethernet hubs are designed to combat the broadcast-based problems of standard Ethernet hubs. They do so by sending packets only to their designated address; all other users on the segment receive only the packet headers, with the data in the packet zeroed out. Such secure hubs are available today from many of the leading network hardware manufacturers.

Ethernet switches, on the other hand, provide similar security by also sending packets only to their destination stations. In this case, all other stations receive no data whatsoever. As a result, Ethernet switches offer significant performance enhancements to Ethernet networks, and we highly recommend their use.

Consider the following examples.

In the diagram, all stations on the network receive all packets—therefore, any of the users on the network (or anyone else who gains physical access to the network infrastructure) may utilize a promiscuous network card to capture all the data traversing the Ethernet segment:

Figure 6.11
Simple network.

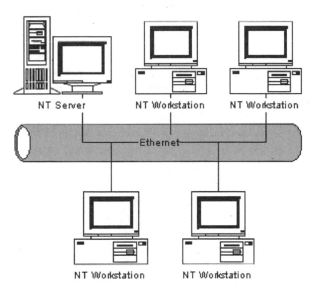

In the following diagram, only the stations which are intended to receive data packets actually receive them; similarly, all other stations on the network see only the traffic which is addressed to them:

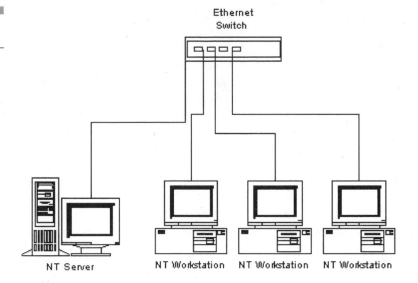

Figure 6.12
Switched network.

Network Browsing and Name Resolution

One of the most useful features of Windows NT networking is the ability to interactively "browse" the network in order to find resources which are of interest. Unfortunately, there is no default security placed on the browsing process. Rather, security comes into play when users actually select resources that they would like to access.

This means that any user on the network may see the names of resources which are available for use—regardless of whether that user actually has rights to use that resource. From a security perspective, this is troubling. After all, users who cannot see those resources to which they do not have access are far less likely to try to gain access to them through illicit means.

Therefore, it is in the interest of security-conscious administrators to limit the advertisement of resources on their systems. Conveniently, Windows NT provides a means to perform this task. As was described in Chap. 3, any file or directory can be shared by creating a file share. Each file share has several attributes, including the sharename, the user rights to the share, and so on.

By default, all Windows NT file shares are explicitly advertised to all other servers and workstations on the network. Shares that have the $ character appended to the end of their sharenames, however, are not advertised. This means that sensitive file shares may be hidden by appending the $ character to the end of their sharename.

In order to do so, simply create the share as described in Chap. 3, then name the share with the $ character at the end. Next, go to the network neighborhood and attempt to browse for the share. If the share was created properly, curious users will not be able to see the sharename.

Note that even though the sharename is not advertised, the share still exists and is fully accessible, assuming that the user knows the name of the share. Any user can explicitly map a drive letter to that share by providing the server name and sharename in the form (\\Server Name\Share Name).

Regardless of the restrictions placed on advertisement of resources, however, security-conscious NT administrators should be aware of the browsing process and its implications for network security. This understanding will permit administrators to be aware of the potential avenues of attack to their networks, on the basis of their service advertisement patterns. Note, however, that this discussion centers on the administrator's ability to limit service advertisements—not on how to secure those advertised resources. For more information on the latter, see Chap. 3.

Browsing Details

Within Windows NT networks, the browsing process is facilitated by a Windows NT system which functions as a browser server. Windows NT domains may contain four types of browser servers: Domain Master Browsers, Master Browsers, Backup Browsers, and Preferred Master Browsers. Both Domain Master Browsers and Master Browsers serve the same function: to serve as the primary browser within their respective networks. Backup Browsers serve to provide some fault tolerance to the browsing process. If a Master Browser fails, the Backup Browser will take over browsing operations.

Note that each Windows NT server within a given domain is a browser server. By default, the Domain Controller for that domain is the Domain Master Browser. All other Windows NT servers in the domain function as Backup Browsers.

In the case of a network with no Windows NT servers, the Windows NT workstations will vote among themselves to select a Master and a Back-up Browser. This voting process is termed a *Browser Election.*

In most cases, it really doesn't matter which system functions as the master browser. In a few cases, however, it is advantageous from a performance standpoint to identify one system as more capable than others. This system is termed the *Preferred Master Browser.*

In order to force the election of a Preferred Master Browser, set the registry key

```
HKEY_LOCAL_MACHINE\SYSTEM\CurrentControlSystem\Services\Browser\
Parameters
```

to a value of 1.

In either case, the Master Browser maintains a list of all resources on the network which may be interactively browsed. This list is called the *Browse List.* The Browse List is populated automatically by computers within the domain who send their resource information directory to the Browse Master. Alternately, the Master Browser can request all servers on the network to register themselves at any given time by sending a *Request Announcement* broadcast.

Within this context, it is important to recognize the fact that the location of master browsers within a network is extremely dependent on the configuration of the network and the protocols employed. For example, let's consider a network with two segments separated by a router:

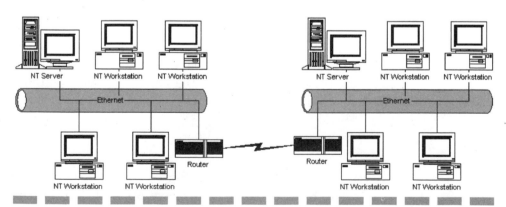

Figure 6.13 Routed network.

For our first example, let's assume that the network utilizes the NWLink/IPX protocol. In this case, the domain controller will automatically be nominated as the Domain Master Browser for the network. When a user on the network wishes to interactively browse the resources available on the network, that user's workstation sends a broadcast name query requesting the names of resources which are available on the network.

On Windows NT networks which utilize the NWLink/IPX protocol, such name query broadcasts are permitted to cross router boundaries—this means that, in our example, any station on the network will be able to contact the Master Browser to permit interactive browsing. This is one of the advantages of using a protocol like NWLink/IPX, whose broadcast packets are typically forwarded across router boundaries.

Therefore, the workstation will be able to communicate with the Domain Master Browser for name query purposes. This allows the Domain Master Browser to populate the user's own browse cache with the required information, allowing the user to browse the network resources.

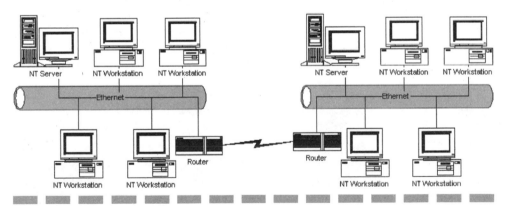

Figure 6.14   Routed network.

Consider, however, a second example. In this case, the network utilizes Microsoft's TCP/IP protocol. As in the former example, the Windows NT server acting as the domain controller will automatically be nominated as the Domain Master Browser.

Unlike the previous example, however, the TCP/IP protocol implementation in Windows NT will not permit name query broadcasts to traverse router boundaries. Specifically, routers in Windows NT networks using TCP/IP typically are not configured to forward name query broadcasts, such that workstations are typically unable to communicate with Master Browsers on other network segments.

In this case, network browsing requires that each network segment maintain an independent network browser. Therefore, in the preceding example, there will be multiple master browsers. The Domain Master Browser will continue to be the Windows NT Server functioning as the domain controller. Within the remote segment, however, the Windows NT systems will elect a browser among themselves.

This browser, in turn, must be aware of the Master Browser on the primary segment. By default, this browser should be able to identify the Master Browser on the primary segment simply by token of the fact that it is the domain controller. Approximately every 15 min, the Master Browser in the remote subnet will automatically synchronize with the Domain Master Browser.

Thus, when a Windows NT system on the remote segment wishes to browse the resources on the network, it will turn not to the Domain Master Browser, but rather to the Master Browser on the local segment. This Master Browser will always be up-to-date within 15 min and allow browsing of all network resources of which it is aware.

Thus, the protocols selected—and the placement of servers on segments—has an enormous impact on the browsing process.

Peer-to-Peer Security

As we have seen, Windows NT is designed to act both as a workstation operating system and as a network operating system. These complementary purposes, while convenient for end users, often significantly increase the complexity of security.

In a pure network operating system, such as Novell's NetWare, the only form of data sharing permitted is from servers to workstations; that is, workstations function only to send and receive data from servers—and not from other workstations. This makes security administration relatively easy. Because all resources which may be shared reside on the server, the security which must be provided becomes extremely focused. By focusing the security on the server, the task of security is quite simplified.

With Windows NT, however, the paradigm changes. Suddenly, each workstation may serve as both workstation and server. As was shown elsewhere, both the Windows NT Workstation and Server products are able to share information over local and wide area network in an effective manner. What does this mean for security-conscious system administrators?

In short, it means that the administrator has lost control. With the new peer-to-peer paradigm, the administrator can no longer control access to all resources over the network. Instead, individual users may control the fate of their own data. This means that while users have greater and greater freedom to share information and work together effectively, the ability of the administrator to secure that data are becoming increasingly difficult.

In a Windows NT network, any given user may share a directory or file with any other group of users. That user may, of course, provide discretionary access control over that resource in order to limit the number of users who may utilize the resource; the question is, "Will they?"

Both human nature and our own experience shows us that few users are concerned about security. Even fewer consider themselves competent to implement security effectively to protect their own resources. The combination of these two factors can wreak havoc on an organization's plans for data security.

The only solution, therefore, is to insist that sensitive data be stored on administrator-controlled Windows NT servers. This permits administrators to control the security in a centralized fashion. In addition, it allows administrators to use all the tools which Windows NT provides, including the system auditing functions. As with access restrictions, few users are likely to check their security logs on a regular basis. Centralizing sensitive data means that administrators can take responsibility for this critical task.

Of course, administrators cannot expect all users to place all their data on centralized servers. Indeed, there are good reasons not to do so, including the implications for large volumes of unnecessary network traffic. Therefore, it is up to Windows NT system administrators to educate their users about the proper methods for sharing data in a secure manner.

As was shown in Chap. 3, on file security, the Windows NT defaults were designed more for ease of sharing data than for robust security. By default, all new file shares are created with only one user permission—the Everyone group is granted Full Control rights to the share. This means that all users, regardless of their security level, by default have full control over the data being shared. This full control extends to reading, modifying, and deleting the data.

Thus, Windows NT system administrators must educate their users to immediately revoke the Full Control rights granted to the Everyone group on creation of a new file share. More specifically, administrators need to ensure that their user communities have an appreciation of the varying levels of security which NT can provide to file shares—and that these levels are actively used.

Still, we believe that truly critical data should be kept centrally on a Windows NT server. This is due to several considerations, including the need to provide proper security and auditing of access to that data as mentioned above. In addition to those reasons, however, is the notion of data availability and integrity.

For example, few users back up their workstations on a regular basis unless provided extremely simple means to do so. Even then, many users will simply ignore the realities of proper system backups, choosing instead to "take the risk" of a system crash.

A better solution is to store mission-critical data centrally, where it can be centrally controlled, protected, and backed up. Although data which reside on remote Windows NT workstations can, in theory, be backed up centrally, the reality is that doing so is extremely difficult to manage effectively. We strongly recommend that organization-critical data be stored, protected, and shared centrally, as opposed to making use of Windows NT's peer-to-peer functionality.

Finally, note that the risks of peer-to-peer functionality also extend to other sharable resources, such as printers. In a manner similar to files, users of Windows NT workstations may share printers which are locally connected to their systems. Much like the file shares, Windows NT does provide for discretionary access control to those printers.

In some cases, printers are less sensitive resources than are files. After all, who cares if a user is permitted to print to a given printer? Is that really a security risk? Well, maybe.

With standard printers, it is likely that there is virtually no risk associated with permitting any given user access. But consider the implications of access to special types of printers, such as printers which contain blank checks for payroll or account payment purposes. In such a case, it is easy to see why access to the printer might need to be very closely controlled and effectively audited.

The default settings for new printer shares are insecure in much the same way as file shares. When a new printer share is created, the Everyone group is granted Print access to it. This means that anyone in the system may print to the printer. In the example noted above, this might lead to potential disaster. We strongly recommend that all users be educated as to the risks of the default values for new printer shares.

Even more importantly, we strongly recommend that printers which contain sensitive documents—such as blank checks or staff evaluation forms—be shared centrally from a Windows NT server, rather than peer-to-peer from a Windows NT workstation. This enables system administrators to effectively set permissions and auditing preferences for the shared printer.

In short, administrators need to be aware of the risks of peer-to-peer networking. *Although peer-to-peer networking is technically no less secure than the more traditional workstation-server interaction, human nature significantly impacts the process.* Very simply, users are less likely to employ the available security mechanisms and utilize them effectively than are properly trained Windows NT system administrators. Because it is not cost-effective to train all users to this level, administrators must take it on themselves to train their users in the rudiments of Windows NT security. Moreover, they must take control of mission-critical assets and provide centralized control and access to them.

PDCs and BDCs

In Windows NT domain-based networks, domain controllers represent a single point of potential failure. If, for example, a domain controller fails and there is no backup domain controller available to take over operations, the entire domain-based security architecture begins to fall apart.

More specifically, if there is no central domain controller to authenticate validate logon requests and validate user rights, users will be unable to perform these necessary tasks. As a result, the network becomes nearly worthless.

Thus, administrators should be aware of the fragility of their domain controllers and protect them accordingly. For example, imagine a potential attack in which a hostile intruder attempts to deny availability of a Windows NT network by flooding a domain controller with excessive traffic. In such a scenario, the network administrator would be well advised to have at least one backup domain controller to take over the load until the primary domain controller was able to come back on line. Although denial-of-service attacks are rare, they can significantly threaten the health of an organization's network infrastructure.

Administrators should also be aware that Windows NT servers can be named domain controllers (primary or backup) only at the time of the operating system installation. Servers which are configured as non–domain controllers cannot ever be converted to the domain controller role. Rather, the entire operating system must be reinstalled to enable the server to act as a domain controller. This is one of the most serious flaws, in our opinion, in the Windows NT administrative model.

Administrative Access

As has been documented elsewhere in this book, the Administrator account is often a focal point for potential system intruders. The reason for this centers around two facts. First, the Administrator account has full control over the system. While it does not have default access to all files or resources within the system, it does possess the ability to take control of any given resource. Moreover, it possesses the ability to set system auditing policies and reset the audit logs. Second, the Administrator account, by default, exists on every Windows NT system. Also, by default, it cannot be locked out because of excessive password failures. Note that this feature is designed to prevent a malicious hacker from using excessive password attempts as part of a denial-of-service attack.

Therefore, the Administrator account makes an inviting target for system intruders—and this is especially true with respect to network-based attacks. As a result, there is a strong need to protect the Administrator account. Within a Windows NT network, there are several possibilities for helping to protect the Administrator Account. These include renaming the Administrator account and restricting network access.

RENAME THE ADMINISTRATOR ACCOUNT. Even though the Administrator account exists on all Windows NT systems, it need not be called "Administrator." Rather, it may be renamed to anything the system administrator desires. To rename the Administrator account, launch the User Manager (or User Manager for Domains). By default, the User Manager resides in the *Administrative Tools* group within the Start menu.

From within the User Manager, select the Administrator account, then select the *Rename...* option from the User menu. Then from within the Rename dialog box, type the new name for the account and press the *OK* button. Note that in large organizations, this change should be documented, so that other system administrators will be aware of the change.

This modification is especially effective in Windows NT because Windows NT by default makes no distinction between failed logons for bad passwords and bad usernames (although it can do so through manipulation of the API set). Specifically, if either the username or password is invalid, Windows NT will return an error indicating that the logon failed, but will not indicate which of the two was invalid. Thus, an intruder may attack the Administrator account without limit, even if the account has been renamed. The intruder will not be informed that the Administrator account no longer exists.

RESTRICT NETWORK ACCESS. By default, the Administrator account may access the system from any station on the network. This permits a valid administrator to log into the system and perform system administration tasks from any network station.

Unfortunately, this also means that it is possible for any user on the network to attempt to impersonate the administrator in the manner described above. Therefore, some organizations choose to limit the stations from which the administrator is granted access. Although this configuration limits the flexibility of the administrator in terms of ease of access, it does significantly increase the security of the system.

There are two principal ways to limit access to the system:

1. The first is by limiting a given user account (such as Administrator account) to explicit network stations. In order to do so, first launch the User Manager (or the User Manager for Domains). By default, the User Manager resides in the *Administrative Tools* group within the Start menu. From within the User Manager, select the account you wish to limit to particular network stations. Then double-click on that account name. This will bring up the User Properties dialog box. From within this dialog box, select the *Logon to* button to bring up the Logon Workstations dialog box. From within the Logon Workstations dialog box, the administrator may name specific workstations from which access will be allowed. To do so, first click on the *User May Log on to These Workstations* radio button. Then, explicitly name the workstations from which access will be permitted. In naming the workstations, enter valid computer names in at least one of the boxes in the dialog box.

2. The second way to limit access is less granular and more global. This method utilizes the user right associated with logging in locally versus remotely. More specifically, there is an explicit user right termed "Access this computer from network." By setting group and user privileges to this right, the administrator can effectively limit access via the network. To do so, first launch the User Manager (or the User Manager for Domains). By default, the User Manager resides in the *Administrative Tools* group within the Start menu. From within the User Manager, select the *User Rights...* option from the Policies menu. Then, using the pull-down list box, select the "Access this computer from network" user right. Once this right is selected, the lower portion of the dialog box will indicate the users and groups which have been granted this right. By default, everyone is granted this right. To change this right assignment, use the *Add...* and *Remove* buttons on the right side of the dialog box.

For more detailed information on setting user rights, please refer to Chap. 2, *Managing User Security.*

Windows NT Naming

As we have seen, much of the Windows NT networking depends on proper system naming. This is because file shares, for example, are a combination of the server name (`\\Server Name`) and the share name (`\Share Name`). When typing a server name, the user expects that server to be the server to which that user is intending to refer—and not some other server masquerading as that server.

Indeed, the issue of impersonation has shown itself to be problematic from a security perspective in other networking environments. This section describes how Windows NT naming works, and how it resists impersonation of servers.

Within a Windows NT network, each system has a valid system name. In the case of a critical system, such as a domain controller, this name is associated with an SID for that domain. In the case of a domain workstation, the name is chosen at will by the owner of that workstation.

The association of the SID with the name of the Domain Controller is intended to make impersonation of the domain controller more difficult.

If a new system comes on line claiming to be the domain controller, Windows NT will deny the server access to the domain. This will cause an event to be placed in the event log.

In the case of a domain workstation, names are not assigned until the system comes on line in the network. At that time, the workstation (or server which is not acting as a domain controller) broadcasts a name registration request over the network. It then waits to see if any other systems on the network have already claimed that name. If no other system has claimed the name, the workstation is permitted to use the name.

If another computer has already claimed that name, however, the other computer will issue a negative name registration response—this indicates that the name is already in use. It is then up to the new workstation to accept the failed name request and prompt the user to choose another name.

By default, Windows NT is configured to "play by the rules" with respect to system (NetBIOS) names; that is, if another system has already claimed a name, Windows NT will accept the failed request. Of course, if you were a malicious intruder, you might program your system to not accept the failed response, but instead attempt to use the name anyway. In such a case, there would likely be a conflict in the network which would yield uncertain results.

Part of this question depends on the protocols being used and the name resolution strategies employed. Let's consider an example:

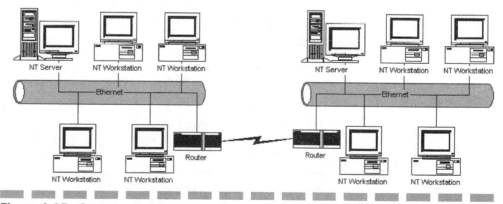

Figure 6.15   Routed network

Imagine the same network as was shown in previous examples. The network consists of two segments separated by a router. The only protocol in use on the network is TCP/IP. Note that this is an extremely realistic example—a large percentage of the Windows NT networks being built today utilize only the TCP/IP protocol suite.

In a TCP/IP network, each node in the network is assigned a unique TCP/IP address. These addresses are associated with a specific machine name, and the combination of both enables any computer on the network to communicate with any other. Therefore, the network requires some way to translate NetBIOS (machine) names to TCP/IP addresses. One way to provide this is to utilize Microsoft's Windows Internet Name Service (WINS), which is part of the Windows NT Server product.

WINS functions to translate TCP/IP addresses to NetBIOS names and vice versa. This is relevant from a security perspective because WINS becomes the arbiter of TCP/IP name and address relationships. Consider the chain of events when a new system comes on line.

Imagine that a Windows NT system configured as a WINS client on the remote side of the network is powered on. When the system boots, it will first attempt to register its name by communicating with the WINS server. Because it has been preconfigured with the TCP/IP address of the WINS server, it can send a directed datagram with the appropriate information. Inside the datagram is information concerning the requested name and TCP/IP address.

When the WINS server receives the datagram, it first consults its database of active names and TCP/IP addresses. If neither the name nor the address is already claimed, WINS will grant the request and send a message back to the client workstation indicating success. If, however, either the name or address is already in use, WINS will attempt to arbitrate the request. Note that this process may occur if a potential intruder attempts to utilize a previously assigned name or address.

If there is already an entry for the computer name requested, WINS will send a message to the system which has already claimed the name. That system, in turn, will send a message back to WINS indicating that the name is, indeed, still in use. Thus, WINS will always permit computer names and TCP/IP addresses to be assigned on a first-come, first-served basis. If WINS receives a request for a name or TCP/IP address already in use, it will verify that the original owner still desires the name/address combination and not permit it to be assigned to the new workstation. In this way, WINS can help reduce the chance of an impostor posing as a known server or workstation.

SNMP Security

With the advent of larger and larger enterprise networks, network administrators have found their jobs to be more and more difficult. As the networks have grown, managing the far-flung regions of the network has become nearly impossible.

Fortunately, both network hardware and software vendors have supported the rapid growth of the *Simple Network Management Protocol* (SNMP), which enables administrators to remotely manage large portions of the network infrastructure. In addition, they can utilize SNMP to provide up-to-the-minute reporting and logging of the health of network infrastructure elements.

Windows NT supports SNMP-based alerts and management. Via SNMP, Windows NT administrators can monitor the health of their Windows NT systems via standard management consoles. At the time of writing, however, they cannot perform significant remote administration of those systems. Microsoft has committed over the long term to providing this functionality.

In addition, Microsoft has committed to providing remote administration tools which enable the use of standard World Wide Web browsers. Using this functionality, Windows NT administrators will be able to remotely configure their NT systems using only a web browser.

Of course, the power that comes with the implementation of significant remote administration also has an accompanying risk. That risk is related to the potential for a malicious user to take over management of network devices, capture network alerts, and so on. Unfortunately, SNMP V.1 was not built with security in mind; rather, it was designed to provide simple, open monitoring and management of infrastructure elements. SNMP V.2 has some additional security functionality built into it, but it has yet to be ratified as a formal standard.

The power and convenience of SNMP- and WWW-based management leads many Windows NT administrators to desire its use. The flip side, however, is that the poor security normally associated with SNMP and the Web poses a significant risk to network security. For those Windows NT administrators who wish to use SNMP-based management and alerting, this section provides some guidelines for enhancing security.

The first stage of securing SNMP is to ensure that the SNMP service has been properly installed. If it has not, consult the Windows NT documentation for information regarding proper network service installation.

Once SNMP is installed properly, select the Network Properties dialog box. This dialog box can be selected by right-clicking on the *Network Neighborhood* icon, then selecting *properties* from the Context menu. Alternatively, you can select the *Control Panel* option from the *Settings* option of the Start menu, then select the *Network* applet.

Figure 6.16
Network configuration dialog box.

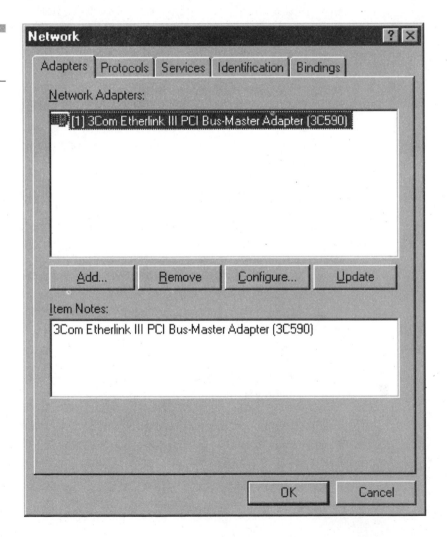

Next, select the *Services* tab, then select the SNMP service from the services list. Double-click on the SNMP service. This will bring up the SNMP Properties dialog box. From this dialog box, select the *Security* tab.

Figure 6.17
Microsoft SNMP properties.

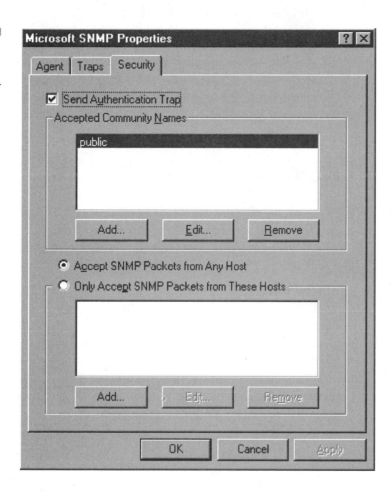

The SNMP Security dialog box permits the administrator to perform two functions:

1. The administrator may elect to initiate an SNMP trap for failed logon attempts. Doing so permits the monitoring of invalid logon attempts from a remote SNMP-capable network monitoring station. In order to configure SNMP authentication traps, click the checkbox marked *Send Authentication Trap* and enter the proper community name in the box below.

2. The administrator may configure the system to only accept SNMP packets from certain hosts on the basis of the remote hosts' TCP/IP or IPX address. This option can be useful in terms of limiting the number of hosts which can communicate with the NT system via SNMP, but in reality provides severely limited security. To configure the system to respond only to SNMP packets from specific hosts, click the checkbox marked *Only Accept SNMP Packets from These Hosts,* then enter the appropriate network addresses in the box below. Finally, click the *OK* button to save the changes.

Remote-Procedure Calls

In order to support complex application architectures, Windows NT natively supports a standard form of the Remote-Procedure Call (RPC). RPCs can be used to provide distributed processing services to complex applications.

Like most of the technology integrated into Windows NT, the RPC architecture is fully covered by the Windows NT security architecture; that is, RPCs are protected using the same methods as are other access methods. Therefore, each RPC requires a valid set of logon credentials, which can be verified using standard Windows NT challenge-response handshakes (when used with a Windows NT client). No further administration is required in order to secure standard Windows NT RPCs.

The Future of NT Networking

Microsoft's networking technologies have evolved considerably from their early attempts with Microsoft LAN Manager. Still, the domain-based network architecture model implemented in Windows NT 3.x shows its heritage from former products. Without question, it pales in comparison to the technology exhibited by other competing network operating systems such as Novell's NetWare.

The next generation of Windows NT networking is still hazy. However, Microsoft has released some information concerning the Cairo project, which is intended to be the follow-on to the current Windows NT product line.

From all indications, Cairo will have a single integrated directory structure (based on the Exchange engine) for the entire network. This will include every element of the network, including servers, users, files, directories, and groups. Everything will be integrated such that a single administration tool can be used to administer any branch of the integrated directory tree.

From a security perspective, the addition of a networkwide directory will assist administrators in creating and maintaining secure Windows NT networks. Today, Windows NT administrators are able to administer remote Windows NT systems with some ease; most NT administration utilities are written to allow the administrator to select a system anywhere on the network to administer. The problem, however, is that each system on the network must be configured individually. With this approach, administrators must constantly switch their focus from one machine to the next in a repetitive process.

With a fully integrated enterprise directory structure, however, an administrator could conceivably set administrative policy—including account policies and user rights—from one central location with a single administrative activity. This would help to ease some of the security management burden currently associated with Windows NT networks.

Moreover, the creation of an integration directory structure would mean that the domain-based structure of current Windows NT networks would fall by the wayside. Rather than having multiple domains, each with unique trust relationships with one another, an integrated directory structure would allow for all Windows NT servers and workstations to work as part of an enterprisewide domain. This would help simplify the security administration of the network—and perhaps lead to greater security.

CHAPTER 7

System Integrity and Availability

But who is to guard the guards themselves?
—*Decimus Junius Juvenalis*

Traditionally, many users and administrators think about computer security only in terms of protecting data from malicious (or curious) unauthorized users. Indeed, much of an average organization's security efforts are focused on protecting data from users—not from Murphy or mother nature.

At the same time, this set of priorities seems rather paradoxical. After all, any reasonably competent computer security expert will tell you that more data is lost to disk crashes and power failures than to hackers.

Of course, protecting against Murphy and mother nature is hardly as sexy or interesting as protecting against a "superhacker"—but statistically, it is much wiser. In short, a proper computer security program must address all three of the classic computer security areas: confidentiality, integrity, and availability.

Disk Integrity and Availability

Although NTFS is quite sophisticated in terms of high-level error handling and crash recovery, it cannot possibly be responsible for handling lower-level system faults. The designers of NT, however, were determined that NT would provide a rock-solid foundation on which to run applications across an enterprise—from end-user workstations to back-end database servers and everything in between. Doing so would require that NT be able to provide high integrity and availability of data, even in the face of significant hardware failures.

NT provides these services through its lower-level disk management technologies. Specifically, fault-tolerance services are provided by the implementation of "hot fixes" within NTFS (see discussion of hot fixes in Chap. 3) and the use of Redundant Arrays of Inexpensive Disks (RAID).

Fault Tolerance and RAID

RAID was originally developed to counter the risk of a single mechanical hard disk failing, thus bringing an entire computer system to its knees. In order to do so, it effectively splits information among a range of relatively inexpensive hard disks to provide some system redundancy. There are five industry-recognized levels of RAID which include some form of system redundancy:

RAID LEVEL 1. RAID level 1 provides for the duplicate storage of data on multiple different physical hard disks. With RAID level 1, all the disks may be fed from the same disk controller (*disk mirroring*) or from two or more identical disk controllers (*disk duplexing*). In the case of a disk failure, a system configured with RAID level 1 will automatically continue operations using the spare copy of the data on the alternate drive. When used in combination with hot-swappable disks, RAID level 1 enables the system to continue operations while the disk is replaced.

There are, however, some drawbacks of RAID level 1. First, disk writes must be performed concurrently on multiple physical disks. In the case of disk mirroring, especially, this may lead to a reduction in overall disk throughput due to a bottleneck in the disk controller. Second, RAID level 1 requires the system to have twice the amount of disk space available than can actually be used; that is, 50 percent of the disk space in the system is unavailable for use because of the redundancy features.

RAID LEVEL 2. RAID level 2 is fundamentally different from level 1. In level 2, the disk array consists of several (at least 3) physical disks linked together to the same controller. This controller then spreads data across multiple disks—there is no notion of putting a single file on a single disk. This process is known as *data striping*. In RAID level 2, data is split at the lowest possible level (bytes) such that not even single disk blocks are guaranteed to be stored together.

At the same time data is written to a disk in the array, the system also writes error-correction code (ECC) to another disk in the array. This error-correction code is mathematically related to the original data in such a way that the original data can be recovered utilizing only the correction code.

RAID level 2 provides somewhat better performance than level 1 because of its ability to spread data among drives as they are able to receive it; in this way, it can yield some additional efficiencies at the drive level. Note that while RAID level 2 may be available as part of the hardware which runs Windows NT, it is not one of the software-based RAID options available to administrators from within Windows NT.

RAID LEVEL 3. RAID level 3 introduces the concept of data parity. The data parity algorithm is used as a replacement for the ECC scheme in RAID level 2. Data is still striped across all disks at the lowest possible level.

Note that the use of data parity does not impact the recoverability of the data; in either case, the system may recover the data on a lost disk by reversing the respective algorithm. With parity, however, the process is made more efficient and requires that less disk space be set aside for recovery information. Note that like level 2, level 3 is not directly implemented in software within Windows NT.

RAID LEVEL 4. RAID level 4 differs from level 3 in two fundamental respects: (1) data is striped across disks at a much higher level (blocks)—doing so yields efficiencies in reading and writing larger volumes of information; and (2) in RAID level 4, parity information is not spread across all disks—rather, it is placed on a completely separate physical disk. In the event of a disk failure, the lost disk can be restored using the parity-block information contained on the parity disk.

Unfortunately, RAID level 4 introduces some inefficiencies in that each write to the disk array must be paired with a write to the parity disk.

Although there is some efficiency in the data portion of the array, due to the availability of many disks to receive data, the parity disk has no such advantage. As a result, the parity disk often becomes a bottleneck to increasing system performance. Note that like levels 2 and 3, RAID level 4 is not directly implemented in software within Windows NT at this time.

RAID LEVEL 5.　RAID level 5 solves the performance bottleneck problems associated with level 4. It does so by striping both the data and the parity information (in blocks) to all the disks in the array. As a result, any disk in the array may contain any combination of data and parity information. RAID level 5 does guarantee, however, that any given piece of data and their associated parity information will be stored in different physical disks.

In many ways, RAID level 5 represents the best of all the other approaches. It has no significant bottlenecks, as any drive in the array may be ready to read or receive data at any given time. Moreover, it reads and writes data in blocks, thus yielding efficiencies in large data transfers such as those common in today's file systems. Finally, it requires only a limited amount of storage space for disk recovery information.

Each RAID 5 array requires at least three physical disks. The algorithm for determining the amount of storage space required for parity in a RAID 5 system is $1/n$, where n is the number of disks in the array. For example, a RAID 5 array of four disks would require one-fourth the space to be allocated to parity information. Therefore, if each disk had a storage capacity of 1 Gbyte, the total usable storage space in the array would be 1 Gbyte/disk $\times$ 4 $-$ 1 disks usable = 3 Gbytes of usable space.

RAID 5 is directly implemented in software in Windows NT. For Windows NT servers and all other Windows NT systems with large amounts of disk storage, RAID 5 is an excellent choice. Its combination of effective management of large volumes of data with on-line recoverability and good throughput make it an optimal choice. We highly recommend the use of RAID 5 whenever feasible.

Implementing RAID

RAID settings are configured using the Windows NT Disk Administrator. The Disk Administrator icon, by default, is found in the *Administrative Tools* group within the *Programs* option in the Start menu. Note that you must be logged into Windows NT as a member of the Administrators group in order to perform RAID conversions and updates.

The first time Disk Administrator is launched, it will not proceed without receiving the user's approval to write an NT signature to the disks to be administered. NT administrators should not be concerned; rather, they should allow Disk Administrator to write its signature, then proceed.

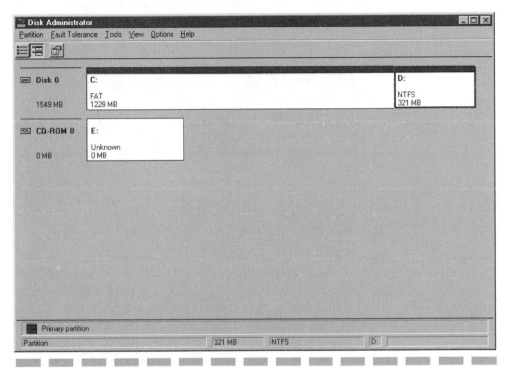

Figure 7.1 Disk administration.

RAID Level 1 (Disk Mirroring)

CONFIGURING RAID LEVEL 1. To configure RAID level 1, administrators should first launch Disk Administrator. From within Disk Administrator, administrators should select the two volumes that they wish to mirror (or duplex). Note that you can select multiple volumes by holding down the control key, then selecting the two partitions with the mouse.

Next, select the Fault Tolerance menu, then the *Establish Mirror* option. This should cause the partitions to be relabeled with the same driver letter. In addition, they should change colors to purple, to indicate the presence of a mirrored disk set.

Then, exit the Disk Administrator and reboot the system. Doing so will commit your changes to the disk. Once the system reboots, the Disk Administrator will display the mirrored disks in the color red, indicating that the initial mirroring process is under way. Once the original data is copied to the mirrored spare, the process is complete. Note that creating a mirrored disk set will affect the information stored on the Windows NT emergency repair disk. As a result, the Emergency Repair disk should be updated as soon as possible following the creation of a mirrored disk set.

To update the Emergency Repair disk, type `RDISK` from the command line. This will launch the Rescue Disk utility, which will allow the administrator to create a new rescue disk or update an old one.

RECOVERING FROM A DISK FAILURE. In the case of a failed mirrored disk, the administrator must manually break the mirror set, then re-create it once an additional disk is placed on line. The first step in the process is to break the mirror set. To do so, first launch the Disk Administrator.

Next, select the mirror set that you wish to break. Then, select the *Break Mirror* option from the Fault Tolerance menu. The mirroring partition will automatically be assigned the next available drive letter.

To make these changes take effect, you must commit the changes to the disk. You may do so by exiting the Disk Administrator and following the prompts as in the previous discussion, or you may do so from within the Disk Administrator. To do so from within Disk Administrator, select the *Commit Changes* option from the Partition menu. This will immediately commit the changes to the disk.

In order to re-create the mirror set, replace the failed disk and follow the instructions shown above for creating new mirror sets. Note that removing a mirrored disk set will affect the information stored on the NT emergency diskette. If a replacement disk is not immediately available, administrators should update the Emergency Repair disk to indicate the absence of the mirror set.

RAID Level 5

CONFIGURING RAID LEVEL 5. RAID level 5 requires at least three disks with sufficient disk partitions to contain the data and parity information. In order to calculate the required disk space for RAID 5, consult the RAID 5 discussion above. To configure RAID level 5, first launch the Disk Administrator.

From within Disk Administrator, select the partitions which will become the disks in the RAID array. Note that you must select at least three equivalent-sized partitions. You may select more than one partition by holding down the control key, then selecting the partitions using the mouse.

Once the partitions have been selected, select the *Create Stripe Set with Parity* option from the Fault Tolerance menu. Next, select the size of the stripe set desired. When the stripe set has been identified, it will appear in the color green within Disk Administrator.

When you have finished making changes, commit your changes to disk either by selecting the *Commit Changes* option from the Partition menu or by exiting the Disk Administrator. Then, restart the system.

After the system is rebooted, the stripe set will take effect. Bear in mind the fact that updating the stripe set will also require updating the NT Emergency Repair disk.

RECOVERING FROM A DISK FAILURE. In the event of a disk failure, the RAID 5 array will continue to read and write data to the remaining disks in the array. Note that the system will continue to function normally without one disk partition by regenerating the information on that disk on the fly as required by the system. This process, however, is extremely CPU-intensive. In addition, operating without one of the disks in the set leaves open the possibility of an entire system failure due to the failure of a second physical disk. Administrators should remember that RAID 5 is unable to provide on-line recoverability for two simultaneously failed disks.

Therefore, we recommend replacing failed disks immediately in a RAID 5 configuration. To replace a disk in a stripe set, first replace the physical disk. Then, launch the Disk Administrator and select the stripe set.

Using the control key and the mouse, select the new disk to be added to the stripe set. Then, select the *Regenerate* option from the Fault Tolerance menu. This will regenerate the stripe set using the new disk. On committing the changes to disk, either by selecting the *Commit Changes* option from the Partition menu or by exiting the Disk Administrator, the system will regenerate the information from the lost disk.

UPS Service

Like most other modern operating systems, Windows NT is designed with a "lazy write" data cache. This means that at any given time, there is likely to be data in memory within a Windows NT system that are awaiting being written to disk. Specifically Windows NT stores data in memory until it finds a "convenient" time to write the data to the disk and thus store it permanently.

Because Windows NT system utilization tends to be "bursty," or occurring in peaks and valleys, the lazy-write cache is able to yield significant performance benefits. The lazy-write cache is, in fact, the primary rationale for the requirement that users shut down the Windows NT environment using the appropriate menu commands—and not simply shut the machine down at the power switch.

Thus, Windows NT systems are constantly vulnerable to data corruption or loss due to power failure. Note, however, that Windows NT systems are not unique in this respect—rather, many other operating systems, including the Mac OS and Novell's NetWare, are also vulnerable to the same power-loss difficulties. Windows NT does, however, provide somewhat superior protection against data corruption in the form of the NTFS file system.

Still, little can be done to protect against data loss from memory. After all, until the data which exist in memory have been written to disk, they effectively don't exist, save for the whims of electricity. Therefore, it is imperative that Windows NT systems are always shut down using the prescribed methods; this will write all data out to the disk and will close all files properly.

In some cases, however, we cannot predict when power failures might occur. Indeed, such power failures represent the bane of some administrators' existence.

The only truly effective means of ensuring that Windows NT systems are not victimized by power failures is to supply each system with an *uninterruptible power supply* (UPS), which is little more than a battery which supplies power to a system when and if a power failure occurs. Should the power go out, the UPS powers the system until either the power is restored or the battery is depleted.

We strongly recommend that all Windows NT systems be powered using a UPS at all times. UPSs of sufficient wattage to power standard desktop PCs cost less than $200, making them an excellent investment as a part of new PC purchases.

Of course, we cannot expect that users will always be in the physical vicinity of their NT systems at the time of power failure. Should the user of the system (or administrator) not be physically present when and if the UPS runs out of power, the system will crash, much as it would have if there were no UPS installed. To prevent this problem, Windows NT has a service to monitor the UPS in order to determine when power is depleted. Immediately before power is depleted, Windows NT can be configured to shut itself down properly, closing all files and writing all data to disk.

The service that performs this operation is termed (rather imaginatively) the *UPS service*. To use the UPS service, you must have a Windows NT system and a UPS with the capability of signaling via a serial cable. Most major UPS manufacturers support this type of signaling, and some vendors supply both their own signaling scheme and support software.

If no Windows NT-specific software is provided with your UPS, you should use the built-in UPS service. To do so, first install the service as described in the Windows NT documentation. Next, proceed with UPS configuration as described as follows. To configure the UPS service, select the *UPS* applet from the Control Panel. The Control Panel can be found within the *Settings* option under the Start menu. To begin configuration of the service, double-click on the *UPS* applet. This will bring up the UPS Properties dialog box.

First, you must tell the UPS service to which serial port your UPS is connected. The UPS should be connected with a standard serial cable. Click the checkbox in the top left corner of the dialog box, then select the proper serial port from the pull-down listbox next to it. Then, set the proper characteristics for your particular UPS.

The first line of the UPS configuration indicates whether the UPS supports sending a signal to the system when power is lost. Note that this is a critical function for proper functioning of the system when and if power is lost while the system is active. More specifically, if the UPS cannot signal the system in the event of a power failure, the UPS service cannot function properly. If the UPS can send a signal on pin 8 of the serial cable [Clear to Send (CTS)], click in this checkbox. Then, indicate the state of the pin when power is lost. This data should be found in your UPS owner's manual.

The second line of the UPS configuration indicates whether the UPS supports a signal to the system when the battery is low. If the UPS can

Figure 7.2
UPS configuration.

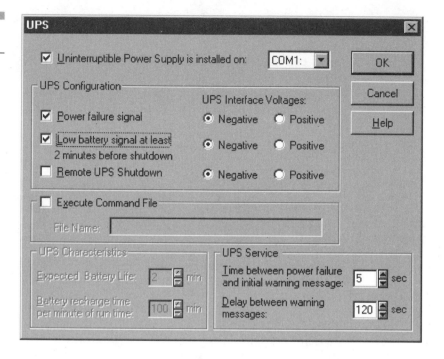

Figure 7.2
UPS configuration.

send a signal on pin 1 of the serial cable [Data Carrier Detect (DCD)], click in this checkbox. Then, indicate the state of the pin when the battery power is low. This data should be found in your UPS owner's manual.

The third line of the UPS configuration indicates whether the UPS supports remote self-shutdown. This is not a critical function for most systems. If the UPS can receive a signal on pin 4 of the serial cable [Data Terminal Ready (DTR)], click in this checkbox. Then, indicate the status of the pin when shutdown occurs. This data should be found in your UPS owner's manual.

Proceeding downward, the next portion of the dialog box indicates whether you would like to run a command file prior to shutting down the system. This command file is a standard Windows NT .CMD (i.e., batch) file, and can perform important system tasks in the moments immediately prior to losing power. For example, many Windows NT Server systems function as database servers. Because of on-line caching, most databases must be shut down cleanly before the system itself is shut down.

The command file option permits the administrator to, for example, automate the closing of a database before system shutdown occurs. Note that some large databases require significant closing time. Also, note that this command file must complete its execution within 30 seconds. Administrators of large databases are likely to find this extremely limiting—as a result, we recommend that administrators who require longer time periods for shutdown scripts utilize third-party UPS monitoring software. Regardless of the software used, administrators should be certain that their UPS is sufficient to handle the power requirements of the system for the time required.

To configure a command file to run prior to system shutdown, click the appropriate check box in the dialog box. Then, enter the name of the command file in the Edit box. Note that for safety, it probably makes sense to include a full file path to the command file you wish to run. After all, it wouldn't help much to get a "file not found" message right before you run out of power and the database comes to a crashing halt!

The final two portions of the dialog box permit the administrator to set the UPS characteristics and the warnings requested from the system. On the left side of the dialog box, the administrator can set both the expected battery life and the charge time per minute of run time. You can calculate the expected battery life by adding up the power requirements of each device connected to the UPS, then referring to the UPS manual to determine the run time (in minutes) of the UPS with your particular power draw. Note that it makes sense to estimate the run time conservatively, especially if your UPS does not support a low-battery warning. Also, the run time of your UPS is likely to decrease over time as a result of battery wear and other factors.

The charge time per minute of run time indicates how long the UPS requires to recharge its batteries. This setting is especially important when intermittent power failures cause a system to transfer back and forth between UPS and standard power. This information should be found in the UPS owner's manual.

On the right side of the dialog box, the administrator can set the relative times for two separate alerts. First, an administrator can set the delay between a power failure and an initial alert being sent to the administrators. Some administrators set this value to 1; that is, they want to know within a second of a power failure. In most cases, however, this is not a good idea. Very often, UPSs switch from standard to battery power and back quickly to supplement small brownouts and fluctuations in the standard power. Although the frequency of these switches depends primarily on the "cleanliness" of the power in your area, it's probably not a good idea to receive an alert 1 second after switchover. After all, by the time you read the alert, the UPS may already have switched back. Therefore, we recommend that this setting be left at the default of 5 seconds.

The final setting is the delay between the sending of warning messages. When power to the UPS has been lost, the system will continue to notify the administrator on a periodic basis. To set the frequency of these warnings, set the appropriate value in the dialog box.

When the UPS service configuration is complete, click the *OK* button to save your changes. Your Windows NT system is now protected by the UPS service. Note that changes made to the UPS service via the UPS applet in Control Panel are placed in the registry, although they are not immediately used by the UPS service. The UPS service reads its registry entries only when it first starts up. Therefore, you must stop the UPS service and restart it before changes will take effect.

The next time power goes out, the UPS service will place an entry in the event log indicating that the UPS is on battery power. Then 5 s later (depending on your settings), it will send a "power out" alert to the system on which the alerter is running and to all domain administrators. These two events will continue to occur on a periodic basis (set by the administrator) until either power is restored or a low-battery condition exists. If power is restored, the UPS service will place an entry in the event log indicating that the UPS has switched back to standard power and will send a "power back" alert to the local system and to the domain administrators.

If the power has not been restored by the time the low-battery signal is raised (or the battery-life counter nears completion), the server will be stopped. Then, the system will send a final power-down message to all users connected to the server and will write an entry in the event log. Finally, it will run the appropriate command file, then shut down the server.

Alerter Service

The Alerter service can be used to send alerts to system administrators or other users. These alerts may be triggered by any number of events, including low-disk-space conditions, problematic network connections, and high resource utilization. Moreover, alerts can be configured to warn about security or other access issues, printing difficulties, and power loss (when the UPS service is active).

By default, the Alerter service is installed on Windows NT server systems and is set to start automatically. On Windows NT workstations, the Alerter service is installed, but is set to manual startup. To ensure that the service is running, check the Services dialog box of the system. The Alerter service is required to be running on any system which will generate alerts to other systems in the network.

A parallel service, called the *Messenger service,* is used on Windows NT systems to receive messages. Note that Messenger service equivalents are available for OS/2, Windows for Workgroups, and Windows 95. By default, the Messenger service is loaded on all Windows NT systems and is set to start automatically.

The first stage in configuring the Alerter service is to indicate a list of users (or computers) who should receive alerts about system functions. In most cases, these users will include system administrators and other IS personnel. To set the list of users or computers, first launch the Server Manager. By default, the Server Manager can be found in the *Administrative Tools* group of the *Programs* option under the Start menu.

From within Server Manager, select the server whose Alert service you would like to configure. Next, double-click on that server, then select the *Alerts* button from the server properties dialog box. This brings up a dialog box from which an administrator can add or remove users or systems to be notified of system events. To add a system or user to the list, type the respective name in the leftmost edit field, then click *Add.* To remove a name, highlight it from the list on the right, then click the *Remove* button.

For more information concerning establishing alert criteria and settings, consult the Windows NT Resource Kit.

Remote-Access Service (RAS) Security

Before I built a wall I'd ask to know what I was walling in or walling out.

—Robert Frost, 1914

This chapter provides information on securing Windows NT networks and systems which are connected to the outside world via the public phone network. While it contains much detailed information on securing the Windows NT Remote-Access Service, it also provides recommendations regarding organizational policy and procedure for other types of dial-up remote access.

Introduction to RAS

One of the most useful utilities included as part of the Windows NT operating system is the Remote-Access Service (RAS). In this age of telecommuting and "information at your fingertips," RAS provides NT users and administrators the ability to link Windows NT systems across a wide variety of telecommunications services in a transparent manner.

To understand both the use and potential security implications of RAS, it first helps to understand the concept behind it. Consider an example of a fictitious company, the Alpha Widget Corporation, which maintains a dedicated sales staff across the country. These salespeople carry notebook computers with Windows NT Workstation and need to maintain connectivity with Windows NT servers in their home offices.

RAS allows the remote salespeople to dial into the corporate network and do all the things that they might be able to do from within the office itself—albeit at a lower speed. As far as the users are concerned, there are no new interfaces to learn, and no new concepts to explain. All the Windows NT system functions, such as mapping drives and browsing the network, are performed using the standard Windows NT tools. For example, File Manager may still be used to create new drive mappings, regardless of whether the user is connected directly to a network or via an RAS link.

Remote-Access Theory

But how does it work? In general, two widespread schemes are used today for providing remote access: "remote control" and "remote node." In the remote control model, a system is dedicated to providing remote connectivity by using itself as a pass-through for information transfer; that is, a remote user may dial into the system and actually take control of a system which physically resides on a network. All the application-level processing is performed on the system which is physically connected to the network—in this case, only the input and output are redirected over the remote link to the user in the field. Products such as Symantec's PC Any-Where fall into the category of remote-control systems.

In the remote node model, on the other hand, a system actually becomes a member of a remote network by attaching itself over a telecommunications link. In this model, the system which physically resides on the network acts as a router for remote nodes—all the network traffic to and from the remote node goes through this system. In contrast to the remote-control model, however, all the standard application processing activity takes place on the remote system. Products such as Shiva's LAN-Rover fall into the category of remote-node systems.

In general, remote-control systems are unable to support more than a single remote user for each local dial-in server. This is because the remote user effectively takes control over the dial-in server in order to perform the remote-control process.

Remote-node systems, on the other hand, can often support large numbers of users on a single physical dial-in server. As was described above, this is because the dial-in server is merely acting as a router for the remote user's network packets. Like the Shiva LANRover, Windows NT's RAS system is a remote-node system. Indeed, this should not be surprising, since Shiva was responsible for much of the development of Windows NT RAS.

Security Implications of RAS

Thus, the Windows NT RAS provides a means to extend your NT network beyond the physical boundaries of your offices. More specifically, users may utilize standard dial-up phone lines [or Plain Old Telephone Service (POTS)], Integrated Services Digital Network (ISDN) lines, or X.25 links to connect to remote NT servers.

The most immediate security implications of utilizing RAS are clear to most administrators; by opening up a link to the outside world, the risk of potential system invasion increases exponentially. In order to fully understand the risk, however, we must understand the tools and methodologies of potential intruders.

Demon Dialing

For example, so-called demon dialing is a favored tactic of system intruders. Let's say that a hacker is looking for new systems to penetrate—either systems at random or certain systems in particular. One way to gain access to these systems is to knock on the owner's front door and ask to be permitted access. Obviously, this tactic is likely to fail.

Another approach is to attack the system by a connected network or by a dial-up extension of that network. Of course, the phone numbers attached to private network access points are rarely published—and are often held as corporate secrets by security-minded organizations.

Therefore, the task of a potential system intruder is to find the access points for the target network. One approach to finding the telephone numbers is to dial every number in a given exchange—then wait to see which are answered by modems. This approach is known as *demon dialing,* and there are dozens of programs available free of charge to perform this task.

Therefore, even if your dial-in access numbers are nonpublished and kept private by your organizations' employees, you cannot be certain that the numbers are unknown to potential intruders. In fact, organizations which use RAS for remote dial-in networking should always assume that the numbers associated with their network access points are known to the entire world—and therefore should be protected accordingly.

RAS Authentication

Because system intruders may be able to gain knowledge of the dial-up access numbers associated with RAS servers, RAS has significant built-in protection to ensure proper authentication. At the administrator's discretion, this authentication can be at least as robust as that for normal Windows NT system logons—and, in fact, probably should be made more secure.

Insecure Communications

Note also that all communications between RAS clients and RAS servers are likely to take place over insecure communications channels such as POTS phone lines. As a result, users and administrators cannot assume that their communications over these channels will not be monitored by third parties. Therefore, the RAS architecture provides for the use of strong encryption technology to ensure that passwords (and other data) cannot be captured by intruders monitoring the communications channel.

Another potential vulnerability associated with intruders monitoring a communications channel is the possibility of a *replay-based attack,* in which an intruder may capture the entire text of an authentication session, then "play" that attack back over the network while claiming to be the authorized end user. Similarly, the Windows NT RAS authentication system provides protection against this type of attack.

Authentication Protocols

By default, RAS offers three choices in authentication protocols. Note that each provides similar functionality—verifying users against the Windows NT SAM—with differing levels of absolute security. Each relies on a different "handshaking" process and potentially different encryption algorithms, but all provide the same functionality. The three authentication protocols are as follows:

CHAP. CHAP, or the Challenge Handshake Authentication Protocol, is generally considered to be the most secure of the authentication protocols available in Windows NT RAS. The Windows NT RAS CHAP implementation is based on an open standard, defined in Internet Request for Comment (RFC) no. 1334 (*PPP Authentication Protocols*). Note that CHAP is not specific to any given encryption algorithm. Windows NT may use two different encryption algorithms when using the CHAP authentication protocol: DES and MD5. Each is described in more detail below.

DES. DES, or the Data Encryption Standard, is a private-key cryptosystem developed for the U.S. government. For several years, DES was the government's primary standard for data encryption. In addition, many of the largest financial institutions in the world rely on DES to protect their financial transactions. Today, however, DES is somewhat dated. The original key lengths utilized for DES are now considered no longer sufficient to protect against a determined attacker. Some variations on DES which are considered secure, however, are not permitted to be exported from the United States under the ITAR regulations. In any case, however, DES probably does provide adequate security for *most* Windows NT implementations.

MD5. MD5 is a proprietary encryption algorithm designed by one of the world's leaders in data encryption: RSA Data Security, Inc. MD5 provides secure hashing functionality, which is essential to ensuring the security of the handshaking process.

The CHAP authentication procedure is used by default with DES encryption when a Windows NT RAS client attaches to a Windows NT

RAS server. This is considered the most secure authentication method available for Windows NT remote access. Other third-party RAS clients may utilize CHAP in conjunction with MD5:

SPAP. SPAP, or the Shiva Password Authentication Protocol, was designed by Shiva Corporation for secure authentication. As was mentioned above, Shiva manufactures one of the most popular remote-node-based access systems in use today—and was central in the development of the RAS system. Generally, SPAP is considered to be less secure than CHAP, but not decisively so. Therefore, SPAP should be considered acceptable for most Windows NT implementations. SPAP is used by default when a Shiva client attaches to a Windows NT RAS server, and when a Windows NT RAS client attaches to a Shiva server.

PAP. PAP, or the Password Authentication Protocol, has no encryption algorithm associated with it; that is, PAP authentication makes no provision for encrypting the authentication stream. Generally, PAP is used only when a third-party client incapable of the other authentication approaches described above attaches to a Windows NT server. We strongly recommend that the PAP protocol not be used in a production environment. This will help to limit the risk associated with setting up a dial-in server.

Note that the Windows NT RAS server can be configured to disallow access from RAS clients which are unable to use either CHAP or SPAP authentication (i.e., those which utilize clear-text authentication). This can be configured from the Remote-Access Setup dialog box. For more information on this option, please refer to the *Configuring RAS Securely* section below.

Additional RAS Security

Arguably, however, the RAS logon authentication is such a critical piece of an organization's security architecture that greater steps should be taken to provide security. More specifically, many organizations are likely to want to implement some other, perhaps hardware-based, form of authentication in order to ensure the security of dial-up servers.

The choices available to system administrators in this arena are quite broad. The majority of these options, however, revolve around some simple concepts. Chief among these is the reasoning behind token-based authentication devices. Such devices are designed to fundamentally increase the requirements for access.

Two-Factor Authentication

Simple passwords, for example, require that a potential user have *knowledge* of certain information. In most cases, the information is a valid username password combination.

Token-based authentication devices, however, require two separate components: something which a potential user knows and something which that user *possesses*. In this case, the potential user must have knowledge of a valid username and must possess an access token in order to be permitted access to the system. Systems which implement this policy are often termed *two-factor authentication devices*.

There are several implementations of token-based authentication devices currently on the market. These include challenge-response units, time-synchronization systems, smart cards, and biometric devices. Each provides differing levels of security at different cost levels.

The most popular access tokens in use today are challenge-response and time-synchronization systems. Challenge-response units work by matching a known "seed," or challenge, with a known response. The relationship between the challenge and the response is based on a secret, proprietary algorithm contained within the token and the security server.

Typically, when a user attempts to access a system protected by a challenge-response system, the server issues a challenge to the user. When the user types the challenge into the challenge-response unit, the unit responds with a predictable response to the entered challenge. This response is then fed back to the server for verification.

Alternatively, some two-factor authentication schemes utilize a time-synchronization approach. In this case, the user is given a token which is time-synchronized with a server-based authentication module. Each side (client and server) also has the same authentication algorithm associated with it. Using the current time as a seed, each side is capable of producing a new password from time to time. As long as the two stay synchronized, they can be assured of producing the same password during any given time period.

Thus, when attempting to access a system protected with a time synchronization authentication system, users merely enter their usernames and the passwords currently displayed on their tokens. The system verifies the password using the same algorithm, and permits or denies access accordingly.

One of the most popular time-synchronization tokens, SecureID from Security Dynamics Corporation, has been fully integrated with the RAS logon process. Working with Microsoft, Security Dynamics has created a DLL-based process which allows the SecureID token to be used for seamless RAS authentication.

Regardless of the type of token used, all token-based devices have some problems associated with them. Not surprisingly, many of these problems revolve around management issues. For example, organizations which utilize physical tokens must make allowances for human fallibility. On any given day, some number of legitimate users are likely to leave their tokens at home, or have their tokens eaten by pets, etc. Organizations must then make temporary tokens available to these users so that they can proceed with their legitimate work.

Moreover, tokens are not a permanent investment. Most time-based tokens last only about 2 to 3 years—after that, they must be replaced. For smaller organizations, this may not be a significant issue. For larger organizations, however, the costs involved might soon become enormous. As an example, consider the costs associated with replacing thousands of $60 tokens every 2 to 3 years.

Because of these problems with cost and management, some token manufacturers are now producing "soft tokens," which are identical in function to, albeit different in form from, standard hardware-based tokens. Rather than encoding their challenge-response or time-synchronization algorithm in a hardware device, the algorithm is placed in a standard executable program. By carrying the program around on the hard disk of a notebook, for example, users need not worry about losing their tokens or replacing them when the batteries go dead.

Secure Communications

Each of these two approaches—traditional challenge response and time synchronization—yields an extremely secure authentication process. A user must not only know something, such as a username, but must also possess something, such as a hardware- or software-based token. Moreover, none of the passwords generated by either of these two approaches is predictable in the abstract. Thus, each password generated is effectively used only once—and is unlikely to be used again in the immediate future. Therefore, the use of these systems provides extremely good security against replay-based attacks.

Above, we discussed the problems of using RAS over insecure communications channels. Indeed, the majority of RAS traffic is likely to traverse telecommunications systems that cannot be considered secure. Therefore, Windows NT also provides significant protection against data capture by providing link-based encryption.

In contrast to the password-based encryption discussed earlier, link-based encryption will perform on-the-fly encryption of all data which traverses a RAS link. In order to do so, it will encrypt all network packets which are bound for a RAS link and decrypt all packets which have been received from RAS links. In this way, NT's RAS link-based encryption provides seamless protection for the entire communications channel.

The algorithm used for providing link-based encryption in Windows NT is RSA Data Security's RD4. In order to configure this option, please refer to the *Configuring RAS Securely* section below.

"Smart" Modems and RAS

Token-based authentication devices, however, are not the only means of providing greater security to a Windows NT RAS implementation. Rather, there are many other strategies available to limit access to dial-up phone lines. Some organizations, for example, utilize dial-back modems in order to enhance security. These modems maintain a list of users, passwords, and phone numbers. Users who wish to use the system dial the modem, then enter their usernames and passwords. The modem then drops the call and dials the user back at a prearranged number. This strategy allows the modem to determine whether a user is legitimate, on the basis of their physical location (i.e., their phone number).

Unfortunately, dial-back modems have some significant problems. First, by definition, they tie a user to a specific geographic location. Because the system must maintain a list of users and their associated legitimate phone numbers, no realistic provision can be made for users who travel frequently. This, therefore, limits the effectiveness of this system for mobile sales staff. Second, dial-back modems have been known to be compromised by various schemes, including call forwarding.

Windows NT also provides a built-in alternative to dial-back modems. The RAS service permits administrators (or users, if configured) to enable RAS to perform dial-back functions. In this case, the modem is not required to support dial-back functionality. Rather, the Windows NT RAS server itself takes care of authenticating users, dropping calls, and calling users back at prearranged numbers. Of course, the implementation of dial-back in the RAS server does not mitigate all the problems noted above; users still must remain at a known phone number in order to authenticate fully. Also, schemes such as creative uses of call forwarding cannot be handled by the Windows NT dial-back service.

To resolve this latter problem, larger and larger numbers of organizations are beginning to use modems which utilize Called Number Identification, or "Caller ID," in order to provide some user authentication. This strategy solves one of the critical problems with dial-back modems mentioned above. At the same time, it still restricts users to a single physical location (except in the case of cellular modems).

Therefore, both dial-back and CID-based modems have significant restrictions attached to them, although both can be useful in limited situations. For example, consider a system administrator who sets up a RAS server to perform routine maintenance from home. In this case, it might be perfectly acceptable to limit access to given phone numbers, namely those at the administrator's home. Thus, Windows NT administrators should consider the use of these technologies where practical.

Configuring RAS Securely

This section describes how to install RAS and enable users to access it in a secure manner. Readers are advised that an understanding of the previous sections will be helpful in the installation process.

When preparing to install and configure the NT RAS, administrators should strongly consider which servers require the use of RAS and which do not. Some administrators install RAS by default on all servers. We, on the other hand, recommend that RAS be installed only on servers which will be required to either support dial-up users directly or those which will be used for outbound access.

Of course, merely installing the RAS server on a given Windows NT server will not automatically permit all users on that system to utilize RAS. Rather, the right to use the RAS must be explicitly assigned by the administrator, and therefore can be centrally controlled. Still, because of the potential risks associated with RAS, we recommend that the RAS server only be installed where there is a legitimate and well-defined need.

In addition, much like the rest of the operating system functionality, use of the RAS service can be audited by the system administrator. We strongly recommend that administrators make use of the logging and auditing facilities available.

RAS Installation

In order to install the RAS server, first click on the Start menu, then select *Settings* and *Control Panel*. From within *Control Panel,* select the *Network* applet. Then, select the *Services* tab, and click on the *Add...* button. Select the Remote Access Service from the list, then click the *OK* button. This will install the Remote Access Service on your system.

Once the Remote Access Service is installed, it must be configured appropriately for your system. In order to do so, select the RAS from the *Services* tab in the *Network* applet of *Control Panel,* then press the *Configure* button. Then add configuration entries for the modems (or other communication devices, such as ISDN terminal adapters) which are attached to your Windows NT system. If you are unsure of the appropriate device driver, select the *Detect* button to attempt an automatic detection of the available devices. Once you have selected the device and entered the proper *Settings...,* you must select whether the device will be used for outbound access, inbound access, or both. Select the appropriate entry from the radio buttons in the lower left corner of the dialog box.

Note that this setting will have a significant impact on the potential security of your RAS implementation. Some administrators configure RAS for both inbound and outbound access in all cases, under the assumption that it's easier to configure once than to have to change it in the future. *We strongly recommend that access be permitted only as is currently required—do not use this setting to "plan for the future."* Should requirements change in the future, this setting is simple to modify.

Figure 8.1
Installing RAS.

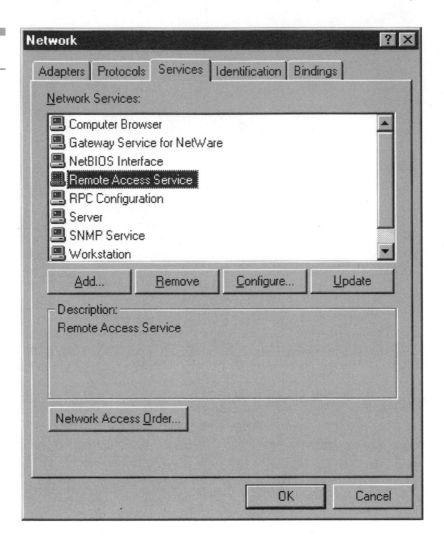

If you do choose to enable inbound access via RAS, you must then select the protocol configurations which will be accepted. Note that all the native Windows NT protocols are fully supported across RAS links. Most organizations, however, limit the number of protocols in use across RAS links because of limited bandwidth availability.

Consider the following dialog box below concerning TCP/IP access:

In this case, the administrator must select whether inbound RAS clients will be able to access resources which reside on the RAS server only, or whether they will be granted access to all the services across the network

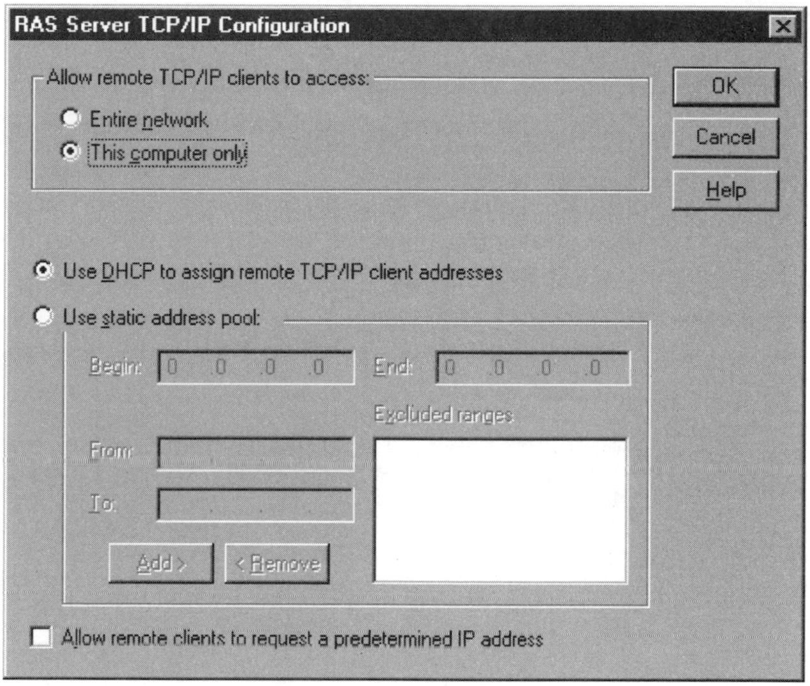

Figure 8.2
RAS TCP/IP configuration.

(to which they have been granted access). This, too, is a critical setting for securing RAS access.

Many organizations choose to place all the resources to which remote users require access on a single server, then permit RAS access only to that server. Doing so helps limit the possibility of an intruder running amok throughout an entire protected network. Note that this setting will not affect the overall security of the RAS authentication and authorization process; rather, it will limit only the potential risk of an organization in the case of a successful RAS penetration. *Whenever possible, we strongly recommend that administrators allow access only to the local RAS server, and not to the network as a whole.*

In addition, the administrator must select a method for assigning remote TCP/IP addresses. Because remote workstations may reside on foreign networks with different TCP/IP configurations, the easiest way to manage RAS-based TCP/IP addresses is via the standard Windows NT DHCP process. This enables administrators to view only one pool of shared TCP/IP addresses, while also limiting the remote clients to a set of known "safe" addresses. This latter point is addressed by the checkbox at the bottom of the dialog box above: "Allow remote clients to request a pre-determined IP address." We recommend that clients not be permitted to select their own addresses, as this helps limit the possibility of an intruder "spoofing" the address of a legitimate user or server.

To configure the protocols which will be available to both inbound and outbound users, select the *Network...* option from the Remote-Access Setup dialog box. This will bring up the following dialog box:

Figure 8.3
RAS protocol configuration.

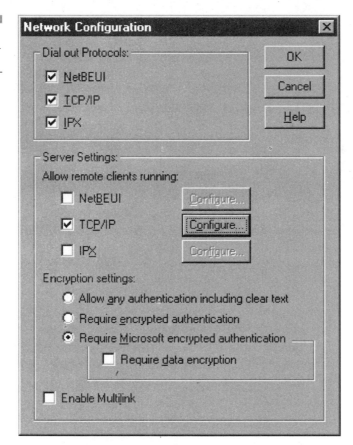

From within this dialog box, the administrator may select both the protocols which will be used on the RAS link(s), as well as setting the encryption and authentication security for those links. The top two parts of the dialog box are concerned with setting up the protocols which will be used. The lower sections refer to the encryption and authentication options.

The protocol options are self-explanatory. For more information on selecting network protocols, please see Chap. 6, *Designing Secure NT Networks*.

Selection of the proper policy for encryption, however, requires more careful thought. The first option, "Allow any authentication including clear text," is not recommended. This will permit any RAS client to use any of the authentication protocols (CHAP, SPAP, PAP) described above. The use of PAP, which is nonencrypted, presents a significant security risk. Therefore, we recommend against using this option.

The second option, "Require encrypted authentication," limits RAS clients to the use of either CHAP or SPAP for authentication. Both CHAP and SPAP provide some level of encryption for the authentication process; neither sends any significant data over the wire in clear form. Therefore, this option is acceptable for RAS servers which will permit access to both native Windows NT RAS and non-Windows NT RAS clients, such as those written by Shiva.

The third option, "Require Microsoft encrypted authentication," limits RAS clients to those which are able to perform native Windows NT authentications using CHAP and DES encryption. This option is most useful for organizations utilizing only Windows NT RAS servers and clients. Doing so will yield the highest possible level of security in a native RAS implementation.

Below the third option is a checkbox which allows the administrator to indicate that all traffic between the RAS server and client will be encrypted using RSA Data Security's RD4 algorithm. As was discussed above, the use of link-based encryption is highly recommended, and will significantly increase the security of the RAS implementation. This option is available only when using RAS with native NT clients and servers; it cannot be used with clients requiring either SPAP or PAP authentications.

The final option on the dialog box enables the use of Multilink PPP. Multilink PPP is a standard for using multiple physical links to provide a larger logical network connection to a remote point. Therefore, instead of using a single large "pipe," Multilink PPP allows the use of several smaller pipes to provide the equivalent bandwidth.

Administering RAS Permissions

After following the steps described above, RAS itself is fully configured. By default, however, users are not permitted access to the RAS server without explicit authorization from the system administrator (or equivalent). To do so, first launch the Remote Access Admin. The Remote-Access Admin can usually be found in the *Remote Access Service* folder in the *Programs* choice in the Start menu.

When using the Remote-Access Admin, administrators should first ensure that the RAS service is running on the server. To start the service, select the *Start Remote-Access Service* option from the Server menu.

Once the RAS service is running, administrators may choose to grant RAS privileges to selected users. To do so, select the *Permissions* option from the Users menu. This will bring up the Remote-Access Permissions dialog box.

From within this dialog box, members of the Administrators group may allow or disallow access to the remote access server. Note that these rights may be assigned on an individual user basis.

To assign dial-in rights to a user, first select the user in the top portion of the dialog box. Then, click the checkbox marked "Grant dial-in permission to user." Next, select whether the RAS server will be using the Windows NT dial-back service. If not, click on the radio button marked *No call-back*.

If dial-back is desired, select either "Set by caller" or "Preset to." The former option will allow users to set the number from which they will be calling, and hence to which they should be called back. The latter choice allows the administrator to set the phone number which should be called back.

RAS for Outbound Internet Access

As more and more organizations seek to provide a presence on the worldwide Internet, RAS has become a popular means for connecting end-user networks and workstations to the Internet. By design, Windows NT RAS supports the TCP/IP Point-to-Point Protocol (PPP), which is widely used for Internet connectivity. Thus, it is possible to connect either a single Windows NT system or an entire Windows NT network to the Internet via the NT RAS.

At the same time, the risks associated with connecting a RAS-equipped Windows NT system to the Internet are significant. For more information on the details of securing a Windows NT system for service as an Internet host, please see Chap. 9, *Windows NT Internet Security*.

Note that while Windows NT RAS can act as an Internet gateway and router, this was not its originally intended purpose. As a result, the performance that you might expect when using Windows NT RAS as an Internet router is far less than what you might expect from dedicated internetworking hardware.

At the same time, the functionality provided is quite useful for small workgroups—if the proper security measures are taken. Indeed, we would not recommend that this method be used for connecting any significant number of users to the Internet—rather, a dedicated Internet connection (with a dedicated Internet firewall!) should be used instead.

Securing Inbound Access with PPTP

The rapid growth of the public Internet has made some organizations rethink their private WAN strategies. After all, they argue, why reinvent the wheel? Why maintain a parallel private network to the public Internet, rather than simply using the Internet to carry corporate traffic?

Up until now, the reasons have been twofold. First, the Internet provides no traffic delivery or performance guarantees; that is, there is no strong reason to believe that any given message will make its way to its intended destination—let alone in an efficient manner. Second, the Internet provides no inherent security for the packets which traverse its segments. Therefore, anyone with the opportunity and the means (and there are many) are able to examine the contents of any and all Internet traffic.

This second problem is being addressed with the implementation of so-called *virtual private networks* (VPNs), which are designed to use parts of the public Internet to transfer private data with security and confidentiality. Often, VPNs between two sites are termed *encrypted tunnels*.

In versions 4.0 and later of Windows NT Server, Microsoft has included the capability to create encrypted tunnels using the *Point-to-Point Tunneling Protocol* (PPTP), which is designed to permit users to easily create and remove encrypted tunnels while leveraging the simple and secure communications afforded by RAS.

Moreover, PPTP supports protocols other than TCP/IP. By packaging these protocols within TCP/IP frames, PPTP becomes a flexible communications protocol. Currently, the PPTP specification supports IPX, NetBIOS, and NetBEUI in addition to standard TCP/IP.

To utilize PPTP to secure Internet communications, both clients and servers must be able to support the PPTP protocol. Over the next 6 months or so, a large number of vendors are expected to introduce products which support the PPTP.

To enable the use of PPTP on Windows NT Server, administrators should first ensure that the TCP/IP protocol is installed correctly. Then, right-click on the Network Neighborhood icon, then select *Properties* from the context menu. Next, select the *Protocols* tab and the TCP/IP protocol.

From within the TCP/IP protocol dialog box, select the button marked *Advanced*. Then, click the checkbox to enable the use of PPTP. *To fully utilize the security provided by PPTP, administrators should also enable link-based encryption for RAS as described in previous sections.*

Securing Enterprise Dial-in Access

As we have discussed above, the Windows NT RAS is extremely effective in providing easy-to-use remote dial-in capabilities. This helps system administrators provide a common means for users to have dial-up access to an organization's network. At the same time, however, it also means that end users who manage their own Windows NT workstations may also use the RAS to provide dial-up connectivity to their own workstations. Because there is no central control over this type of dial-in access, allowing users to do so may lead to a significant security breach.

We strongly recommend that the dial-in use of RAS be centralized. Because a Windows NT server can support a large number of active RAS sessions, centralization is both feasible and cost-effective. Moreover, it provides the administrator with greater control over system security and the end users with more professionally managed dial-in access.

Consider the implications of users providing their own dial-up access from their desktops. First, not all users are likely to provide good password security on their systems. Moreover, some users are likely to have accounts on their systems which have no passwords at all. Finally, some users might configure RAS to allow clear-text authentication.

Each of these potential configurations of RAS provides suboptimal security for the enterprise. And, if the system providing RAS dialup is connected to a large Windows NT network, the security risk goes far beyond the exposure of a single Windows NT workstation.

Securing the Point of Access

One of the prerequisites for users to provide dial-up access to their systems is access to an appropriate phone line. Today, many organizations use digital phone systems for intraoffice communications. These digital signals are then converted to analog signals before being sent out to the public phone network.

The use of digital phone systems provides an unexpected advantage to security-conscious system administrators. Unlike analog devices, digital telephony hardware is not necessarily interchangeable. More importantly, it is not at all compatible with standard analog modems. Therefore, organizations which provide only digital lines to their employees are at limited risk from unauthorized RAS dial-up servers.

Note that the risk is limited, although not completely eliminated. This is because there are some modems which do support digital phone systems. Also, there are devices which convert digital signals to analog and vice versa. As a result, a determined user may be able to use either a standard or a nonstandard modem on a digital office line.

Thus, there is virtually no way to limit Windows NT workstation users' ability to provide their own RAS dial-in capability, especially if analog phone lines are provided to the desktop. Most organizations must therefore rely on policy to prevent potential security risks.

Administrators can, however, take some measures to detect the use of RAS dial-in servers on Windows NT workstations. They can, for example, use demon dialers of their own to dial their organizations' phone numbers on a regular basis. This is an excellent way to find modems connected to outside phone lines—and hopefully to do so before hackers find them.

CHAPTER 9

Windows NT Internet Security

He that is secure is not safe.

—*Benjamin Franklin, 1748*

Over the last year or so, the growth in the worldwide network of networks, the Internet, has exceeded every expectation. Indeed, most people can no longer pick up a newspaper or watch television without seeing reference to the Internet.

The Internet has been positioned as the new medium for business and communication in the 1990s and beyond. Analysts anticipate on-line buying and selling of goods and services to reach billions of dollars by the next century. Moreover, the advent of high-bandwidth communications is likely to lead to video on demand and live videoconferencing over the Internet.

Each of these new uses of the Internet depends on a similar foundation: that the Internet can provide robust and secure communications. If the Internet cannot be made secure, it cannot be used for the tasks mentioned above.

This chapter discusses the steps Windows NT administrators can take to help ensure the security of their Windows NT systems used as Internet servers. Note, however, that this chapter does not constitute a primer on Internet security. Rather, the suggestions mentioned here for securing Windows NT systems for use as Internet servers should fit within the context of a greater enterprisewide Internet security plan. That being said, however, note that more and more Windows NT systems are being used as "Intranet" servers—providing Internet-like services to users within a private organization. This chapter also addresses the security implications of using a Windows NT system in this way.

Internet and Windows NT Services

To understand how Windows NT can make an effective Internet server, it helps to understand a bit more about the Internet and the standard services which it provides. Generally speaking, the Internet is simply a large network of computers which communicate using a known protocol (TCP/IP) and use a more-or-less standard set of applications. These applications, such as FTP, Telnet, and HTTP (the World Wide Web), are merely different uses of the same underlying TCP/IP network. Therefore, while these services are traditional uses of the Internet, they are far from the only services which might be provided.

This means that virtually any service which can run over TCP/IP can be used over the Internet. This includes services such as native Windows NT networking. As was discussed in previous chapters, Windows NT networking is based on NetBIOS frames (NBFs), which can be encapsulated in other protocols. Therefore, Windows NT native networking services can be provided over TCP/IP networks such as the Internet simply by encapsulating NBFs within TCP/IP packets.

At the same time, however, it is not altogether clear that doing so is either a proper—or a safe—practice. As we have seen, Windows NT provides a significant number of services through its native networking technology. These services may well be far more than an administrator might wish to supply to the worldwide audience of the Internet. Indeed, there is strong reason to believe that it's probably best to stick with the traditional Internet applications which provide both known functionality and known potential risk.

These traditional services were pioneered on non–Windows NT–based systems. Indeed, the vast majority can trace their roots to various flavors of UNIX and its derivatives.

In more recent times, however, many traditional Internet server services have been ported to the Windows NT platform. Today, all the core Internet services can be provided by Windows NT servers using native technologies, third-party tools, or any combination of either. Regardless of the derivation of the services which it can provide, it is becoming apparent that Windows NT makes a strong Internet server platform. The combination of its performance, manageability, and ability to run on relatively inexpensive hardware is making it one of the top choices for new Internet servers.

As you might expect, however, not all is completely rosy. Traditional UNIX-based Internet servers have a far longer history of use in the Internet, and therefore have a longer track record of providing secure Internet access and service. Windows NT, on the other hand, is a relative newcomer to the Internet market. Therefore, some observers question NT's ability to withstand the security challenges faced by Internet systems. In truth, only time—and the successful or unsuccessful efforts of Internet hackers—will tell the tale.

One final note—keep in mind the fact that implementing many of the security suggestions made throughout this book, in addition to those mentioned in this chapter, will help improve the security of your Windows NT Internet server. On the basis of the current Internet hype, some readers are likely to turn directly to this chapter to find out quickly how to securely configure an NT server for use on the Internet. We strongly caution against using this chapter in that manner; rather, we strongly suggest that readers understand and implement the security recommendations made in the preceding chapters as well. Only by doing so will readers be able to fully understand the implications of the recommendations made here.

In addition, readers should be aware that this chapter addresses only the common user-oriented Internet services. Other services, such as DNS, NNTP, and XNTP, have their own security implications which are not discussed here.

FTP Services

In its native form, Windows NT provides only a single significant Internet service: the Windows NT FTP server. The FTP server is a part of the core operating system and can be installed as an option when the TCP/IP protocol suite is installed.

With the addition of the freely available Internet Information Server for Windows NT, however, administrators can now choose among two "semi-native" FTP servers. Each provides extremely similar functionality: the ability for remote users to navigate a directory tree and both send and receive files from that tree using platform-independent standard tools.

For those administrators looking for an integrated set of Internet services with reasonably strong security features, we strongly recommend that the Internet Information Server be used. For those administrators who require only FTP services with limited security features, the native FTP service may be sufficient. In either case, however, there are some important things to consider when using the FTP servers, including the following:

Directory permissions and privileges. Administrators should be aware that both of the available FTP servers require users to connect to a specific user account, regardless of whether anonymous logons are used. The rights granted to this account are, in turn, granted to each user who logs into the FTP server. Therefore, administrators should ensure that this account has proper privileges and directory permissions associated with it.

Passwords in clear. Administrators should be aware that both the native Windows NT FTP server and the FTP server in the Internet Information Server support the use of unencrypted passwords. When configured in this manner, all user logons which occur over the Internet will occur in clear-text form. Therefore, anyone using an Internet packet sniffer may be able to view the usernames and passwords of users in real time.

Administrators should also be aware that the Computer Emergency Response Team (CERT) and others have verified dozens of incidents of packet sniffers being used on the Internet.

FTP Recommendations

FTP services can be extremely secure if configured properly. When configured improperly, however, the FTP server may open up a Windows NT server to a significant security risk. In order to mitigate the risk and provide secure access, we recommend the following:

ANONYMOUS LOGONS. As was mentioned above, neither the native Windows NT nor most other implementations of FTP servers or clients support encrypted logons. As a result, all logon information which is transferred between the client and the server may be viewed by anyone watching traffic on the network. In the case of the Internet, this means that user IDs and passwords may be vulnerable to network hackers.

There are two possible ways to limit the risk associated with sending FTP passwords in the clear. The first is to require users to utilize one-time passwords. One-time passwords are good only for one particular logon session (or for a short time duration). Such products are available from third-party vendors. Alternatively, administrators may choose to use public-domain one-time password strategies such as SKEY.

The second possible choice is to not permit the use of any user IDs and passwords. Rather, administrators may force all users to log into the FTP server using an anonymous account. Of course, this choice also has significant drawbacks. First, it does not permit effective auditing of user's activities. Because users are not individually identifiable, the system cannot effectively log their activities. Second, it does not permit the administrator to assign differing levels of access rights to different users. Indeed, the precise opposite is true—it forces all users to have exactly the same access.

In some cases, these two limitations are acceptable. For example, consider a company which wants to set up an FTP site to distribute public documents or free updates to software. In cither case, the system need not provide user-level auditing and need not require different levels of security.

Thus, some cases are ideal for the use of anonymous logons. Whenever possible, we strongly recommend that administrators configure their systems to use anonymous logons, either in conjunction with regular logons or alone. When regular logons are required, we strongly recommend the use of one-time passwords.

NT NATIVE FTP SERVICE. To configure anonymous logons using the native Windows NT FTP server, first right-click on the *Network Neighborhood* icon. Then, select *Properties* from the context menu.

Figure 9.1
Installing the Native
FTP service.

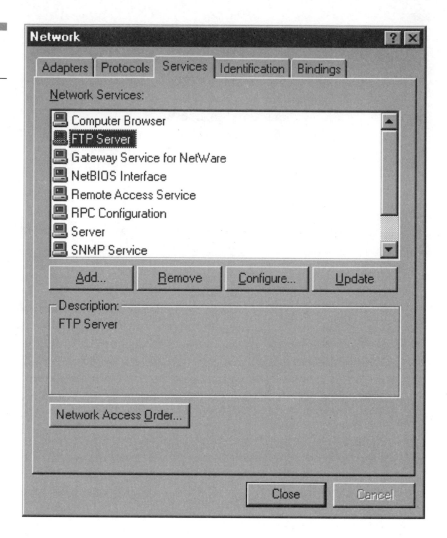

From within the Network Properties dialog box, select the *Services* tab and the *FTP Server* option. Double-click on the *FTP Server* to bring up the FTP Server Properties dialog box.

In order to enable anonymous connections, click on the checkbox marked "*Allow anonymous connections.*" If you want to disallow all regular logons, click the checkbox marked "*Allow only anonymous connections.*"

Note that when using anonymous connections, you must specify a user name under which anonymous users will be connected; that is, even though anonymous users need not use a username and password to log

Figure 9.2
Native FTP Service
properties.

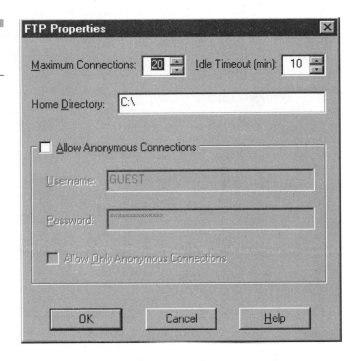

into a specific user account, they must inherit the privileges of a user account. By default, this user account is the Guest account.

Administrators should note that on versions 4.x and later of Windows NT, the Guest account is disabled by default. Also, note that when using anonymous logons, administrators must ensure that there is no user named "anonymous." When anonymous logons are enabled, the anonymous username becomes a reserved logon name.

Clicking the *OK* button twice will save the FTP server information. To ensure that settings take effect, administrators should shut down and restart the FTP server from the Services dialog box.

INTERNET INFORMATION SERVER. In order to enable anonymous logons using the Internet Information Server, first launch the Internet Service Manager. By default, the Internet Service Manager can be found within the *Microsoft Internet Server* group of the *Programs* option in the Start menu. From within the Internet Service Manager, select the FTP server whose warning messages you would like to modify. Then, double-click on this server. Next, select the *Services* tab from the FTP Service Properties dialog box.

Figure 9.3
IIS FTP properties.

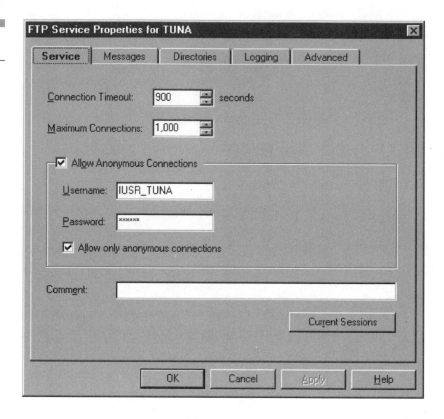

From this dialog box, click the checkbox marked "Allow anonymous connections." If you wish to limit connections to only anonymous users, click the checkbox marked "Allow only anonymous connections."

As was mentioned above, you must specify a username under which anonymous users will be identified when using anonymous FTP logons. Unlike the native FTP server, the IIS by default installs a special account for FTP clients to use. This account is called IUSR_Server_Name, where Server_Name is the name of the server on which IIS is running.

By default, this user account is a member of the Guests and Domain Users account. Moreover, the IUSR_Server_Name user is not permitted to change the password, and the password for this user account is set to never expire.

Administrators should be aware that the password associated with this account is chosen randomly by Windows NT. Although the likelihood is that this password is reasonably secure, there is a possibility that the chosen password might be insecure. Therefore, administrators are free to change this password to one they know to be secure against standard attacks, and we recommend that administrators follow this course of action.

Also, administrators should note that the `IUSR_Server_Name` account may be created either in a Windows NT domain or within a single Windows NT server. If the IIS is installed on a Windows NT server acting as a primary or secondary domain controller, the account will be created in the domain database. If the IIS is installed on any other type of NT server, the account will be created in the local server database. To save these settings, click the *OK* button.

VOLUME PERMISSIONS. By default, both the native FTP Server Service and the Internet Information Server require the administrator to identify a home directory for FTP users. This is the directory into which users will be placed once they are authenticated to the FTP server.

When using the native FTP service, users, permissions to files and directories are protected by two different settings. The first is the file and directory security provided by the operating system and file system.

Therefore, one of the most effective ways to provide security is to use the NTFS file system. *In fact, we strongly recommend that administrators use the NTFS file system when using the FTP service.*

In addition to the volume-based security, the FTP Server Service also contains volume-level security restrictions which can be configured from the FTP Server Security dialog box.

Figure 9.4
IIS FTP volume
security.

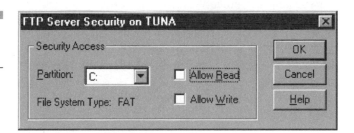

To open this dialog box, first ensure that the FTP service is running on the Windows NT system by checking the Services dialog box. Then, launch the Server Manager (or Server Manager for Domains). By default, the Server Manager can be found within the *Administrative Tools* group within the *Programs* option of the Start menu. From within the Server

Manager, select the Windows NT system containing the FTP service you would like to configure. Then, select the *FTP Service* option from the FTP menu. From this dialog box, select the *Security...* button.

From within the FTP Server Security dialog box, administrators can set volume-level read and write permissions for each volume in the system. Note that these permissions act in addition to any permissions set at the file system level. In addition, and more importantly, administrators should note that these permissions function regardless of the volume type. Therefore, administrators can set read and write security permissions on all types of volumes including FAT.

At the same time, however, note that these permissions are hardly granular; that is, they provide only high-level control over the volumes in the system. Therefore, the only effective way to use these permissions on a FAT system is to ensure that sensitive information is stored only on discrete volumes and that permissions to those volumes allow neither read nor write access. Although this solution is technically feasible, we still strongly recommend that administrators utilize the NTFS file system whenever possible. Moreover, we strongly recommend that administrators separate volumes on which operating system files and utilities are stored from those which permit FTP access.

Note that with respect to traversing the file system, the native FTP service works exactly as does the standard command prompt. This means that users are permitted to traverse the directory tree (using the CD command) to the full permissions allowed them by the file system and the read/write permissions assigned to the volumes they traverse. No further restrictions are placed on the FTP user.

With this in mind, consider the implications of the default settings for the native FTP service. If anonymous logons are permitted, any user may log into the system using the default guest account (assuming that it has been enabled for the FTP service). When using this account, remote users have Full Control rights over most of the operating system files and utilities. In this configuration, an anonymous user may be able to compromise an NT system over the Internet using a trojan horse attack, as described elsewhere in this book. *NT administrators should be extremely careful to separate anonymous users from access to sensitive files, using either the NTFS file system or separate volumes for anonymous FTP users (or both!). Moreover, administrators should be aware that permitting anonymous FTP users to upload files to an NT system may lead to a potential denial-of-service attack.*

When using the FTP server included with the IIS, however, some of the configuration details described above change significantly. Unlike the native FTP service, the IIS FTP server is relatively sophisticated in its directory and file permissions. At the same time, however, the complexity associated with configuring directory permissions for the IIS FTP server may lead to administrative errors.

Much like the native FTP service, the IIS FTP server permits the use of a default home directory. This is the directory into which users will be placed immediately after logon authentication.

Unlike the native FTP service, which treats the home directory as any other, however, the IIS FTP server views the home directory as the "root" of all other allowable directories. This means that users may traverse any and all directories which exist below the home directory (according to file and directory permissions), but cannot change to directories above the home directory. Contrast this to the native FTP service, which permits tree traversal to the limits of the user account permissions.

In this way, the IIS FTP server provides a simple, default way to easily recognize which directories in the file system are potentially vulnerable to FTP clients. To make the FTP service more useful, however, the IIS FTP server permits the use of virtual directories. *Virtual directories* are directories which are not children of the FTP root directory, but may be traversed by FTP clients.

Using virtual directories, administrators may permit FTP access to any directory in the system, regardless of whether the directory actually exists as a child directory of the FTP root directory. This has implications for both system utility and security. From a utility perspective, it means that any directory in the system may be used as a source or target directory for FTP clients. From a security perspective, however, it means that the simplicity associated with the default IIS FTP root directory may disappear.

Administrators should be aware of two significant factors with respect to calculating effective FTP user rights for their file systems when using the IIS FTP server. First, all virtual directories act very much like their own root directories. That is, FTP clients will not be permitted to change directories to the parent directories of virtual directories. They will, however, be granted access to traverse child directories of the virtual directories. Second, all directory traversal rights must also be put into the context of the underlying file system. When using the NTFS file system, for example, it is possible to limit users' access to directories using file and directory-level permissions. These permissions also apply to FTP clients.

Thus, when using the IIS FTP server, we recommend that administrators utilize the FTP root directory — and its children — to the greatest extent possible. Whenever possible, all files which are available to FTP clients should be placed in the FTP root or one of its children. While virtual directories provide additional flexibility, they also require that administrators keep track of multiple directories and permissions to ensure the security of the entire system.

If administrators do choose to use virtual directories as a part of their FTP directory hierarchy, we recommend that they utilize both NTFS- and IIS-level permissions to provide a dual safety net. To configure IIS-based protection for virtual directories, select the *Directories* tab from the FTP Server Properties dialog box.

Within the *Directories* tab, click the *Add...* button to add a virtual directory. Then, add the name of the directory and the location on the disk to the following (Directory Properties) dialog box. Note that the virtual directory need not exist on the system running the IIS. Rather, it may exist on another system to which the IIS system has access via a file share. If the directory exists on a remote file share, you must also enter a valid username and password for an account with access to that file share—otherwise, the link will not work. Once this information has been added, select the type of permissions you would like to associate with that directory. IIS can support either read-only, write-only, or any combination of the two types of access.

FTP LOGGING.   Elsewhere in this book, we have emphasized the importance of proper auditing and logging of user activities. The FTP service is certainly no exception to this rule. In fact, logging of FTP operations can be critical to ensure the security of the system and to provide an after-the-fact record of system penetration.

NATIVE NT FTP SERVICE.   By default, the native FTP Server Service provides relatively limited—yet functional—logging capabilities. The native FTP service can log three types of activity:

- Logons by anonymous users
- Logons by nonanonymous users
- File accesses by any user

Each of these three types of log settings can be set up via the Registry Editor. To do so, first launch the Registry Editor as described above. Then, select the HKEY_LOCAL_Machine on Local Machine master key.

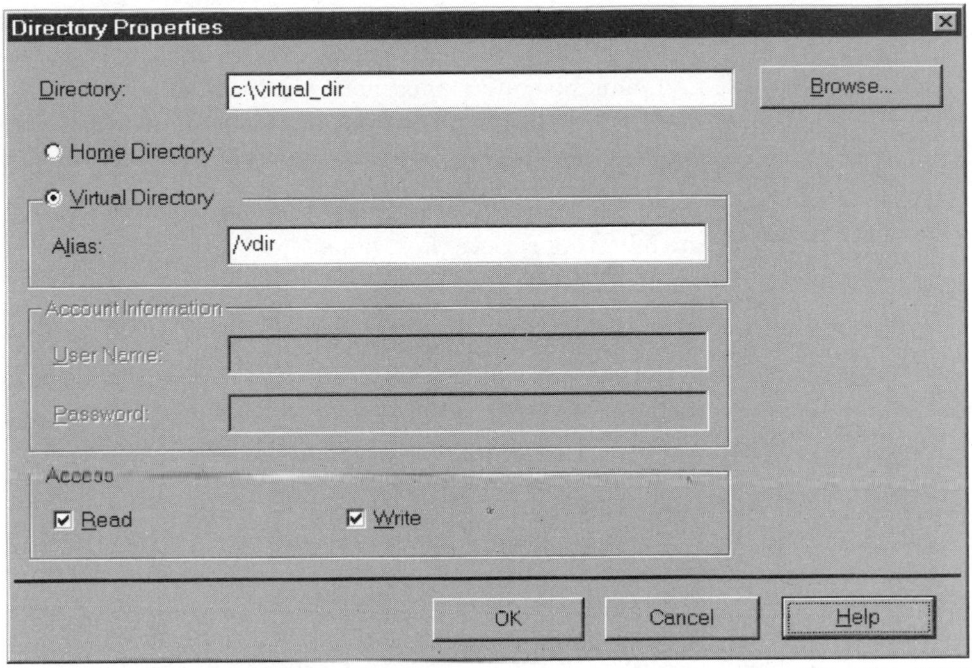

Figure 9.5 IIS directory properties.

The key

```
\System\CurrentControlSet\Service\ftpsvc\Parameters\LogAnonymous
```

controls whether Windows NT will create log events when anonymous users log into the system. Setting this key with a value of 1 will cause an audit event to be generated when an anonymous user logs into the native FTP service. Setting this key with a value of 0 will prevent the system from generating audit events for anonymous logons. By default, this key is set with a value of 0. We recommend that this key be set with a value of 1 to enable full logging.

Another key,

```
\System\CurrentControlSet\Service\ftpsvc\Parameters\LogNonAnonymous
```

controls whether Windows NT will create log events when nonanonymous users log into the system. Setting this key with a value of 1 will cause an audit event to be generated when a nonanonymous user logs into the native FTP service. Setting this key with a value of 0 will prevent the system from generating audit events for nonanonymous logons. By default, this key is set with a value of 1; we recommend keeping the default setting.

Each of the two keys discussed above will cause audit events to be generated in the standard Windows NT event log. Because of this integration, administrators need not keep track of an extra log for FTP logons. For FTP file logging, however, administrators must monitor an external log file.

To enable FTP file logging while using the native FTP server, create the following registry key value:

`\System\CurrentControlSet\Service\ftpsvc\Parameters\LogFileAccess`

Setting this key with a value of 1 will enable logging of file accesses. Setting the key with a value of 0 will cause no file logging to occur. By default, this key value does not exist; therefore, there is no FTP file logging by default.

When file logging is enabled, administrators should be aware that file access audit events are not sent to the standard Windows NT event logs. Rather, they are sent to a file called `FTPSVC.LOG`, which by default exists within the `%System_Root%\System32` directory. This file is a standard text file and therefore cannot be viewed using the Event Manager. Also, this file may be vulnerable to tampering unless protected with a proper ACL on an NTFS volume. *We strongly recommend that administrators protect this file appropriately using the file ACLs.*

Within this file, the audit events generated for each file access include the following information:

- Username
- Client IP address
- File operation (open, append, etc.)
- Filename
- Date
- Time

INTERNET INFORMATION SERVER. The IIS FTP server, on the other hand, provides somewhat more robust logging capabilities. To configure the IIS logging capabilities, first launch the Internet Service Manager. By default, the Internet Service Manager can be found within the *Microsoft Internet Server* group in the *Programs* option in the Start menu.

From within the Internet Service Manager, select the FTP server you wish to configure. Then, double-click on the FTP server to view its properties. From the Properties dialog box, select the *Logging* tab.

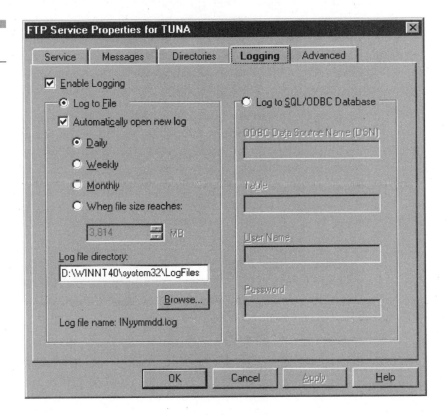

Figure 9.6
IIS FTP logging.

Unlike the native FTP service, the IIS FTP server permits a choice of logging repositories. By default, the IIS FTP server will send its logs to a file generated on a daily basis. These log files reside, by default, within the `%System_Root\System32\LogFiles` directory. Note that new log files may be generated on a daily, weekly, or monthly basis according to the needs of the system administrator.

Moreover, new log files may be generated when the file size exceeds a value set by the administrator. To set these options, click the appropriate checkbox from within the FTP Server Properties dialog box shown above.

When logging to a file is enabled, log files will be created within the specified directory with the name syntax `INyymmdd.log`, where `yy` stands for the year, mm stands for the month, and dd stands for the day. Therefore, a log created on January 1, 1997 would have a filename of IN970101.log. Note that this log file will be used for all the services provided by the Internet Information Server (FTP, WWW, Gopher), and not just for the FTP service. In this way, the IIS provides some integrated logging capabilities. It is not capable, however, of integrating directly with the Event Viewer.

Alternatively, administrators may choose to send their log files to an on-line database. This database must be able to communicate using the Open Database Connectivity (ODBC) service and you must install version 2.5 or later of the ODBC drivers. Not surprisingly, Microsoft recommends the use of the Windows NT-based SQL (Structured Query Language) Server database.

Logging to a database can have several significant advantages. First, logging to a database can provide additional security for the log files. Because they are stored in an unknown file format, modifying them is difficult—if not impossible—without accessing them through the database (and via the database security). Second, storing the logs in a database allows administrators to parse and query their logs in a robust manner. Doing so allows for analysis not possible with simple log files.

To log to a database, you must create a proper table in your database (as documented in the IIS documentation), then supply the IIS with the information needed to connect to that database and table. Finally, fill in the appropriate boxes in the FTP Service Properties dialog box.

ALLOWING ACCESS BY ADDRESS. The Internet Information Server also permits administrators to filter FTP clients by their client TCP/IP addresses. In this way, administrators can restrict access to only a handful of remote client addresses, or they can restrict access from a given range of addresses. Note that the native FTP server offers no such option.

In order to configure address-based access, first launch the Internet Service Manager. By default, the Internet Service Manager can be found within the *Microsoft Internet Server* group in the *Programs* option in the Start menu. From within the Internet Service Manager, double-click on the FTP server you wish to configure. Then, select the *Advanced* tab.

By default, all TCP/IP client addresses are permitted access to the IIS FTP server. To limit those addresses, administrators may specify either

Figure 9.7
Limiting IIS bandwidth.

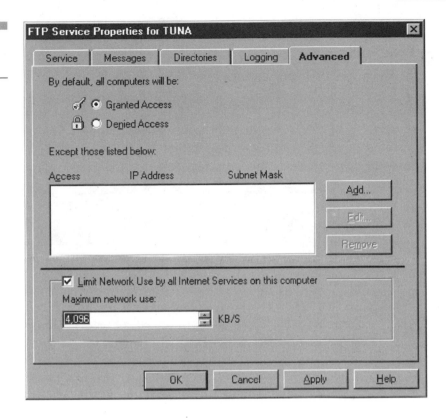

those addresses which are acceptable for access or those which are not acceptable. In the former case, any address which is not explicitly named will not be permitted access; in the latter case, any address not explicitly named will be permitted access. Note, however, that the two may be used in combination with one another. In the case of a conflict, the more restrictive rights apply. Therefore, if a system is explicitly denied access, it will be denied access regardless of other settings which might permit access. To configure either type of address-based access, select the proper radio button from the FTP Server Properties dialog box. Then, add the list of TCP/IP addresses and subnet masks using the *Add...* button.

Note that you can add either single addresses or entire subnetworks to the list. To filter on an entire set of computers, enter the address for the network on which those computers reside.

Once valid entries have been made, the FTP Server Properties dialog box will indicate whether access has been granted or denied for that computer or network. Click the *OK* button to save your changes.

Figure 9.8
Denying access.

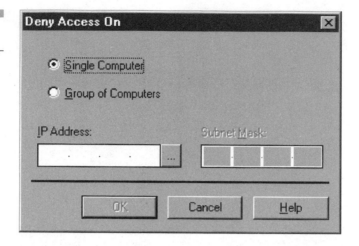

Figure 9.8
Denying access.

Administrators should be aware, however, that basing security on the client TCP/IP address provides only limited security. Indeed, any determined system intruder will not be stopped by this type of security. There are several well-known methods of subverting the client TCP/IP address restrictions, including the use of TCP/IP spoofing and TCP/IP loose source routing. In many cases, however, the use of TCP/IP address restrictions will simply provide one more level of difficulty for potential system intruders.

PREVENTING DENIAL-OF-SERVICE ATTACKS. Over the last several years, denial-of-service attacks have become increasingly popular among Internet hackers. Although it is impossible to fully prevent denial-of-service attacks, the IIS FTP server and the native FTP server do provide some means of limiting the possibility of a successful attack. Each can limit the number of concurrent FTP sessions, and the IIS provides even more granular support for monitoring bandwidth utilization.

Both the IIS and the native FTP servers provide a means to limit the number of users which can concurrently connect to the FTP server. In the absence of such a limit, an attacker might simply open a large number of FTP sessions to the server, effectively using all the bandwidth and CPU capacity of the server such that the system becomes unusable. By limiting the number of concurrent sessions, an administrator can mitigate the risk from this type of attack.

To limit the number of concurrent users of the native FTP service, first right-click on the *Network Neighborhood* icon. Then, select *Properties* from the context menu. Finally, select the *Services* tab and double-click on the FTP Server.

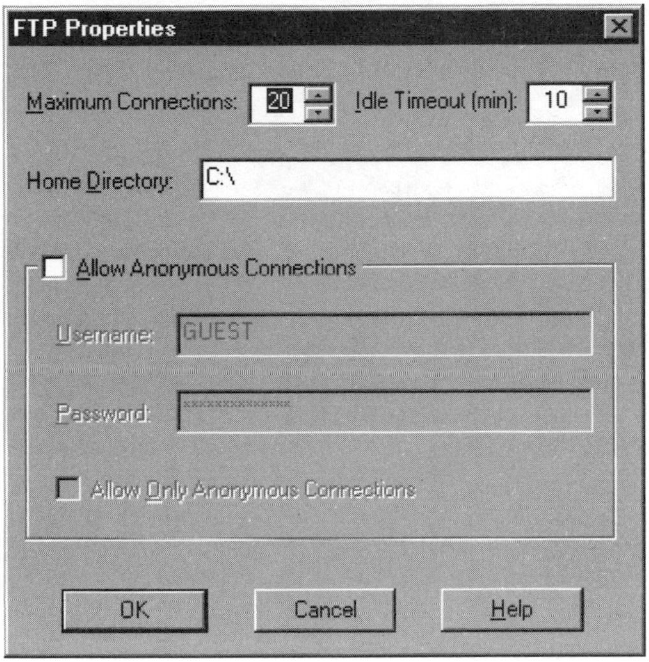

Figure 9.9
Native FTP service
properties.

This will bring up the FTP Server Properties dialog box. From this dialog box, the administrator can set the number of concurrent users and the timeout period after which sessions are terminated. Click the *OK* button to save your changes.

To limit the number of concurrent users of the IIS FTP server, first launch the Internet Service Manager. By default, the Internet Service Manager can be found within the *Microsoft Internet Server* group in the *Programs* option in the Start menu. From within the Internet Service Manager, double-click on the FTP server you wish to configure. Then, select the *Service* tab. From this tab, administrators may set the number of concurrent users as well as the timeout period, much as in the native FTP service.

In addition, the IIS FTP server also permits administrators to select the total amount of network bandwidth which the IIS will use. Thus, it is possible to limit the IIS to only a subset of the available network bandwidth in order to provide both a safety margin as well as guaranteeing

Figure 9.10
IIS FTP server configuration.

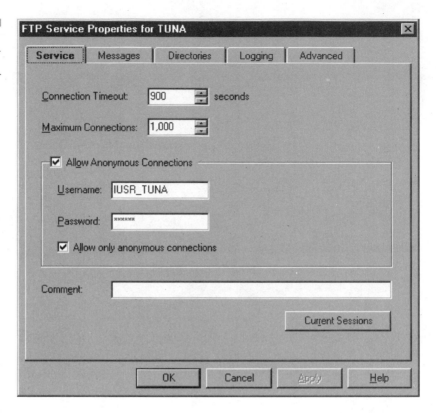

Figure 9.10
IIS FTP server configuration.

bandwidth for other applications. To do so, select the *Advanced* tab from the FTP Service Properties dialog box.

Then, click the checkbox marked "Limit network use by all Internet services on this computer." Finally, select the amount of bandwidth you wish to allocate to the IIS servers. Note that you cannot set bandwidth limits for specific service (e.g., FTP), only for the entire IIS.

LEGAL WARNINGS. Both the native FTP server as well as the IIS FTP server support the presentation of a legal warning to users on logon. This warning may be presented to all users, regardless of whether they are using anonymous or specific user ID logons. Many legal experts recommend that organizations place a warning message on all their system logon screens to warn potential intruders of the private nature of the systems being used. This may assist in the prosecution of computer hackers.

INTERNET INFORMATION SERVER. To set up this warning message using the Internet Information Server, first launch the Internet

Figure 9.11

IIS FTP access denial.

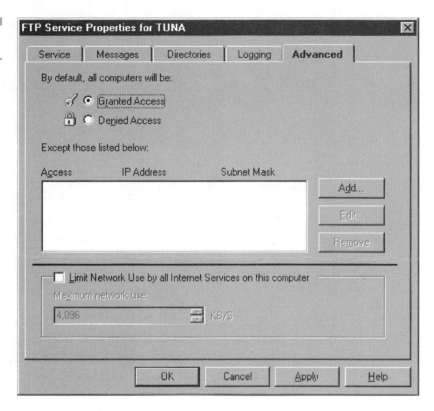

Service Manager. By default, the Internet Service Manager can be found within the *Microsoft Internet Server* group of the *Programs* option in the Start menu. From within the Internet Service Manager, select the FTP server whose warning messages you would like to modify. Then, double-click on this server.

Select the *Messages* tab from the top of the dialog box. This dialog box then permits the administrator to add three separate warning messages. The first (and the largest) will be presented to FTP clients immediately after they have been authenticated to the system. The second will be presented to all users when they log out of the FTP server. The final message will be displayed to users when the maximum user count has been exceeded and they are denied access as a result. By default, each of these messages are blank.

NATIVE NT FTP SERVER. Administrators using the native FTP service, unfortunately, have a slightly more difficult task to set the

Figure 9.12
IIS message.

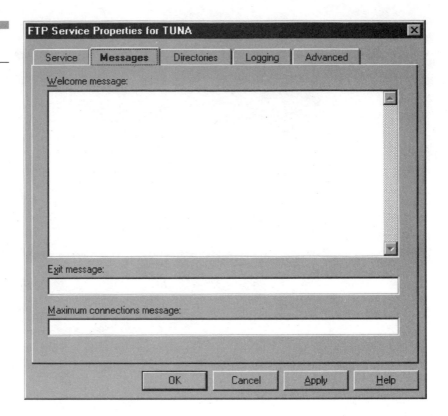

warning messages. To do so, administrators should first launch the Registry Editor. The key

```
HKEY_LOCL_MACHINE\SYSTEM\CurrentControlSet\Services\ftpsvc\
Parameters\GreetingMessage
```

controls the greeting message which will be presented to users immediately after logon authentication. Note that this key permits a string which is not as long as that provided by the IIS. Therefore, if you require an extremely long warning message, you should probably use the IIS. By default, there is no greeting message set in the registry.

Another key

```
HKEY_LOCL_MACHINE\SYSTEM\CurrentControlSet\Services\ftpsvc\
Parameters\ExitMessage
```

controls the message which will be displayed to the user immediately before the FTP session ends. The default sign-off message is "Goodbye."

A final key

```
HKEY_LOCL_MACHINE\SYSTEM\CurrentControlSet\Services\ftpsvc\
Parameters\MaxClientsMessage
```

controls the message which will be displayed to users who are rejected logons because of an overflow of users.

WWW Services

The explosion in popularity of the World Wide Web (WWW) over the last 18 months has caused many NT users to configure their NT systems to provide WWW services. These WWW services may be provided by third-party WWW servers (such as the Netscape Commerce Server) or via the Internet Information Server. This section addresses some of the general security concepts associated with WWW services, then addresses some of the more detailed approaches taken to security in the IIS. Users of third-party WWW servers are advised to consult with their server vendors regarding security.

One of the most important features about the web in terms of security is that it is "stateless," meaning that a web session is really just a large number of very small transactions, in which the web browser requests specific information from a specific web server. Therefore, any authentication or authorization that is to occur must occur for each independent transaction.

In general, most web servers require no specific authentication; rather, they support anonymous access to all users. Indeed, most of the data residing on the public web is intended to be free to all who wish to see it.

Increasingly, however, organizations are using web technology to provide access to sensitive information, either within or among organizations. The growth in web-enabled interfaces for industry-standard databases has led to a trend toward greater use of the web for publishing information which previously was accessible only via proprietary tools.

This, in turn, means that sensitive data may now be more vulnerable to prying eyes than ever before. By reducing the requirements for client access to the least common denominator (i.e., the browser), organizations may have inadvertently created a much larger potential audience for their sensitive data. Of course, few organizations intend to publish their sensitive information on the Internet, but rather place it on private internal "intranets."

These intranets, although more secure than placing data on the public Internet, still carry significant risk. Administrators should remember that the majority of security violations are due to internal personnel, not outside hackers.

WWW AUTHENTICATION.   While specific-user authentication on the World Wide Web is relatively rare today, it is fast becoming a requirement for many new web sites. Note that the native high-level protocol of the web, the HyperText Transfer Protocol (HTTP), does support rudimentary authentication. By embedding a user name and password within the headers of an HTTP request, a client may authenticate to a given server.

This authentication scheme, however, suffers from many of the same risks as does the native FTP authentication scheme described above. More specifically, native HTTP authentication occurs in clear text; that is, no encryption (or even scrambling) is provided, yielding a free-for-the-taking username and password combination for anyone sniffing packets on the network.

Given the relative simplicity of capturing passwords in this manner, we strongly recommend against using HTTP clear-text authentication, unless other steps are taken to ensure the limited use of those passwords. One way to do so is to utilize one-time passwords. Schemes for doing so are described elsewhere in this book.

For more robust authentication, however, one of several more proprietary schemes must be used. For example, the Microsoft Internet Information Server supports standard anonymous logons, clear-text HTTP logons, and the more proprietary Windows NT Challenge-Response logons. Note that the latter choice, Windows NT Challenge-Response, is the most secure and the least standard of the three.

The primary drawback of using a proprietary logon standard is that the standard must be supported by both the WWW server and the client browser. At the time of writing, only the Internet Explorer WWW browser supports the Windows NT Challenge-Response protocol. More popular browsers, such as the Netscape Navigator, may support NT Challenge-Response at some point in the future. Note that this is primarily a concern for public Internet sites; those organizations using web technology only internally may not be concerned about the support from large numbers of outside browsers. Indeed, the lack of support from other browser manufacturers may be seen by some as an additional security measure.

To configure the IIS to provide the desired authentication, administrators should first launch the Internet Service Manager. By default, the Internet Service Manager can be found within the *Microsoft Internet Server* group in the *Programs* option in the Start menu. From within the Internet Service Manager, select the WWW server you wish to configure, then double-click on it.

Figure 9.13
IIS WWW properties.

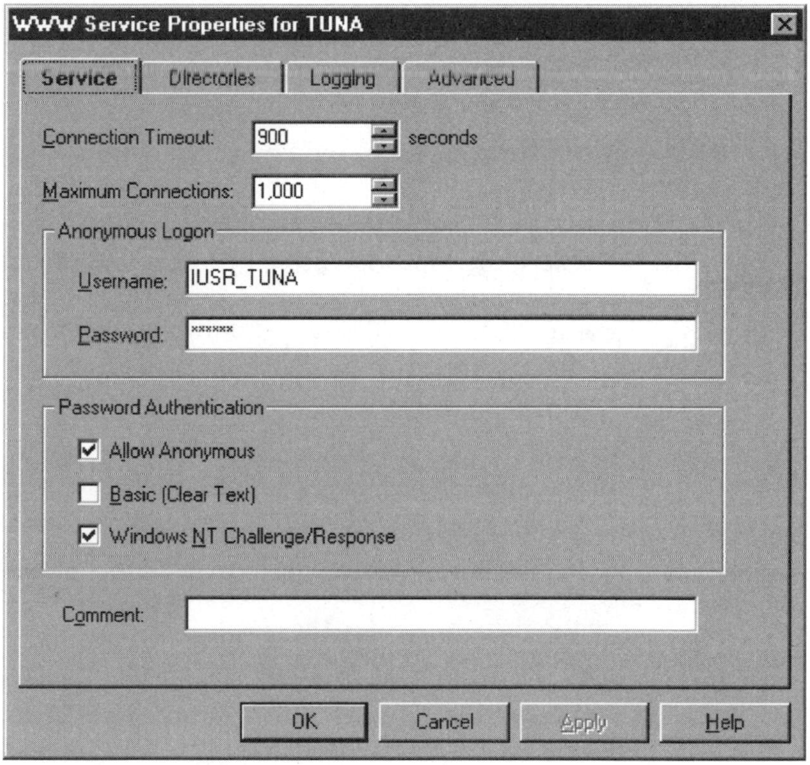

This brings up the WWW Service Properties dialog box. From within this dialog box, administrators may select the types of authentication which will be permitted to the WWW server. By default, both anonymous and Windows NT Challenge-Response authentications are permitted. Note that by default, clear-text authentication is expressly denied.

We recommend that most administrators maintain these settings. In any case, clear-text authentication should never be permitted, especially across the public Internet. In some cases, administrators may wish to disable anonymous logons entirely, opting only for Windows NT Challenge-Response authentication. This will provide greater security at the cost of reduced standardization across multiple brands of browsers.

When anonymous logons are used, users will be authenticated against the system using the account shown in the dialog box. By default, this account is the same as was described above for the IIS FTP server. Note that this user must be privileged to log onto the system locally. Moreover, this account must be privileged to read all directories containing web pages and scripts which the administrator wishes to make accessible to anonymous users.

IIS WWW Authentication Process

When an authentication request is received, Windows NT first checks on the type of identification presented. If the connection is anonymous, the anonymous account described above is used for access. Should this account not have sufficient rights to complete the operation, the server will send a message back to the client indicating the other types of authentication supported. Users may then be prompted to enter a username and password for further access.

If the connection attempt contains valid credentials (i.e., a username and password), the IIS will attempt to access the requested WWW resources using those credentials. If the username-password combination provided is unable to provide access to the requested resources, the server will return an error to the client.

In the case of the Windows NT Challenge-Response authentication, however, the process is slightly different. Currently, only the Microsoft Internet Explorer supports this functionality, although other browsers are expected to do so over time. When an Internet Explorer user connects anonymously to an IIS WWW server, the server will attempt access using the anonymous account described above. If the attempted access fails and the IIS is configured to permit Windows NT Challenge-Response authentication, however, the Internet Explorer will be queried for a username and password.

Note that this transition from anonymous logon to NT Challenge-Response happens automatically; there is no requirement for the user to be queried or enter logon credentials. Rather, the credentials are passed from the local client operating system. This is convenient for some users, as they need not log into both their local systems and remote web systems separately. Other users, however, may wish to maintain separate user accounts and may be inconvenienced by this feature.

Note also that the account which is obtained from the client workstation must be valid for the server on which the IIS WWW server resides. In the case of a Windows NT domain, the user account must exist within the domain.

For corporate intranets, these requirements regarding user accounts and client browsers are probably insignificant. Indeed, the Microsoft model appears to scale well to organization-based intranets of closely controlled web servers, browsers, and centrally defined user accounts.

On the Internet, however, none of these things can be taken for granted. Therefore, the NT Challenge-Response authentication is unlikely to make a great impact on the Internet marketplace until the technology reaches a critical mass.

Systems developers should also be aware that the WWW authentication schemes described above are merely implementations of the Internet Server API (ISAPI). Using the ISAPI Software Development Kit (SDK), system developers may write their own authentication schemes.

Session Security

Of course, simply providing secure, encrypted authentication methods will not ensure secure use of a web site. Indeed, much of the information which flows between a web browser and a web server may well be sensitive data. Consider the implications of a web server designed to process credit card data for on-line purchasing. It takes little imagination to see the potential security problems with an authentication-only security architecture.

To address this problem, there are several competing standards to supply session-level encryption of WWW activity. One scheme implements a secure version of the most popular WWW protocol, HTTP, called Secure HTTP. Another uses an encrypted lower-level protocol in order to encrypt all traffic over a WWW session. This latter scheme, called Secure Socket Layer (SSL), is implemented in the IIS WWW server.

To use the SSL features of IIS, you must first generate a key pair (used for encryption). The Key Manager application included with the IIS is used to generate these keys. By default, keys generated using the Key Manager are 1024 bits long, although shorter key lengths can be used. We strongly recommend the use of 1024-bit keys.

To generate a key, first select the server for which you would like to generate a key. Next, select the *Create New Key...* option from the Key menu. This will bring up the following dialog box:

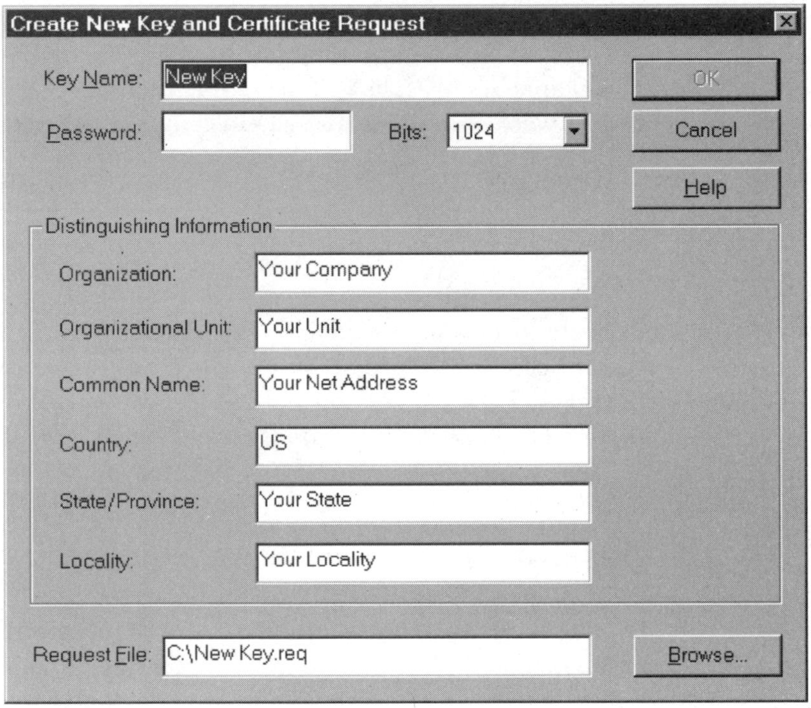

Figure 9.14
IIS SSL key
generation.

Fill the appropriate information into this dialog box, then click *OK*. Note that this will produce a file (shown at the bottom of the dialog box) which you may send to a key certifying authority.

Once a key set has been generated, it must be certified by a certifying authority before it is valid for use on the Internet. Currently, Microsoft is working with VeriSign to provide signature certificates for use with SSL on the Internet. Administrators may contact VeriSign at http://www.verisign.com for information on receiving certificates.

Once a certificate has been received, Key Manager is once again used to install the certificate. To do so, first select the key whose certificate you wish to install. Next, select the *Install Key Certificate* option from the Key menu.

Once the key pair has been generated and a certificate installed, SSL may be enabled for any of the home or virtual WWW directories in the IIS. To enable SSL on a given directory, select the proper WWW server from the Internet Service Manager. Then, double-click on that server to bring up the Properties dialog box.

Within the Properties dialog box, select the *Directories* tab. Within this tab, select the checkbox marked "Require secure SSL channel." Note that doing so will deny access to users who are not using SSL-enabled browsers. Moreover, administrators should be aware that Microsoft recommends setting up multiple content directories for secure and nonsecure content. Doing so will help administrators avoid having a WWW directory not protected by SSL as a parent for a secure directory.

IIS WWW Security Recommendations

This section provides some detailed recommendations for using native Windows NT functionality to improve the security of your WWW server.

AUTHENTICATION.   We recommend using the default IIS settings for security authentication in most cases. The default settings permit both anonymous logons and Windows NT Challenge-Response logons. Clear-text basic logons should not be permitted, as they risk the potential compromise of passwords over the network.

Organizations which use the Internet Explorer—or other NT Challenge-Response-compatible browsers—exclusively may wish to also eliminate the use of anonymous logons. Doing so will provide additional security, albeit at the cost of requiring users to have identical logon information for the system on which they work as they do for the WWW server. In a domain-based network, this is likely to be the case.

USE SSL WHERE POSSIBLE.   Merely providing adequate authentication will not ensure the security of a WWW session. Rather, an additional level of session encryption is required to keep other sensitive session data out of the hands of network snoopers. Technologies including

SHTTP and SSL provide this capability. We strongly recommend that users of the IIS utilize the SSL functionality built into the WWW server.

UTILIZE NTFS VOLUMES. As has been stated elsewhere in this book, data on non-NTFS partitions cannot be protected. Therefore, we strongly recommend that all WWW data and scripts be stored on NTFS volumes and protected with appropriate access control rights. Note that one user in particular, by default the `IUSR_MachineName`, must be able to access those resources which you wish to make available to anonymous users. Note also that the same user must have the user right to log on locally.

ADHERE TO CGI BEST PRACTICES. This book is not intended to provide a deep explanation of the potential security risks associated with all WWW servers. At the same time, administrators should understand that the risks associated with WWW servers often apply to such servers on all platforms. For example, much like under other operating systems, administrators should be careful about the executable files (including command interpreters) which they place in CGI binary directories. For more information on such topics, consult a reference on WWW servers in general, or specifically on those hosted on Windows NT.

Telnet Services

Much like FTP, Telnet is a service typically provided on many different platforms in order to provide platform-independent connectivity among systems. More specifically, Telnet permits a user to obtain a terminal session on a remote system.

As most users of Windows NT will recognize, the vast majority of Windows NT administration takes place via GUI (graphic user-interface) tools, not command-line utilities. Although there are some command-line equivalents for some administrative functions, it is nearly impossible to administer a Windows NT system using only the command line. There are, however, some utilities which can be used effectively in a terminal session. These include utilities such as the AT utility to schedule batch jobs, and the CACLS utility to modify file and directory permissions.

By default, there is no Telnet server which ships with Windows NT Workstation or Server. Several third-party vendors, however, are now producing quality Telnet servers for Windows NT. When using these products, NT administrators should be aware that Telnet inherently suffers from the same security weakness as does FTP: unencrypted passwords traversing the network. *We strongly recommend that administrators who choose to use Telnet servers utilize either one-time passwords or some form of link-based password encryption.*

Windows NT as a Firewall Platform

Today, most organizations which connect to the Internet use some form of "firewall" to isolate their private network from the public Internet. The design and construction of secure Internet firewalls is a topic which is far beyond the scope of this section; readers who need to provide firewall services should refer to the many excellent other volumes on building and maintaining Internet firewalls.

That being said, however, we should also note that Windows NT is becoming an increasingly popular platform for firewall construction. Many of the leading firewall vendors either have ported or are in the midst of porting their firewall solutions to Windows NT. In addition, Microsoft has announced the release of Catapult, a Windows NT–based application gateway firewall, which was released in late 1996.

Some of these products will run on native NT configurations. Others, including those which provide more optimal security, are designed to exist on a dedicated Windows NT server with all unnecessary services either disabled or removed. In addition, versions of Windows NT prior to version 4.0 had some significant security limitations in the TCP/IP implementation (loose source routing, etc.). Some of the leading firewall products for Windows NT are designed to plug these known holes.

Because of the speed at which the firewall market is currently developing, we recommend that readers keep up with the latest product releases and vendor analyses before making a selection regarding either firewall products or platforms.

NT Native Networking

As was mentioned above, few administrators will want to supply standard Windows NT networking services over the Internet. Doing so will allow users with Windows NT, Windows 95, or Windows for Workgroups networking clients to connect to file and printer shares directly.

Note that even if Windows NT networking services are not supplied to the Internet, these services can still be supplied to other internally connected networks. This permits the server to connect, for example, to a database server elsewhere on the internal (or DMZ) network.

There are two primary ways to limit Windows NT networking services over the network:

1. Administrators can limit access to the TCP/IP ports used for Windows NT networking. These ports should be blocked at the point of Internet connectivity through a firewall or packet filtering router. The ports used include ports 137, 138, and 139 for both TCP and UDP traffic.

2. In addition, we recommend that administrators remove the Windows NT networking bindings from the interfaces which lead out to the Internet. This will provide a safety margin in case the packet filtering fails or is disabled. To do so, remove the NetBIOS over TCP/IP bindings from all network interfaces which connect to the Internet. These bindings may be found in the Network Properties dialog box in the *Bindings* tab. It's also a good idea to make sure that your bindings properties are correct by attempting Windows networking connections to that interface before connecting it directly to the Internet.

To provide additional security, we also recommend that, where feasible, all administration be performed from the system console. In cases where physical access to the console is feasible, we recommend that administrators revoke network access permissions for all users. To do so, first launch the User Manager (or User Manager for Domains). By default, the User Manager is located in the *Administrative Tools* group within the *Programs* option of the Start menu.

From within the User Manager, select the *User Rights...* option from the Policies menu. Then, select the user right entitled "Access this computer from network." Revoke this right from all users by clicking the *Remove* button as necessary. Alternatively, revoke this permission from all except one user account which can be used for remote administration. If this latter option is used, we recommend that the password be both resistant to dictionary-based attack and changed on a regular basis. Administrators should be aware, however, that the user account associated with the IIS must have rights to log on locally.

Windows NT Packet Filtering

In Windows NT 4.0 and later, administrators may also filter TCP/IP traffic when using NT as a router. To set up rudimentary filters from within NT, first right-click on the *Network Neighborhood* icon. Next, select the *Protocols* tab and double-click on TCP/IP. Then, select the *Advanced* button.

This brings up the Advanced IP Addressing dialog box. From within this dialog box, click the checkbox marked "Enable security," then press the *Configure* button. This brings up the TCP/IP Security dialog box.

Figure 9.15
TCP/IP packet
filtering.

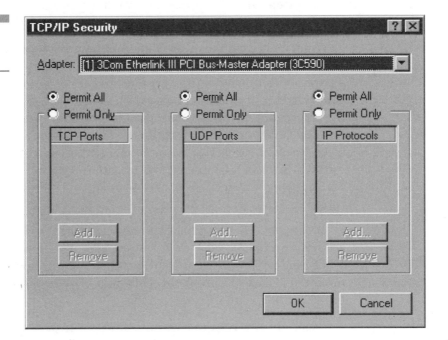

As this dialog box indicates, administrators may limit TCP/IP traffic based on TCP and UDP port numbers. Unfortunately, Windows NT permits only two possible choices for packet filtering—either all packets are passed, or only those packets with the named port numbers are passed. There is no option provided to exclude small sets of port numbers. As a result, we strongly recommend that administrators rely on packet filtering routers for their primary filtering requirements.

Final Advice

In the world of Internet security, most experts agree that it is nearly impossible to create a system which is impenetrable to Internet hackers. There are large numbers of things, however, which can make the hacker's job more difficult. Herein lies the task for the Internet system administrator.

Windows NT presents a bit of a unique case in the Internet world. Traditionally, most Internet hosts have been based on some variant of the UNIX operating system. As a result of this exposure, UNIX has been the target of innumerable attacks—many of them successful. Over time, however, system architects and administrators have learned from these attacks and have changed UNIX to make it more impervious to attack.

Windows NT, on the other hand, is a relative newcomer to this arena. While the fundamental security model is extremely strong, it's still not altogether clear what will happen when NT becomes the target of significant numbers of Internet hackers. The likelihood, of course, is that it will remain secure in the face of most—but not all—Internet attacks. Much like the UNIX variants which have come before it, there are likely to be some holes in the NT security implementation. Therefore, we strongly recommend that NT Internet system administrators keep track of the latest developments in Windows NT security and obtain and apply security-related patches when released.

In the past, Microsoft has been criticized for the slow speed with which security problems were dealt. More recently, however, Microsoft has made concerted efforts to issue patches within days or hours of being informed of security problems. It is up to system administrators, however, to obtain and apply those patches.

There are several good ways to find out about Windows NT security problems. One is by tracking the CERT and FIRST mailing lists, where many general computer security announcements are made. Another is to follow the NT Security mailing list. To subscribe to this mailing list, send the text "Subscribe NTSECURITY" in an e-mail message to NTSecurity-Request@iss.net. Note that this list has no official connection to Microsoft.

APPENDIX A

KERBEROS AUTHENTICATION

As the complexity of the enterprisewide information infrastructure increases at a rapid rate, more and more system administrators are being called on to provide security across a heterogeneous mix of hardware and software platforms. Few technologies available today are able to address the discrete and varied needs of a far-flung enterprise infrastructure. Unfortunately, Windows NT also fails in this regard. Although Windows NT does provide extremely credible security within the Windows NT environment—and it does run on a wide range of hardware platforms—it does nothing to help secure other types of systems.

As a result, there has been a call for Windows NT and other widely used operating systems to fit into a larger enterprise-capable security architecture. NT provides support for this type of effort through its support of the standardized *Distributed Computing Environment* (DCE), which was designed by the members of the Open Software Foundation (OSF) to provide significant integration among widely varying hardware and software combinations.

One of the primary elements of DCE is support for an integrated security architecture. This architecture is a slight modification of the widely published Kerberos architecture used at MIT. Conveniently for Windows NT administrators, the Windows NT security scheme can be integrated with DCE Kerberos today using third-party products. Moreover, Microsoft has made a commitment to providing native support for the DCE security architecture over the long term.

This appendix will help administrators understand the general architecture of Kerberos, then focus on the version of Kerberos implemented in the current release of DCE.

Overview

Kerberos—once known only as the three-headed dog who guarded Hades in Greek mythology—has returned to life. This time, however, he guards not the underworld, but rather the distributed security systems of corporate and academic America.

275

In the last three decades, we have observed a paradigm shift in the use of computing resources. Similarly, we can identify a parallel shift in the security requirements for those systems. As we move from timesharing systems to networked personal computers and on to distributed systems, the security challenges we face grow as a function of system complexity.

Distributed computing systems are, by nature, notoriously difficult to secure. As information spreads and becomes decentralized throughout an organization, identifying *where, when,* and *how* to secure it becomes an almost herculean task. Often, *managing* the security for ongoing support is even more difficult.

Kerberos is one of the few technologies available today which readily addresses the unique challenges of distributed security. In doing so, it helps centralize many of the security functions and ease the management burden.

Brief History of Kerberos

Kerberos was first created in the mid-1980s as a part of the MIT Project Athena. The original intent was simple: to create a protocol for both authentication and authorization which would be secure over a wide range of distributed computing platforms. The Kerberos protocol is intended to allow any two computers on a network to conduct secure and trusted communications, even when the network is known to be penetrated by intruders and neither computer has any intrinsic reason to trust the other.

To allow for this level of security, very few assumptions were initially made regarding the relative security of the various platforms on which it would run. Indeed, in designing Kerberos, the MIT architects assumed that it is *next to impossible* to ensure that any given workstation on a given network is secure. Now in version 5.0, Kerberos provides all this functionality and more. It still assumes little about the relative security of the platforms and communications infrastructure on which it depends (see *Kerberos Fundamentals* section, below). Indeed, while there are some potential weaknesses in the Kerberos architecture, it has become a de facto standard for securing heterogeneous distributed computing networks.

The importance of Kerberos has grown still further in the last few years with the inclusion of a modified version of Kerberos in the DCE public release. With several industry-leading companies poised to push

DCE onto the networks and desktops of corporate America, Kerberos is likely to enjoy new-found prominence in mainstream computer security.

Kerberos Fundamentals

The Kerberos protocol itself is conceptually quite simple. It relies on a few fundamental principles: *limited assumptions, private-key encryption,* and *a secure security server.* Each is described in greater detail below.

Limited Assumptions

As noted above, Kerberos makes few assumptions regarding the relative security of the computing infrastructure on which it runs. For example, it assumes that

- There is no authentication provided by the host operating system.
- There is no trust to be placed in the network address.
- There is no other network security required.
- All servers do not have to be physically secured.

Note, however, that while Kerberos makes no assumptions about these criteria, their presence will not materially affect the Kerberos implementation. Assume, for example, that the local operating system requires authentication on login. This would merely add a layer to the overall security of the network, and would not have any effect on the central Kerberos security protocol.

At the same time, adding additional layers of security will serve to decrease the possibility of network penetration. Indeed, there are some security steps which Kerberos does not require, but will be considered mandatory for most implementations. For example, while Kerberos does not require that all servers be physically secure, common sense (and the bottom line!) might require otherwise.

Private Key Encryption

Private key encryption has been in use in various forms for hundreds, perhaps thousands, of years. The most modern iteration of it is one of the foundations of the Kerberos protocol.

Private key encryption assumes that a given message can be modified in a completely predictable way known only to the holders of a private "key." Only those who have access to the key will be able to understand the messages encrypted with it.

By assigning each element (e.g., users and servers) in the Kerberos network a unique private key, the Kerberos server can positively identify any element at any time. The private keys are shared only between the element and the Kerberos server; no other network element ever sees or needs to have detailed information about the private key of another element. Thus, the Kerberos server acts as a trusted independent third party (see *Secure Kerberos Server* section, below).

Because private keys must remain confidential to network elements and the Kerberos server, key management becomes a critical issue. Once initial keys are assigned, key updates are generally handled within the protected shell of the protocol itself; that is, new keys are sent to network elements within the protection of the old private key. Unfortunately, this cannot be secure if one of the private keys is compromised.

In theory, a network intruder who covertly obtains the private key of a Kerberos element would be able to receive the key updates as they are passed along the network. Therefore, key updates of known compromised accounts must be handled outside the network itself. Those considering Kerberos implementations should be aware that this might lead to a long-term administrative burden for system maintenance.

We should also note that the Kerberos specification does not require any *specific* encryption algorithm. Rather, nearly any private key cryptosystem can be adapted for use with the Kerberos protocol. The U.S. government's Data Encryption Standard (DES) is used in many commercial Kerberos implementations.

Secure Kerberos Server

The Kerberos protocol was designed to work over networks that were known to be penetrated by system intruders. It was not, however, designed to remain secure in the face of a compromised Kerberos Key Distribution Center (KDC) server.

Understanding private key encryption provides the answer to why this is so (see *Kerberos at Work* section, below). The KDC *must* function as a "trusted third party," as it is the negotiator of all secure communications links within the Kerberos-secure network, and therefore the linchpin of the security architecture.

As mentioned, Kerberos was the three-headed dog who guarded the entrance to Hades in Greek mythology. Analogously, the Kerberos server is actually three separate servers in one, although all typically reside on a single computer. The three components are the *Authentication Server* (AS), the *Security Database* (SD), and the *Privilege Server* (PS).

The AS is tasked with providing authentication services to users logging into the network. Usually, this consists of providing properly encrypted packets to workstations on request. The PS is a ticket-granting server which either allows or disallows access to specific network services. The SD is a resource for both, in that it contains information about each registered user and the privileges those users are allowed for any given network service.

Note that the SD may be distributed across several Kerberos slave servers on a large enterprise-level network. Of course, each of these slave servers must then be secured in the same way as the master.

We should also be aware that the availability of the network depends on the availability of the Kerberos server(s). Should the primary Kerberos KDC server, for example, drop off the network, no user would be able to access any Kerberos-protected network service. *Therefore, it is imperative that there be significant redundancy built into this part of the network infrastructure.*

Kerberos at Work

With an understanding of the preceding assumptions, the underlying Kerberos protocol becomes clear. This section serves to make the connection between these assumptions and the inner workings of the protocol itself.

When a user logs into a Kerberos-secured network, there follows a predictable series of events. This series of events is required to establish the identities of both clients and servers as well as establishing authorization levels. Generally, the process proceeds as follows.

Kerberos Authentication and Authorization

STEP 1. The user sends a request for credentials to the Authentication Server (AS) in order to access an Application Server (AppServer). This may happen in one of two ways:

a. The user sends a clear-text request to the AS. The reply will be sent back encrypted with the user's private key (see step 2).

b. A user who is already logged into the network (authenticated) and simply needs access to additional resources (authorization) sends a Ticket Granting Ticket (TGT) to the Ticket Granting Server (TGS). This ticket contains her authentication information and the name of the server to be accessed (AppServer).

STEP 2. The AS (or the TGS) responds with credentials for the AppServer, encrypted with the user's private key. The credentials consist of two pieces of information:

a. A ticket for the AppServer. This ticket is encrypted with the users' private key and contains two items: (1) the users' identity and (2) a unique one-time session key.

b. The same unique one-time session key, encrypted with the AppServer's private key.

STEP 3. The user sends the ticket and a copy of the session key to the AppServer.

STEP 4. The session key is used to authenticate the user. In addition to checking for the proper authentication, the server may also check the time stamp on the ticket to make sure it was issued "recently" and is not a "replay" of a captured session. At this point, the common session key has securely been shared between the server and the client and may be used for session encryption, to exchange a subsession key, or to provide authentication for the server.

Important Features

Several important features come to light, including the following:

■ Passwords are never transmitted across the network.

- Both clients and servers are subject to authentication. This means that it is impossible for an intruder to masquerade as a server.

- Packets may be time-stamped in order to avoid replay attacks.

- Packets contain network addresses embedded within the private key shell, allowing the network to disallow logins from unauthorized workstations or servers.

Beyond the mandatory security measures, however, lies a critical trade-off between security and performance. Unlike some other security protocols, Kerberos allows for system tuning based on the security-performance mix.

Thus, different security and performance parameters can be established for different installations. For some installations, the former is all-important. For others, system performance plays a central role. In any case, once initial authentication is completed, administrators have an array of choices available to them.

Thus, Kerberos provides a robust security model with the ability to adapt to the security requirements of various organizations. Security may be taken from the client level to *either the server or the application level*. As a result, there exists the possibility for close cooperation between system applications and the network security framework.

Authentication and Authorization Vulnerabilities

The Kerberos authentication-authorization process is quite formalized and thought to be quite secure. There are, however, some known vulnerabilities. These are discussed in the *Kerberos Limitations* section, below.

Kerberos Standards

Specifications for Internet-standard Kerberos implementations are available from the Internet Engineering Task Force (IETF) as a series of Requests for Comment (RFCs). The most current RFC pertaining to Kerberos is RFC 1510 (Kerberos V5), dated September 1993. Other RFCs that have relevance to Kerberos include those for the Generic Security

Services Application Programming Interface (GSS-API; RFCs 1508/1509).

The Kerberos RFCs, however, provide only the framework for a Kerberos implementation. They describe many of the low-level issues (wire protocol, etc.), but do not address all the higher-level issues. For example, there is

- No standard client implementation
- No standard for data encryption
- No standard administration protocol
- No fully accepted code base

In fact, little more than the overall architecture has been standardized. Some pseudocode is included with the RFC to help in the implementation process; however, even this is not mandatory for any given implementation. The only widely distributed code samples are those from MIT itself, although individual users often modify the code for use on their systems.

Various vendors, however, have written their own commercial code implementations. Unfortunately, this means that there is the potential for limited interoperability among Kerberos implementations from different vendors.

Kerberos and DCE

The current version of the OSF Distributed Computing Environment (DCE) utilizes a slightly modified version of Kerberos V5. By placing the security foundation of DCE on the Kerberos protocol, OSF has validated Kerberos as a security model. While other security enhancements are under consideration for version 1.2 of DCE, clients can rest easy knowing that Kerberos has satisfied the near-term security concerns of the DCE system architects.

DCE Kerberos

Because DCE is designed to allow for processing models fundamentally different from those found in some of today's distributed networks, Kerberos has been forced to evolve into a more finely grained protocol.

For example, DCE allows for the use of *Remote-Procedure Calls* (RPCs), which allow a client to execute a procedure on a remote server. To establish whether the client has authority to perform the requested procedure call, Kerberos must establish a security "identity" for the request. By doing so, Kerberos can maintain security among clients, servers, and the procedure calls that flow between them.

Thus, DCE Kerberos has evolved a version of the RPC termed an *Authenticated Remote-Procedure Call* (ARPC). To make an RPC, a user first receives authentication and authorization for the action from the KDC, then receives an ARPC, which is, in turn, passed to the remote server. Throughout this process, both the application and the user are shielded from the underlying security mechanics.

DCE Kerberos Security Server Architecture

As shown in the following diagram, the architecture of the DCE Security Server is analogous to that of the traditional Kerberos server:

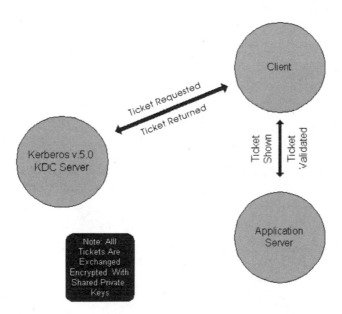

The User/Group registry server is very similar to the traditional Kerberos Security Database, while functionality of the Privilege Server and the KDC server map nearly precisely to the functionality of their identically named counterparts in Kerberos V5.

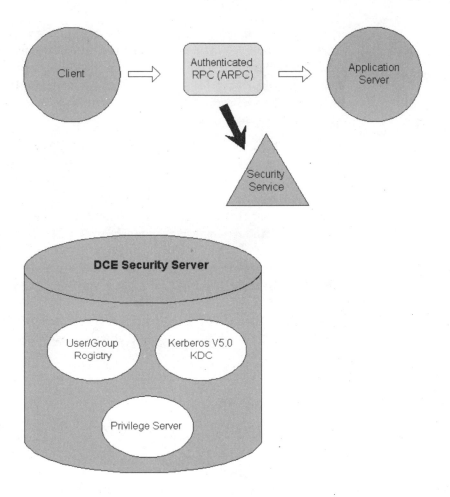

Kerberos Limitations

While Kerberos addresses several common network vulnerabilities (spoofing, replay attacks, etc.), it fails to address several others. When used in combination with other technologies, however, Kerberos can provide the basis for an extremely well secured network. Some of the known weaknesses are identified below.

Key Management

One inherent weakness of the Kerberos system is the requirement to keep the private keys of each network element secret at all times. The entire security framework of Kerberos rests on the assumption of key secrecy; therefore, any compromised keys might destroy the security of the entire network. As a result, key management becomes an all-important (and often burdensome) task. Specifically, provisions must be made for issuing new keys (or having users choose their own), deauthenticating lost or stolen keys, and so on. Over time, this may be a significant task.

Some new Kerberos-like security protocols are now using public key cryptosystems. With such a system, there is no requirement for secret keys to be shared among multiple network elements. Rather, public key cryptosystems work with two related keys. The first key, termed the *private key,* is kept secret to only the network element which owns it. The second, termed the *public key,* is freely distributable to all network elements. Messages encrypted with the public key are only decryptable using the private key of the network element owner. Therefore, key management becomes a relatively simple task.

Other Authentication Weaknesses

Also, the secret keys of users (e.g., passwords) must be chosen such that they are not vulnerable to non-Kerberos attacks. For example, there is no security restriction placed on the initial contact between the client and the Kerberos server. Therefore, any user may obtain a packet sealed with the secret key (i.e., password) of any other user. Once this packet is obtained, it may be subjected to an off-line dictionary attack in which thousands of possible passwords are used to attempt to decrypt the packet. If the password which seals the packet is not strong, it may fall to this type of attack.

Some more contemporary Kerberos implementations are using preauthentication technologies in order to ensure that passwords are not susceptible to easy dictionary attack. With these technologies in place, users are not permitted to change their passwords to easily guessable words or phrases. Organizations using Kerberos in its password-only form without some form of alternate authentication technology are strongly advised to use preauthentication features.

Many organizations, however, will need to implement some authentication technology other than the simple password. The use of such technologies makes dictionary attack virtually impossible, and several Kerberos vendors have announced direct support for them.

Examples of these technologies include password generators, challenge-response systems, smart cards, and biometric systems. For more information on these technologies, consult App. D (*Single Sign-on Security*) in this book.

Scalability Issues

While Kerberos is designed to provide security across multiple geographically separate domains, some users have reported significant problems with distributing Kerberos over too wide an area. The primary issues are performance and administration.

On the performance side, Kerberos administrators should be aware that each user must request access from the TGS on a regular basis. Therefore, geographically distributed networks must have either (1) extremely wide bandwidth, or, more efficiently, (2) a series of Kerberos slave servers to manage each local domain.

Until Kerberos V4.0, Kerberos domain servers acted as direct Kerberos principals in domains other than their own. Thus, when Kerberos users required the use of resources outside of their home domain, the local Kerberos server would authenticate itself to the remote domain server, then pass along the request of the local user. This required each Kerberos server to maintain valid secret keys for each remote Kerberos server. Over time, the number of secret keys required quickly became unmanageable.

In contrast, the Kerberos V5.0 architecture allows for the use of a single multidomain Kerberos server which interacts with each of the local Kerberos domain servers. Thus, any user who requires remote services merely directs the local Kerberos server to contact the multidomain server, which processes the request by passing it along to the appropriate domain server. As a result, each Kerberos domain server is required to share only a single secret key with the multidomain server.

The geographic spread of Kerberos-secure networks also raises difficulties in the area of time synchronization. Because Kerberos tickets are both time-stamped and time-sensitive, both Kerberos KDC and other Kerberos-aware servers must be regularly synchronized. The amount of synchronization necessary is a function of the time constraints imposed by the system administrators. Many corporate users might wish to use a "loose synchronization" scheme in which tickets are valid for several minutes, such that synchronization becomes less of a problem. Organizations more concerned with security are likely to limit the valid life of Kerberos tickets to no more than 1 or 2 min.

Peer-to-Peer Difficulties

By its inherent design, it is apparent that Kerberos was designed for networks with clearly delineated clients and servers. Because each network element which communicates with another network element requires a shared secret password, Kerberos is ill-suited to peer-to-peer-style networks.

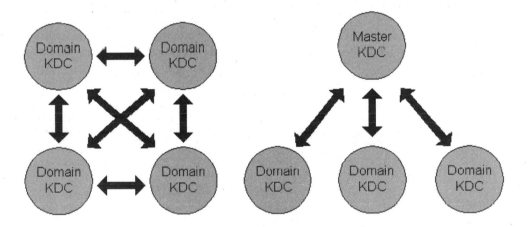

The original Project Athena specification assumed anonymous, dataless workstations and large-scale file and mail servers. As a result, Kerberos is best suited to this type of network architecture. Indeed, this "thin client" paradigm continues to work best with Kerberos today.

Denial of Service

One type of attack not addressed at all by the Kerberos architecture is the so-called denial-of-service attack. In such an attack, the intent is not to compromise the security of the information being carried by the network. Rather, the intent is to ensure that the network will not function, and thereby bring all network traffic to a halt.

Some security protocols are designed for fault tolerance, and are therefore less vulnerable to this type of attack. As we have seen, however, Kerberos depends on the security of a single Kerberos master server. Should this server be the target of attack—either physical or electronic—the entire distributed network might come to a grinding halt.

As a result, the Kerberos server must be (1) well-protected from both physical and electronic attacks and (2) the focus of significant redundancy planning, should a server outage occur. Only when these two criteria are met will the network become reasonably reliable.

MIT Athena

For information on the latest releases of MIT Kerberos, join the Kerberos Discussion List on the Internet. For more information, send electronic mail to Kerberos-Request@MIT.EDU.

APPENDIX B

This appendix describes a program designed to help you test the security of your Windows NT implementation. Many readers may be familiar with the UNIX-based "Crack" program, used to check the security of users' passwords. Passcrack for Windows NT performs a similar function, but with some slightly different implementation details.

The Passcrack for Windows NT utility was written by Jude Sylvestre, an information technology consultant.

Background

To understand the purpose behind—and the use of—the Passcrack for Windows NT tool, we must first understand the underlying technology. Passcrack-like programs were first written to exploit a well-known vulnerability in some versions of UNIX. These UNIX versions permitted all users to gain access to the password files, which contained data associated with user IDs and passwords. Of course, this wasn't originally thought to be a security vulnerability.

At this point, some readers are probably scratching their heads and trying to figure out whether the UNIX system architects were dumb or just stupid. Well, the answer is probably neither—they were, however, perhaps a bit naive.

While the password files (stored as `\etc\password`) were freely available to any user who asked for them, they were thought to be of little use. This is because the contents of the password file (or at least the passwords) were encrypted using a relatively sophisticated one-way hash.

This means that the passwords are transformed from their raw format into an encrypted version. The one-way algorithm used in the encryption nearly guarantees that the encryption cannot be reversed. Therefore, there is no simple way to work backward from the encrypted version of the password to the original unencrypted version.

But what about performing password verification? It would seem that if the encryption algorithm is truly one-way, then there would be no way to reverse the algorithm for the system to verify passwords. Indeed, this is the case. Therefore, the system actually performs password verification on *encrypted,* not *unencrypted,* versions of the passwords.

Let's consider an example. Assume that my user ID is `cbr` (it is) and my password is `buymorebooks` (it isn't). When I first enter my password, most versions of UNIX will encrypt it, yielding a password such as `hdu937d13`. This encrypted password is then stored in the password file. The next time I attempt to log in, I merely type my username and password. Of course, `buymorebooks` doesn't equal `hdu937d13`. So, the operating system must first encrypt the password I have entered and compare it to the previously stored value. This is the process by which most modern operating systems perform authentication.

The use of this type of one-way algorithm, however, does open up a security hole. In UNIX, for example, if I am able to obtain the password file, I can perform a brute-force or dictionary-based attack on it. To do so, I can merely encrypt any given word, then compare it to the values stored in the file. If, for example, I encrypt an entire dictionary of words, I might well find any given password. The moral of the story is *don't ever use passwords which might be found in the dictionary.*

As you might expect from the previous discussion, Windows NT password authentication works much the same way as does UNIX authentication. In much the same way, Windows NT will permit users to compare passwords against an encrypted database of passwords in an attempt to crack users' passwords. This is the purpose behind the Passcrack for Windows NT program.

Windows NT Password Details

The Security Account Manager database within a Windows NT system actually stores two passwords for most accounts in the system. The first is designed for backward compatibility with Microsoft's LAN Manager series of products. The second is designed natively for Windows NT.

The LAN Manager password is fully compatible with previous versions of the LAN Manager product; this allows LAN Manager clients to interact with Windows NT servers. The Windows NT password, on the other hand, is far more flexible and considerably more robust. Consider the differences in the two password sets listed in the following table.

Characteristic	LAN Manager Password	Windows NT Password
Character set	OEM	Unicode
Case-sensitive?	No	Yes
Maximum length	14	128
Encryption (one-way)	DES	MD-4

For each password stored by the system, Windows NT performs a double encryption before storing it in the SAM. The first encryption process uses the algorithm noted in the table above: DES or MD-4 for LAN Manager and NT passwords, respectively. This encryption is considered to be fully secure, because of the properties of the one-way function. The second encryption uses the user's relative ID (RID), using a published algorithm and the previously encrypted password as a seed. According to Microsoft, this second layer of encryption is merely for obfuscation. *It is unclear to us that this process yields significant security value.*

Note that two passwords are stored for each account in most—but not all—situations. For example, Windows NT native passwords which are created using an NT system and cannot fit into the requirements of the LAN Manager specification (i.e., more than 14 characters, or requiring the Unicode character set) have no associated LAN Manager password.

Windows NT Passcrack

Unlike UNIX, Windows NT does not maintain a password file which users may access. Rather, all the account information (including passwords) associated with Windows NT users is stored in the Security Account Manager (SAM) database.

Fortunately, the Windows Win32 API set provides access to this SAM database in a useful way. This is fortunate for legitimate system administrators for two reasons: (1) it means that programs like Passcrack for Windows NT are possible, thus yielding the potential for greater security;

and (2) it means that the use of these APIs is fully auditable within the Windows NT environment.

As a result, it is likely that the type of attack described above would fail in a real-world environment with pragmatic logging, auditing, and proper account and password policies. Contrast this to the UNIX environment, in which it is relatively easy to remove password files (even shadowed password files) for off-line attack.

Prerequisites

To use Passcrack for Windows NT, you must have a file of passwords to use as a source file. Preferably, this should be a large text file with tens of thousands of English words and/or common passwords. Several examples of these files can be found on the Internet. To use this type of file with Passcrack for Windows NT, the file should contain only text and should contain a single password per line.

Note also that Passcrack for Windows NT is capable of producing extremely large numbers of audit events. This is by design—if the program is run against an active Windows NT system, the administrator should be aware of its operation. At the same time, the program does have the ability to quickly fill audit logs of any size. This can be especially dangerous when the registry key

```
HKEY_LOCAL_MACHINE\System\CurrentControlSet\Control\Lsa\
CrashOnAuditFail
```

is set to a value of 1 and the system is set to never overwrite events in the security log. These are the settings which we recommended in earlier chapters. Administrators should be aware that when this is the case, the system will halt when it is unable to continue writing to the security log, as may well be the case after running Passcrack for Windows NT.

In addition, users must have the following rights in order to run the Passcrack program effectively:

- Log on locally.
- Log on as a service.
- Access computer from network.
- Act as part of the operating system.
- Replace a process level token
- Increase quotas

Using Passcrack for Windows NT

To launch Passcrack for Windows NT, either type the path and command line (NTCRACK.EXE) from the Start/Run menu, or select the program from the Windows NT Explorer.

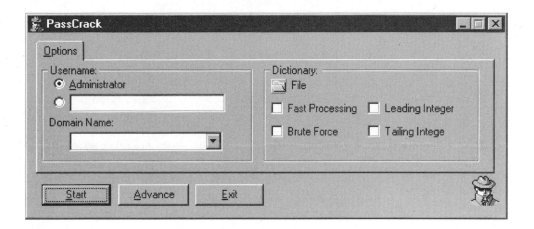

The main Passcrack window contains several options. On the left side of the dialog box, you can select the account you would like to attempt to crack. The default choice is the Administrator account. Note that we strongly recommend that the administrator account have a password which is not a word found in the dictionary attack files. *Moreover, we strongly recommend that the administrator account be renamed to something else* using the User Manager (or User Manager for Domains). This prevents an attacker from succeeding in a brute-force attack against your system, as the administrator account cannot be locked out. Alternatively, you may select a different account to crack by selecting the lower radio button and typing the account name in the Edit box provided.

The lower Edit box should contain the domain name for the users' account you wish to attempt to crack. Note that if the Passcrack for NT program is running on a domain controller, this field is unnecessary. Otherwise, using Passcrack in a Windows NT domain environment requires a valid domain name against which to search for the password.

Next, select the dictionary file containing passwords which you would like to try. To select this file, click on the file icon on the right side of the dialog box. This will bring up a file selection dialog box—keep in mind that the dictionary file you choose must be a pure text file with a single password per line.

If you do not have a password file available, you may also use the Passcrack for Windows NT program in brute-force mode. This mode will attempt all combinations of characters using the characters A to Z and 0 to 9. Note that passwords which contain other characters not in this set will not be vulnerable to this attack. Also, be aware that brute-force attacks are extremely time-consuming and therefore far less likely to succeed in the real world.

To select brute-force mode, click the checkbox in the Passcrack for Windows NT dialog box marked "Brute." You need not select a dictionary file when using Passcrack for Windows NT in brute-force mode.

Normally, Passcrack for Windows NT acts as a well-behaved Windows NT application. Like all well-behaved applications, it will respond to mouse clicks and other events while running, permitting the user to interact with the program, even while intensive processing occurs. Under some circumstances, however, administrators might wish to gain the additional performance which comes with eliminating the event processing loop. Passcrack for Windows NT has an option which will eliminate the event processing loop.

To gain the maximum speed from Passcrack for Windows NT, select the checkbox marked "Fast" from the main dialog box. Note that this will effectively "lock up" the application once the cracking process begins. If you wish to stop the process, you may stop it from the task list.

Sometimes, users add leading or tailing numbers to their passwords in order to make them more secure. This is common in organizations which require users to change their passwords frequently.

For example, I might set my password to be `hobart` (it isn't). Then, the next time I'm forced to change the password, I might change it to `hobart1`, or `hobart2`, and so on. In this way, some users try to subvert the password change process by merely adding an integer.

Passcrack for Windows NT contains an option to check for these types of passwords. When selected, Passcrack for Windows NT will add either leading or trailing integers to each of the words in the dictionary. By default, it uses only the numbers 0 to 9. Therefore, selecting this option will slow down the processing by a factor of 10. To select the leading/tailing integers, click on the appropriate checkbox.

Using Passcrack for Windows NT in Batch Mode

In an ideal world, operating systems would be able to perform Passcrack-like functions at the time of password selection. If this were the case, new passwords would be accepted or rejected when they were first selected by the user. Therefore, bad (read "crackable") passwords would never make it into the password database.

Unfortunately, Windows NT does not provide a native function to check passwords at the time of selection. Therefore, many administrators run Passcrack-like programs on a regular basis to check passwords over time. Of course, running Passcrack for Windows NT on a loaded domain controller during production hours is probably a bad idea; Passcrack is extremely processor-intensive, and is therefore likely to have a negative impact on the user population. With this in mind, Passcrack for Windows NT can also be run in a batch mode. Moreover, Windows NT provides the Scheduling services, which can be used to schedule Passcrack for Windows NT jobs during off-peak hours.

Passcrack for Windows NT supports the following command-line syntax:

```
Passcrack /U = Filespec /P = Filespec /O = Filespec
[/D = <Domain Name>]
[/F = ON/OFF] [/L = ON/OFF] [/T = ON/OFF]
        /? = Help Dialog
        /U = : File containing usernames
        /P = : File containing passwords
        /O = : Output filename
        /D = : Domain Name
        /F = : Fast Mode. Default is OFF
        /L = : Leading Numbers. Default is OFF
        /T = : Tailing Numbers. Default is OFF
```

To schedule Passcrack for Windows NT jobs, first ensure that the Windows NT Scheduler service is installed and active. If it is not, install it from the installation media and start the service using the *Control Panel / Services* option.

Next, identify the precise mode in which you would like to use Passcrack for Windows NT and construct the proper command line. For example, many administrators might use the command line

```
Passcrack /U = <username file> /P = <dictionary file>
/O = <log file> /F = ON
```

to provide a fast search for bad passwords of a subset of the user accounts. The primary administrative burdens associated with using the Passcrack for Windows NT program in this manner are twofold. First, administrators must update the file of user names on a regular basis; second, administrators must examine the log file after each run.

Next, schedule the job using the AT command. The syntax of the AT command to schedule the same Passcrack run is as follows:

```
AT 0200 /every:Sunday Passcrack /U = <username file>
/P = <dictionary file>
/O = <log file> /F = ON
```

This command line will run Passcrack with the options described above every Sunday at 2:00 A.M.

Also, note that the Windows NT resource kit includes a graphic version of the AT utility. This utility provides the same functionality as the command-line version, albeit with a graphic interface. In order to use the graphic version, first install the Windows NT resource kit. Then, run the program called WINAT.EXE This will launch the graphic AT utility.

From within WINAT, click the *Add...* button in order to add a scheduled event. Then, from the Add Command dialog box, enter the proper command line for the Passcrack program as described above. Then, select the frequency with which you wish to run the program and click *OK*.

Cautions and Recommendations

This program is provided with this book for legitimate system security evaluations. We ask that you do not use it for purposes other than those for which it was written.

Of course, some users will be tempted to use this program for illicit or unethical purposes. We can't prevent this from happening—nor can we prevent hackers from writing their own similar tools, some of which have already been written. We can, however, offer you this tool to check your own system. After all, if you can secure your system against this type of attack, it really doesn't matter whether this type of attack is used against your system. To be forewarned is to be forearmed.

As was described above, we recommend that Windows NT system administrators use the Passcrack for Windows NT (or equivalent) tool to ensure the security of the passwords on their systems. Although some operating systems provide a means for verifying the relative quality of passwords chosen by users at the time of password selection, Windows NT supports no such option. Therefore, bad passwords cannot be eliminated on a proactive basis. Rather, the administrator must locate bad passwords on a regular basis and request that they be changed by the users.

APPENDIX C

This appendix lists the security-related audit events which may appear in the Windows NT security event log.

Account Management Events

Account Management events include changes to user and group accounts, including creation, deletion, modification, and group membership changes. Note that more detail on some of these events may be recorded as Object Access events.

Within the Account Management events category, each event may contain the general information listed in the following table.

Entry	Description
Caller Domain	The name of the computer from which an account management call is made. If the computer is in a domain, this may be the domain name.
Caller Logon ID	The session ID assigned to the calling user at the time of system logon.
Caller User Name	The username of the user making the account management call.
Member	The SID (Security Identifier) of the account being added or removed from a group.
Target Account ID	The SID (Security Identifier) of the account or group being modified.
Target Account Name	The username of the account or group being modified.
Target Domain	The name of the computer which contains the account being modified. In the case of a built-in account on a Windows NT workstation, the username will be Builtin. In the case of a built-in account on a Windows NT Server, the username will be the name of the domain.

299

The following table lists valid entries for the Account Management security event category.

Event	Event ID	Description
User Account Created	624	Indicates that a new user account has been created successfully. Administrators should note that there is no parallel failure event for the creation of a new user account.
User Account Changed	642	Indicates that an existing user account has been successfully modified. Administrators should note that there is no parallel failure event for the modification of a user account.
User Account Deleted	630	Indicates that an existing user account has been successfully deleted. Administrators should note that there is no parallel failure event for the deletion of an existing user account.
Global Group Member Added	632	Indicates that an existing user account has been added to a global user group. Administrators should note that there is no parallel failure event for the global group membership addition.
Global Group Member Removed	633	Indicates that an existing user account has been removed from a global user group. Administrators should note that there is no parallel failure event for the removal of a global group member.
Local Group Created	635	Indicates that a new local group account has been created. Administrators should note that there is no parallel failure event for the creation of a new local group.
Local Group Member Added	636	Indicates that an existing user account has been added to a local user group. Administrators should note that there is no parallel failure event for the local group membership addition.

Event	Event ID	Description
Local Group Member Removed	637	Indicates that an existing user account has been removed from a local user group. Administrators should note that there is no parallel failure event for the removal of a local group member.
Local Group Changed	639	Indicates that a change (other than those noted above) has been made to a local group account. Administrators should note that there is no parallel failure event for the modification of a local group.
Local Group Deleted	638	Indicates that a local group account has been deleted. Administrators should note that there is no parallel failure event for the deletion of a local user group account.

Detailed Tracking Events

Detailed Tracking events provide (as the name suggests) low-level tracking of things such as program activation and indirect object accesses (such as when an object uses its inherited security token to access another object). Within the Detailed Tracking event category, each event may contain the general information listed in the following table.

Entry	Description
Creator Process ID	The Process ID of the process which is spawning a new process.
Domain	The name of the computer, or the domain in which the computer resides.
Image File Name	The filename of the executable file containing the spawned process.
Logon ID	The session ID assigned to the user on initial logon. Note that this ID can be used to correlate events.

(Continued on next page)

Entry	Description
New Process ID	The ID assigned to each new process at the time the process is started.
Process ID	The Process ID of the process which is exiting.
User Name	The username of the user who is attempting to spawn a new process. Note that processes spawned by Windows NT will run under the SYSTEM username.

The following table lists valid entries for the Detailed Tracking events category.

Event	Event ID	Description
New Process Has Been Created	592	Indicates that a new process has been created. Can be useful for tracking the activities of users; however, certain audit policies can generate large numbers of this type of audit event.
Process Has Exited	593	Indicates that a process has completed. Can be useful for tracking the activities of users; however, certain audit policies can generate large numbers of this type of audit event.
Handle Duplicated	594	Indicates that a duplicate object handle has been created which has the same or less access than the previous object. Note that this event will be generated only if the original event generated an audit event according to the event policy.
Indirect Access to Object	595	Indicates that an object attempted access to a Local-Procedure Call (LPC) port via another object.

Logon/Logoff Events

Logon/Logoff events are created for each logon/logoff attempt. Administrators may choose whether to audit successes or failures. *We strongly rec-*

ommend that both successes and failures be recorded. Within the logon/logoff event category, each event which appears within the security event log may contain the basic information listed in the following table.

Entry	Description
Authentication Package	The name of the authentication package being used by Windows NT. By default, the Windows NT authentication package is `Microsoft_Authentication_Package_V1_0`.
Domain	The name of the entity which stores the user's account—either the system name or the domain name.
Logon ID	A session identifier which is assigned at logon time. This can be used to correlate with other security events.
Logon Process	The process which generated the logon/logoff request. For local logons, this is `User32`. For network logons, this is `NTLanMan`.
Logon Type	The method used to log on to the system. A value of 2 indicates an interactive logon, while a value of 3 indicates a network logon.
Reason	The cause for the event generation.
User Name	The username of the user attempting logon or logoff.

The following table lists valid entries for the logon/logoff security event category.

Event	Event ID	Description
Successful Logon	528	Indicates a successful logon.
Unknown Username or Bad Password	529	Indicates that an attempt was made to log onto the system with a bad username-password combination. This may be due to an invalid username or a bad password for a valid username. Note that the presence of this event may indicate an attempted system intrusion.

(Continued on next page)

Event	Event ID	Description
Account Currently Disabled	531	Indicates that an attempt was made to log onto the system using an account which was disabled. Note that the presence of this event may indicate an attempted system intrusion.
Logon Type Restricted	534	Indicates that an attempt was made to log onto the system in a method which is not allowed for that particular user account. For example, this may occur when a less-privileged user attempts to log into the console of a Windows NT server.
Password Expired	535	Indicates that an attempt was made to log onto the system using an account whose password has expired. In most cases, this event does not indicate an attempted system intrusion.
Unsuccessful Logon	535	Indicates that an attempt was made to log on and failed for some reason not defined. This occurs when a logon is denied or fails for a reason other than those listed in this table.
User Logoff	538	Indicates that a user has logged off the system successfully.

Object Access Events

Object Access events are among the most common of events found in the event log. They are created when a user attempts to access an object within the Windows NT system or across a Windows NT network. While auditing the success of this operation will yield extremely large security logs and, as a result, is not recommended, *we strongly recommend auditing failures on object access.* Although some of the high-level activity captured by the object access events are also captured by other types of events, Object Access events are perhaps the most useful in providing a detailed picture of user activity. Within the Object Access event category, each event will contain the basic information contained in the following table.

Entry	Description
Accesses	The type of access which was requested, such as `File_Read_Access` or `File_Read_Attributes`. Note that multiple types of access might be requested in a single event.
Client Domain	The name of the system or the name of the domain in which the client user's ID resides. Note that in this terminology, the *client* may ask the *primary* to perform an operation using his security token (impersonation).
Client Logon ID	The session ID assigned when a user logs into the system.
Client User Name	The username of the user whose rights are being used (either by the user or some process acting on the user's behalf).
Handle ID	The handle ID to the object being accessed.
Object Name	The name of the object being accessed (i.e., a file-name).
Object Server	The identity of the subsystem which initiates the audit event. In many cases, this will be the Security subsystem.
Object Type	The type of object being accessed (e.g., a file).
Operation ID	An identifier used to associate multiple audit events with a single user operation.
Primary Domain	The name of the system (or domain, if the account resides in a domain) from which the primary user requests the operation.
Primary Logon ID	The session ID assigned to the primary user upon system logon.
Primary User Name	The username of the person (or process) who is actually performing the operation. In the case of impersonation, this person will be the user acting on behalf of another.
Process ID	The identifier assigned to the client's process within Windows NT.

The following table lists valid entries for the Object Access category.

Event	Event ID	Description
Object Open	560	This event indicates that either (1) an object was opened successfully or (2) a user attempted to open an object and failed. Administrators should pay careful attention to the type field, which will indicate whether the event signifies a Success Audit or a Failure Audit. A pattern of Failure Audits may indicate an attempted attack against the system.
Handle Closed	562	This event indicates that the handle to an object has been closed. Note that this event will appear only for events which generated open events as per the system audit policy.

Policy Change Events

Policy Change events are captured whenever a change is made to the security policy database. Because of the sensitive nature and far-reaching effects of all changes to the security policy database, all attempted policy changes (both successful and unsuccessful) should be logged. Within the Policy Change event category, each event may contain the general information contained in the following table.

Entry	Description
Assigned to	The SID of the account to which a special right is being assigned.
Domain	The name of the computer. If the computer is in a domain, this may be the domain name.
Logon ID	The session ID assigned a user on logon.
New Policy	A chart indicating the auditing which has been enabled by the system administrator.
Removed from	The SID of the account from which a special right has been revoked.
User Name	The username of the user requesting a policy change.
User Right	The user right which is being assigned to removed from a given user.

The following table lists valid entries for the Policy Events category.

Event	Event ID	Description
User Right Assigned	608	Indicates that the specified user right has been assigned to a specific user or group in the system. Note that there is no parallel failure version of this audit event.
User Right Removed	609	Indicates that the specified user right has been removed from a specific user or group in the system. Note that there is no parallel failure version of this audit event.
Audit Policy Change	612	Indicates that the system audit policy has been modified. The event record will indicate the new policy with a table within the record.

Privilege Use Events

Privileged Use events are generated when users exercise the rights that have been granted to them and contain some data regarding the assignment of specific user rights. Failed attempts which generate Privileged Use events should be logged. Within the privilege use event category, each event may contain the general information listed in the following table.

Entry	Description
Assigned	Indicates the special privileges assigned to a given user.
Client Domain	The name of the client user's computer (or domain in which the user account exists). Note that in this terminology, the *client* may ask the *primary* to perform an operation using his security token (impersonation).
Client Logon ID	The session ID assigned to the user when that user logged into the system.

(*Continued on next page*)

Entry	Description
Client User Name	The username of the user for whom the primary is exercising rights.
Domain	The domain name of the computer on which the activity is taking place.
Logon ID	The session ID assigned a user during the logon process.
Object Handle	The handle to the object being accessed.
Object Server	The name of the subsystem which is generating the audit event. In many cases, this will be the security subsystem.
Primary Domain	The name of the primary user's computer (or domain in which the user account exists).
Primary Logon ID	The session ID assigned to the primary user at the time of system logon.
Primary User Name	The username associated with the primary user for this activity.
Privileges	Special user privileges that are invoked to accomplish object access tasks.
Process ID	The process ID assigned to the client user's process.
User Name	The username of the user logging on or off.

The following table lists valid entries for the Privilege Use security event category.

Event	Event ID	Description
Special Privilege Assigned	576	Indicates that a right has been assigned to a user which is not auditable on an individual use basis. In most cases, this is because the right is often used and would therefore flood the audit logs with useless information. It is provided merely to alert the administrator that the right has been granted. The rights included in this category are ■ SeChangeNotifyPrivilege ■ SeAuditPrivilege

Event	Event ID	Description
		■ SeCreateTokenPrivilege
		■ SeAssignPrimaryTokenPrivilege
		■ SeBackupPrivilege
		■ SeRestorePrivilege
		■ SeDebugPrivilege
Privileged Service Called	577	Indicates that a user has attempted (successfully or unsuccessfully) to use a privileged right to accomplish a privileged system function (e.g., setting the system time). Note that a number of unsuccessful audit events of this type may indicate an attempted system penetration.
Privileged Object Operation	578	Indicates that a user has exercised a right (successfully or unsuccessfully) to use a privileged function on a given object. Note that a number of unsuccessful audit events of this type may indicate an attempted system penetration.

System Events

System events are generated when the system detects something which may affect the security of the entire Windows NT system or audit log. This includes the nonremovable event generated when an administrator clears the security log. Within the System events category, each event may contain the general information contained in the following table.

Event	Event ID	Description
System Restart	512	Indicates that a system has been rebooted. When this event appears in the log, administrators should observe whether there was a previous paired System Shutdown event. If not, the system likely crashed and some audit events might have been lost.

(*Continued on next page*)

Event	Event ID	Description
System Shutdown	513	Indicates that a system is shutting itself down and attempting to close the audit log and all other open files in a clean manner. Note, however, that this presents a catch 22—the system cannot guarantee that the log was closed correctly, because it cannot write an event to the log once it is closed.
Authentication Package Load	514	Indicates that the Local Security Authority (LSA) has initiated the load of an authentication package. This package, by default, is the `Microsoft_Authentication_Package_V1_0`.
Logon Process Registered	515	Indicates that a valid logon process has registered itself with the LSA and is ready to receive logon requests. In most cases, the logon process for Windows NT will be WinLogon.
Some Audit Event Records Discarded	516	Indicates that some audit events have been discarded, either before or after being in the audit log. This may indicate that the internal queue for recording events has been overflowed, or may indicate that some older events in the even log have been overwritten. Finally, it may indicate that auditing has stopped before all events have been written to the log. Note that the presence of this event may indicate a system problem or suspicious activity.
Audit Log Cleared	517	Indicates that the audit log has been cleared. This event will automatically appear whenever the log is reset. Note that this event cannot be removed from the log. Administrators should note the time and date each time they reset the log, then compare this event to that recorded information the next time the log is reset. A discrepancy may indicate suspicious activity.

APPENDIX D

SINGLE SIGN-ON SECURITY

As is discussed in Chap. 6, *Designing Secure NT Networks,* Windows NT supports extremely large networks spanning both local and wide area links. As part of the built-in networking security, NT supports the use of a single sign-on (SSO) to all of the distributed network resources within a single (or trusted) domain.

Specifically, this functionality is provided by the NetLogon service, which runs on all Windows NT systems within a domain. Conceptually, the use of NetLogon to provide SSO across an enterprise is simple—although the implications of this use are not.

The use of the SSO functionality does not come without risk. This appendix discusses the concepts of SSO in general, then with an emphasis on the potential security implications for Windows NT and Windows NT Server.

Overview of SSO

In this modern age of the heterogeneous distributed network environment, it has become more and more difficult to both utilize and manage the security required for large-scale mission-critical applications. As networks grow larger and larger, finding ways to effectively navigate and manage their security will become essential to the effective use of distributed systems.

Today, users find themselves required to repeatedly prove their identity to different elements of the network, including LAN servers (NT servers), host systems (NT workstations, and others), gateways, and applications. From an efficiency standpoint, little could be worse.

Similarly, the management of distributed security leaves much to be desired. Maintaining user passwords and user IDs for multiple systems quickly becomes an administrative nightmare, and in many organizations, it is not even *possible* to determine which users have access to which systems. As a result, distributed system auditing becomes nearly impossible.

311

Single Sign-on (SSO) provides a mechanism by which a user logs into a distributed environment once and is automatically given access to all those resources to which that user has authority, regardless of where on the network they reside. Contrast this to the more typical environment in which users must explicitly log into each new system they want to access.

For the user community, the benefits are readily apparent. Users need only remember a single password [or PIN (personal identification number)] and can always be assured instant access to the resources they need. For management, SSO provides a simple means of deauthenticating users, security auditing, and user ID management.

There are, however, some barriers to implementation. Along with the increase in ease of use offered by SSO comes greater responsibility with regard to access control management. Much of this responsibility is discussed in greater detail below.

Security Problems

It can be argued that from a security perspective, SSO provides no real benefit. In fact, by this way of thinking, SSO probably does more harm than good. The reason is obvious: with a single authentication procedure and a single point of entry, the number of resources endangered by a single compromised account grows tremendously. Given the well-known and documented problems with password security today (see Chap. 1, *Security Architecture*), placing a single password on what might amount to the entirety of an organization's information resources seems a step backward, not forward.

Still, the security problems associated with the current state of affairs also needs to be weighed into the equation. When users are asked to have user IDs and passwords for more than a few systems, their ability to maintain discrete and secure passwords becomes jeopardized. Consequently, users have been known to write their passwords down next to their computers, with obvious end results.

Neither scenario affords great confidence in the ability of organizations to secure their data stored on distributed networks. We should note, however, that we *can* achieve excellent security by designing system security in from the beginning, rather than adding it on later as an afterthought. Unfortunately, few organizations are willing or able to redesign their computing infrastructure in order to accommodate security needs. Indeed, it might be argued that few organizations *should* do so, even if they were able.

SSO, as implemented today, allows for a middle ground between complete redesign and the status quo. With a healthy dose of planning, SSO can be delivered for nearly every system likely to be running today in a distributed network environment.

Implementation Requirements

In planning to utilize the SSO functionality provided by Windows NT, we must be aware that our reliance on individual security components grows at a pace equal to the spread of SSO-capable network elements. That is, *all our security concerns are magnified with respect to SSO*. We must be more aware of how strong our passwords are, regardless of whether we have inactivity timeouts implemented, how we manage the administration of security, and so on. This section will help identify some of the problems and some of the solutions associated with an SSO implementation.

Authentication

Because SSO relies on a single point of authentication, that point must be robust enough to guarantee security for the entire network. Therefore, simple IDs and passwords may not be sufficient. Rather, many organizations might wish to use some combination of token-based, smart card, or biometric authentication systems.

Drawbacks of these latter systems include increased costs and increased administration time. The additional security they provide may or may not be cost-efficient, depending on the level of security required.

PASSWORDS. If passwords are to be used as the primary means of identifying and authenticating users, organizations must both implement and enforce proper password policy. This may include, but not be limited to, the following:

Password aging. Users should be forced to change their passwords over time. A proper length of time for password changes may be as frequently as twice a month, or as infrequently as twice a year, depending on the level of security necessary. At the same time, users should not be allowed to change passwords more frequently than every other day or so (see *Password rotation* entry in this list).

Minimum password length. Users should be forced to use passwords long enough to help avoid brute-force attacks. The proper length of a password might range from 5 characters to 12 or more, depending on the level of security necessary.

Non-English passwords. Users should not be permitted to use passwords that appear in dictionaries of English words. By preventing the use of such passwords, systems are less vulnerable to dictionary-based attacks.

Password rotation. Users should be forced to use different passwords over time. They should not be permitted to use their previous 2 to 10 passwords, depending on the level of security necessary.

Account lockout. Although not specifically geared to password security, organizations who implement SSO should also implement some form of account lockout. This means that accounts with large numbers of login failures should automatically be locked out of the system for some period of time. The appropriate number of invalid login attempts might vary, as might the lockout time period, depending on the level of security necessary.

TOKEN-BASED SYSTEMS. Token-based authentication systems provide a much greater degree of security than do passwords alone. In contrast to password-only systems, token-based systems (including smart cards) require the user to *possess* something which allows them access. Examples of lesser-known token-based systems include password generating tokens and challenge-response units.

Note that Windows NT provides operating system "hooks" to allow for the use of alternate authentication technologies, including token-based systems. For more information, see Chap. 1, *Security Architecture*.

Challenge-response units work by providing a one-time password based on a "seed" provided by the system. Thus, a user attempting to log into the system would be challenged by a string of numbers or characters. The user would then enter this challenge into a *challenge-response unit*, which looks much like a handheld calculator, complete with a number pad and an LCD (liquid-crystal display) panel. The unit returns a response to the user, which the user then types into the system in order to gain access. Personal identification numbers (PINs) can be used to secure the response units for greater security. Usually an attacker is unable to obtain both the physical response unit and the PIN and thus will be unable to access the network.

Password generators, on the other hand, are more sophisticated (and slightly more expensive), and provide greater ease of use. Very often, they are time-based units which provide a different one-time password every minute or so. Thus, to log into the system, users would enter their PINs into their generator (which looks much like a challenge-response unit), and be given a current one-time password. This would be verified by a similar unit on the other end of the network, and the user would be given access.

Besides incorporating a *possession* into the authentication process, both of the systems described above also provide for the use of one-time passwords. Therefore, neither system is vulnerable to a "playback" attack in which an intruder captures network sessions, then replays them later in order to gain access. Password-only systems are, unfortunately, often vulnerable to these attacks.

One of the major drawbacks of any type of token-based system is the cost and time of administration. Provisions must be made for users who leave their tokens at home, for replacing lost tokens, for decertifying stolen tokens, and so on. In addition, some password generators are good only until their batteries die (usually about 2 years). At the end of this time period, organizations must purchase new tokens for their users.

In recent months, however, some vendors have introduced software-only versions of their challenge-response systems. These software packages provide the same functionality, but avoid the use of physical tokens.

SMART CARDS.   As noted above, the perceived decline in the relative security of passwords as a primary access-control method has led to an accelerated pace of development of alternate technologies. Smart cards, despite having been developed several years ago, are only now gaining limited acceptance.

Smart cards are considered more secure than passwords (perhaps on a par with other token-based systems), simply because the user must have both the card and the PIN in order to access the system. They are considered less secure than biometric access controls (discussed below). At the same time, they are more expensive than passwords, yet less expensive than biometric controls. Therefore, they lie somewhere in the middle of both the cost and relative security spectrums.

Current-generation smart cards contain their own independent processors and operating systems. They can be used to store passwords, personal information [name, SSN (Social Security number), etc.], digitized fingerprints, pictures, and other data. They are designed such that once sensitive information is placed on the card, it cannot be read by any device. Access is provided by a simple API set which allows for verification of PINs and other sensitive information.

Perhaps the greatest barrier to the introduction of smart cards to the mass market is the requirement that each workstation have a smart-card reader. For large organizations, the cost of these readers quickly becomes an impediment to cost justification.

One new type of smart card, however, requires no special reader. Fisher International Systems has placed smart-card technology into what appears to be a 3.5-in floppy diskette casing. With this system, any standard 3.5-in diskette drive can read the new "smart disk."

BIOMETRICS.   Biometric controls are perhaps the most positive identification method available today. Passwords, for example, only ask the simple question "What do you know?" Smart cards and token-based access control devices ask two questions: "What do you have?" and "What do you know?" Biometrics get right to the heart of the issue. They ask "Who are you?"

Examples of current biometric technologies include fingerprint readers, retinal scanners, voice verifiers, hand geometry devices, signature recognition systems, and keystroke pattern recognition. Although many of these systems are reminiscent of James Bond, the technology has developed such that many may become more common over the next 5 years or so.

Current drawbacks of biometric technologies include cost, processing time, error rates, and a lack of standardization. Still, manufacturers of some of these products claim error rates of less than 1 percent, and advances in hardware speed are expected shortly. This will be a quickly developing market in the future.

Unfortunately, it is unclear whether the near-term development in this field will allow for cost justification within mainstream corporate

America. Each of the biometric systems noted above suffers from the same problem as smart cards: the requirement for an additional hardware device at each workstation. Therefore, biometric controls are likely to remain in government installations and on the silver screen—at least in the near term.

Central Management Functions

The advantages of SSO can be roughly grouped into two categories: time savings for the users and administrative savings for the organization. Robust central management functionality is critical to achieving the latter objective. Indeed, if the central management functionality of an SSO implementation is weak, many of the inherent advantages of SSO (easy deauthentication, usage tracking, etc.) disappear.

Specifically, the system security administrator should be able to obtain a logical view of systemwide rights and privileges. The fact that security is centralized means that such information should be available. Fully developed SSO solutions might include a GUI interface, and should be ported such that they are native to the platforms used by system administrators.

The SSO functionality provided by Windows NT Workstation and Windows NT Server, unfortunately, is today useful only within those contexts. There are few third-party products available today which make use of the functionality. Over the longer haul, however, more products may take advantage of the secure authentication and the open API set associated with the NT products.

On exceptionally large networks, some provision must also be made for management of multiple security servers. Given such a network, it is unlikely that a single security (or file/security server combination) would be able to administer security across the entire network. Therefore, the logical structure and management of multiple servers must be considered. Some vendors offer a master-slave system in which security databases are replicated over time. Others offer other (peer-to-peer) systems of exchanging updated information.

As with any system, there must be some account privileged to "manage" the network. In this case, there must be some users empowered to create and remove accounts, each with their own respective security profiles. Therefore, this account should be protected with even greater care than others. It is recommended that some form of non-password-only authentication be used, if only for this account (or group of accounts).

Audit Logs

Effective system auditing is essential to the success of an SSO implementation. Fortunately, Windows NT provides excellent event auditing capabilities. We strongly recommend that system auditing be configured as recommended in Chap. 3.

Audit logs are designed to serve two general functions: (1) they serve to deter potential system intruders by helping to make them accountable for their actions and (2) they serve as after-the-fact indications of a security problem. In the traditional sense, they serve as a record of attack, perhaps providing information which might be used to find and remove security vulnerabilities for the future.

AUDIT ALERTS.   With current technology (although not yet found in Windows NT products), however, it is possible to use audit logs in a more *proactive,* rather than *reactive,* manner. By tailoring an auditing system to trigger an "alert" on the basis of certain criteria, the audit log becomes a real-time tool that may be used to stop system intrusion before it becomes serious. With SSO in place, such a proactive approach might be even more useful. Because of the "magnifying" effect of SSO mentioned above, quick response is needed to ensure system security.

The alerts provided by such a system are limited only by today's technology. For example, a large number of invalid login attempts from a particular workstation might prompt a lockout of the account, followed by an alert to a system manager. This alert might be delivered by electronic mail, network message, pager message, and so forth.

Encryption

As noted previously, the advent of SSO means that individual login information becomes more valuable and, hence, needs greater protection. One of the most effective ways to prevent the capture of login information is to use one-time passwords, such as those described above (under *token-based systems*). Another is to use encryption for protecting passwords and login information both as they traverse the network and as they reside on the client workstation.

Network cabling is also vulnerable to network "snooping," in which an attacker uses a network protocol analyzer or similar tool in order to "spy" on the traffic passing through the network cable. Although some cabling systems are difficult to tap covertly (e.g., fiber), most are not difficult. If passwords and other login information is passed over these cables in clear text, they will be vulnerable to network snooping. Therefore, they should be protected with some form of encryption. By default, Windows NT does use a proprietary encryption scheme to prevent password snooping.

Cost Justification

To accept SSO, organizations will have to show that there is a tangible cost savings. We have already identified some of the possible cost advantages, such as a savings of user time, a centralization of management functions, and the ability to quickly deauthenticate users. The following charts indicate one way of calculating the potential return on investment of SSO.

Standard Logons:

Category	Events	Totals
Average time to sign on	30 s	—
Average number of logon IDs	4 systems	2.0 min
Average sign-ons per day	3 times	6.0 min
Average pay	$20.00/h	$2.00 daily
Workdays	225 annual days	$550 annual cost

Single Sign-on

Category	Events	Totals
Average time to sign on	30 s	—
Number of logon IDs	1	30 s
Average per day	1	30 s
Average pay	$20.00/h	$0.17 daily
Workdays	225 annual days	$38.25 annual cost

APPENDIX E

As you now know if you've read this book in its entirety, there are innumerable settings and configuration changes which can be made to a Windows NT implementation in order to make it more or less secure. After a while, the configuration choices begin to run together, yielding a difficult mental challenge for those of us who don't have genius intellects.

Therefore, we've created this appendix to help to sort through some of the confusion. In this appendix, we've listed many of the most common security configuration setting which Windows NT administrators should consider when securing their NT systems.

As we've stated throughout the book, each of these settings has distinct advantages, disadvantages, and other implications for security and usability. So, we cannot simply recommend that all administrators go down this list and make the recommended changes. Rather, each administrator must consider the local administrative and security policies within the context of Windows NT in order to hit on the right mix of security and usability.

User Security

On Windows NT 3.51 systems and earlier, the most prevalent security hole is the presence of the default Guest account. On Windows 4.x systems, the Guest account is installed by default as a disabled account—it must be manually activated by the administrator to be used. We recommend that users of versions 3.51 and earlier disable the Guest account.

Administrators should also be conscious of the account policies they set for their systems. We recommend the settings for the user account policies listed in the following table.

Policy	Recommendation
Maximum password age	≤45 days
Minimum password age	1 day
Minimum password length	6–7 characters
Password uniqueness	6–8 password history
Account lockout	Lockout after 5 failed attempts; lockout for at least 45 min; reset failed lockout count every 45 min
Forcibly disconnect users	Yes, during nightly backups if possible
Logon to change password	Require logon to change password

Finally, administrators should be aware of the security implications of frequently misunderstood user rights such as the Backup/Restore right. Using the Backup/Restore right, a user may open any file in the system, regardless of whether it is protected with NTFS-based ACLs. Therefore, access to this user right should be firmly protected using the user manager. Note also that the use of this user right should be audited at all times.

Files and Printers

Much of an administrator's time is often taken up with assigning user rights to files. Indeed, this should be the case—rights to files represent the most clear security barrier in the Windows NT (or any other) system. Administrators should remember several things about assigning user permissions:

1. First, remember that permissions can be assigned only to files which reside on NTFS volumes. As a result, we strongly recommend that all volumes which will contain either operating system files, shared applications, or sensitive data reside on NTFS volumes. FAT volumes may be used for other data.

2. The default settings for all file shares grant Full Control rights to all users. As a result, we strongly recommend that you periodically monitor your file shares and ensure that new file shares are modified with appropriate file permissions for specific users.

3. Both the system directories and other directories containing frequently used executable files may be targeted for trojan

horse–based attacks. Therefore, administrators should ensure that users are not permitted Write rights to these directories. If this is not possible, executable files should be protected by individual file-based ACLs to prevent modification.

The Registry

The registry is one of the most useful—and frightening—pieces of the Windows NT architecture. Although it provides a single repository for all the significant configuration data for a Windows NT system, it does so in a rather obscure and difficult-to-understand manner. While administrators may set specific permissions on individual registry keys (and sets of keys), it is seldom clear which permissions should be set and why. In this arena, Microsoft has provided little guidance—and it seems that some guidance will be required to make the registry fully secure.

Moreover, administrators are able to perform detailed auditing of keys which reside in the registry. Similar to the permissions, however, the implications and results of these auditing options are rarely clear to administrators. Indeed, it is difficult to determine, simply from reviewing the security audit log, whether changes made to the registry represent malicious activity or merely normal operation.

There are, however, some registry keys whose values are quite significant for system security. A great number of these keys are discussed in some detail in Chap. 5, and therefore won't be repeated here in their entirety. A few keys, however, are critical to system security. They are reproduced below.

AUTOMATIC LOGON.   We believe that Windows NT systems should *never be set for automatic logon*. To ensure that automatic logon is not used, set the registry key

```
HKEY_LOCAL_MACHINE\Software\Microsoft\WindowsNT\CurrentVersion\
WinLogon\AutoAdminLogon
```

to a value of 0.

DISPLAY LAST LOGGED-ON USER.   By default, the username of the last user logged into the system is displayed in the Logon dialog box. We recommend that the last username not be reported; doing so merely provides a potential intruder with one of the two pieces of information required to penetrate the system. To ensure that the last user name is not displayed, set the registry key

```
HKEY_LOCAL_MACHINE\Software\Microsoft\WindowsNT\CurrentVersion\
WinLogon\DontDisplayLastUserName
```

to a value of 1.

AUDITING OF BACKUP RIGHTS.   Normally, the use of backup rights is not audited by the system. Because of its potential for abuse, however, we recommend that auditing be enabled for this function. To enable such auditing, set the registry key

```
HKEY_LOCAL_MACHINE\System\CurrentControlSet\Control\Lsa\
FullPrivilegeAuditing
```

to a value of 1.

In addition to monitoring the permissions and values for the keys listed above and in Chap. 5, administrators should also enable auditing of other registry events. See below (*Logging and Audit Trails* section) for more information.

REMOTE REGISTRY ACCESS.   Unfortunately, Windows NT 3.x lacks the ability to easily prevent remote users from accessing registry keys. Under these versions of the operating system, each part of the tree must be manually locked using registry ACLs.

With Windows NT 4.0, however, Microsoft has added a way to disable remote access to the registry to all users except administrators. By setting the key

```
HKEY_LOCAL_MACHINE\System\CurrentControlSet\Control\
SecurePipeServers/WinReg
```

adminstrators can ensure that only administrators have remote access to the registry. We strongly recommend that administrators set this key with a value of 1. Note that it exists by default on Windows NT Servers—it can, however, be added to Windows NT workstations.

Remote-Access Service

The Remote-Access Service (RAS) provides a simple, useful, and potentially secure way to provide remote dial-in capability to a Windows NT network or workstation. Implementing proper remote access security, however, may necessitate the use of additional authentication devices beyond those provided by Windows NT. Nevertheless, there are some configuration settings which administrators can make within the RAS that will help improve security, including the following:

1. Administrators should limit the number of users who are granted rights to dial into the RAS server. Some administrators simply grant dial-in privileges to all users; we recommend that users who require this service be granted access, while all others be denied. Administrators should maintain this policy over time by monitoring usage.

2. We strongly recommend that the most secure encryption (CHAP with DES) be used for authenticating logons. Administrators should configure their authentication such that clear-text authentication is explicitly denied.

3. We recommend that administrators configure the link-based encryption whenever possible. Although the encryption and decryption of all data which traverse the wire will impose a performance penalty, the performance loss is well worth the security gain. Note, however, that the link-based encryption is available only when a Windows NT RAS client attaches to a Windows NT RAS server.

4. Much of the administrative burden associated with supplying a secure enterprise dial-up capability can be reduced to eliminating insecure means of entry, as opposed to fortifying authorized entry points. Nearly all desktop operating systems (including Windows NT Workstation) now support either native or third-party dial-in solutions which users may run from their own systems. In the majority of cases, these dial-in solutions will be far less secure than well-planned and secured centralized dial-in solutions. Therefore, administrators should use both policy and enforcement to ensure that insecure dial-in points do not exist in their networks.

Logging and Audit Trails

One of the basic requirements of a secure operating system is that it provides a means to audit the activities of all users, including system administrators. This auditing serves a dual purpose: (1) it discourages users from stepping beyond their granted rights, as they know that their activities are being monitored; and (2) it provides an after-the-fact trail to follow if there is a system intrusion.

Windows NT provides this capability significantly. By default, however, Windows NT does not audit any of the significant system events for which Windows NT administrators should watch. We recommend that auditing be enabled for user rights as shown in the following table.

Event	Success	Failure
Logon/Logoff	X	X
File and Object Access		X
Use of User Rights		X
User and Group Management	X	X
Security Policy Changes	X	X
Restart, Shutdown and System	X	X
Process Tracking		X

Further, we recommend that auditing for registry events be enabled as shown in the following table.

Event	Success	Failure
Query Value		X
Set Value	X	X
Create Subkey	X	X
Enumerate Subkeys		X
Notify		X
Create Link		X
Delete	X	X
Write DAC	X	X
Read Control		X

Finally we recommend that auditing for file access be enabled as shown (in the following table) on sensitive files (such as system files).

Event	Success	Failure
Read		X
Write	X	X
Execute		X
Delete	X	X
Change Permissions	X	X
Take Ownership	X	X

System Policy Editor

In version 4.0 of Windows NT, Microsoft introduced the System Policy Editor, which is designed to permit administrators to change system policy settings—including most of those described above—using a single graphic utility. Also, the System Policy Editor enables users to maintain multiple sets of policies and switch easily among them.

For more information on the System Policy Editor, consult the documentation included with Windows NT 4.0 and later.

Third-Party Vendors

There are several vendors currently producing products to enhance Windows NT security. Several of them have been mentioned throughout this book. Listed below are two vendors who are currently producing innovative utilities for NT security:

- *Mission-Critical Software.* Software designed to increase the granularity of NT security.
- *SomarSoft.* Software designed to analyze and help make sense of NT security logs (among other things). Http://www.somarsoft.com.

INDEX

About the Author

Charles Rutstein is a Principal Consultant with Price Waterhouse LLC. Mr. Rutstein has extensive front-line computer security experience, and is a recognized expert in the field of computer viruses. He has 7 years' experience in both systems security and the detection, prevention, and removal of computer viruses, and he is the author of a book on the subject.

In addition, he is a frequent speaker to corporate and industry groups, including talks at corporate sites, government agencies, and institutions of higher education. He has been featured prominently in the national media, including appearances on the *MacNeil-Lehrer News Hour*, CBS, ABC, NBC, and Canadian Radio News. Currently, he specializes in the field of distributed systems security.